POWERBASIC IN PLAIN ENGLISH

Chuck Butkus

ScottForesman
ProfessionalBooks
An Imprint of ScottForesman

For Mom

Cover photo courtesy of Image Bank
Cover photo screen image courtesy of Borland International

PowerBASIC is a trademark of Spectra Publishing.

Library of Congress Cataloging-in-Publication Data

Butkus, Chuck.
   PowerBASIC in plain English / Chuck Butkus.
      p.   cm.
   ISBN 0-673-46006-1
   1. BASIC (Computer program language)   2. PowerBASIC (Computer
program)   I. Title.
QA76.73.B3B87   1991   90-35833
005.26′2--dc20   CIP

ISBN 0-673-46006-1

Notice of Liability
The information in this book is distributed on an "As Is" basis, without
warranty. Neither the author nor Scott, Foresman and Company shall have any
liability to customer or any other person or entity with respect to any
liability, loss, or damage caused or alledged to be caused directly or indirectly
by the programs contained herein. This includes, but is not limited to,
interruption of service, loss of data, loss of business or anticipatory profits,
or consequential damages from the use of the programs.

Preface

Ever read a book that taught you how to read? Write? Study? Research? I haven't.

I've read a lot of books on computer languages. Most didn't clearly explain each statement (sentence) or key word of the language. Examples were too simple to show how the statement could be used. None told me why I should use one statement instead of another. The books barraged me with "tons" of computer statements in each language, most of which I would never use. Today, after twenty-five years of writing programs, I still don't see why over half of the statements in many languages are needed, or wanted.

As a consultant, I worked with hundreds of "veteran" programmers from a variety of companies. I saw three people who were great programmers. The rest, even after years of programming experience, wrote programs that were difficult to read, debug (make error-free), or change (even by the authors). Program structure was not consistent, and they didn't even use the same commands or statements to accomplish the same task in two different programs.

While teaching computer science to college students, I realized that I did not have access to any written approach that would teach students *HOW TO WRITE PROGRAMS*. So I began my own approach. This book reflects the first part of my approach to programming. It describes in detail, without using "computerese," the few statements I consider essential to program writing in PowerBASIC. Most of the book is taken up with examples of each statement's use in programs and routines (small sections of a program). All the statements and programs are related to real-life examples. It gives you, in the most down-to-earth writing that I can put out—

- a program structure to base your program writing upon
- a means to design your program, then translate the design into a program structure
- a thorough understanding of the use of PowerBASIC and the selected PowerBASIC statements
- the guidelines that can start you on the path to becoming a great (or greater) programmer

in any computer language.

Chuck Butkus

Contents

CHAPTER 1   About BASIC (It's Not as Basic as You Think)   **1**

    1.1 LEARNING THE HARD WAY   1

    1.2 LESSONS TO LEARN THE EASY WAY   2

    1.3 HOW TO USE THE BOOK   5

    1.4 BASIC AND COMPUTER PROGRAMMING   7

    1.5 A BIT ABOUT BASIC   9

    1.6 A DEFINITION OF A PROGRAM   11

    CHAPTER SUMMARY   11

    THE BOTTOM LINE   12

CHAPTER 2   A BASIC Picture (Is Worth a Few Statements)   **13**

    2.1 BIKES PEAK   14

    2.2 BASIC PROGRAMS   15

        2.2.1 Four Statements We Need for Our First Programs   15

            2.2.1.1 *PRINT*   15
            2.2.1.2 *INPUT*   16
            2.2.1.3 *GOTO*   17
            2.2.1.4 *Calculations*   17

2.2.2 Numbering the Lines   18

    2.2.2.1 Why Use Numbers?   19
    2.2.2.2 Why Use Names?   19

2.3 A NOTE ON CONVENTIONS   19

    2.3.1 Conventions in the BASIC Programs in This Book   20

    2.3.2 Conventions in the Keyboard Instructions   20

    2.3.3 Conventions in the Text of This Book   21

2.4 A SIMPLE PROGRAM TO AVERAGE THREE NUMBERS   22

2.5 A NOTE ON READING PROGRAMS   23

2.6 WHAT A MENU PROGRAM DOES   24

2.7 BIKES PEAK MENU PROGRAM   25

CHAPTER SUMMARY   27

THE BOTTOM LINE   28

EXERCISES   28

CHAPTER 3   PowerBASIC (Your First Workout)   29

3.1 STARTING PowerBASIC (AND BAILING OUT)   31

3.2 TYPING IN A PROGRAM   33

    3.2.1 Guidelines for Typing in PowerBASIC Programs   35

    3.2.2 Writing a Routine within a Program   36

3.3 SAVING A PROGRAM   38

3.4 OPENING AN EXISTING PROGRAM   40

3.5 TESTING A PROGRAM BY RUNNING IT   42

    3.5.1 It Runs!   43

    3.5.2 If It Doesn't Run. . .   43

3.6 THE PowerBASIC ENVIRONMENT   45

3.7 SETTING PowerBASIC OPTIONS   45

CHAPTER SUMMARY   48

THE BOTTOM LINE   48

EXERCISES   49

CHAPTER 4   Programming Logic and Diagrams (Errors Are Usually in Thinking, Not in Programming)   50

4.1 PROGRAM "FLOW" AND LOGIC   51

    4.1.1 Rocks and Routines   51

    4.1.2 Watergates and IF . . . THENs   52

    4.1.3 Pumps and Loops   53

4.2 THE NATURE OF PROGRAMMING   58

4.3 PRECISION OF THE BASIC LANGUAGE   59

4.4 THREE SECRETS OF GOOD PROGRAMMING   60

4.5 THE PROGRAM BLUEPRINT   61

    4.5.1 Sample Blueprint #1   63

    4.5.2 Sample Blueprint #2   65

    4.5.3 Sample Blueprint #3 Through . . .   66

4.6 BIKES PEAK PROGRAMS   66

4.7 POWERBASIC—SKIMMING THE MENUS   67

    4.7.1 The File Menu   67

    4.7.2 The Edit Selection   68

    4.7.3 The Run Selection   69

    4.7.4 The Compile Selection   70

    4.7.5 The Options Menu   70

    4.7.6 The Debug Menu   71

    4.7.7 The Break/Watch Menu   73

CHAPTER SUMMARY   74

THE BOTTOM LINE   75

EXERCISES   75

CHAPTER 5   Types of Data and Names (Stick to the Rules, or There's Chaos)   **77**

5.1 WHAT DATA IS, AND WHY IT'S NEEDED   79

5.2 THE NEED FOR DATA NAMES   81

5.3 DIFFERENT DATA TYPES   84

5.4 POWERBASIC AND NAMING DATA   86

5.5 RULES FOR DATA NAMES   87

5.6 THE DATA DICTIONARY   89

5.7 THE REMARK STATEMENT   92

5.8 A LITTLE HELP ON POWERBASIC HELP   94

CHAPTER SUMMARY   95

THE BOTTOM LINE   96

EXERCISES   97

CHAPTER 6   Organizing the Program (It's a Routine Process)   **98**

6.1 THE ROLE OF THE ROUTINE   98

6.2 ORGANIZING A PROGRAM   99

    6.2.1 The Major Routines   100

    6.2.2 The STUB   102

    6.2.3 The END   103

6.3 THE TEN-PART CLASSIC PROGRAM   104

6.4 ROUTINES FROM NOW ON   110

6.5 FROM BLUEPRINT TO ROUTINES   111

6.6 FILE COMMANDS—(BACK TO THE POWERBASIC ENVIRONMENT)   113

CHAPTER SUMMARY   115

THE BOTTOM LINE   117

EXERCISES   117

CHAPTER 7 Control of Routines (Getting Data in and out of the "Windows") 118

7.1 ROUTINES 121

7.2 SUBROUTINES (MAJOR FLOW DIVERSIONS) 121

7.3 PROCEDURES (MINOR REPEATED TASKS) 125

7.4 THE ROUTINE-SELECTION TEST 128

7.5 AN ARBITRARY DECISION 129

7.6 GLOBAL AND LOCAL DATA 130

7.7 DATA INTO AND OUT OF SUBROUTINES 131

7.8 DATA INTO AND OUT OF PROCEDURES 132

    7.8.1 The Data "Window" 133

7.9 THE GOTO "PROBLEM" 135

7.10 NOTES ON USING THE MENUS 137

7.11 FILE MENU DETAILS 138

    7.11.1 Load 138

    7.11.2 New 139

    7.11.3 Save 139

    7.11.4 Write To 140

CHAPTER SUMMARY 140

THE BOTTOM LINE 141

EXERCISES 142

CHAPTER 8 The PowerBASIC Editor (You've Got a Friend) 143

8.1 WHY YOU NEED AN EDITOR 144

8.2 USING THE EDITING KEYS 144

8.3 FIND 147

8.4 FIND AND REPLACE (CHANGE) 148

8.5 CUT AND PASTE   149

   8.5.1 Move Selected Text   150

   8.5.2 Copy Selected Text   150

   8.5.3 Delete Selected Text   150

8.6 PRINTING PROGRAM BLOCKS   151

8.7 READING AND WRITING PROGRAM BLOCKS   151

8.8 SYNTAX CHECKING   152

8.9 EXAMPLE OF USING THE EDITOR   153

   8.9.1 Find and Replace   153

   8.9.2 Create a Procedure   156

   8.9.3 Move Text   156

   8.9.4 Changing Variables   157

   8.9.5 Adding Statements   158

   8.9.6 Back to the Main Module   158

CHAPTER SUMMARY   160

THE BOTTOM LINE   161

EXERCISES   161

CHAPTER 9   IF Statements (IF You Skip This Chapter, THEN You'll Never Write Good Programs)   162

9.1 THE PURPOSE OF IF STATEMENTS   164

9.2 IFS AND PROGRAM FLOW   165

9.3 THE THREE TYPES OF IF STATEMENTS   169

9.4 THE ELSE STATEMENT   170

   9.4.1 ELSE Statements and Alternative Process Selection   171

   9.4.2 ELSE Statements and Flow Diversion   174

9.5 BLOCK ELSE STATEMENTS   175

9.6 COMPLEX IF STATEMENTS   176

9.7 TWO BASIC DECISION-MAKING RULES   178

9.8 MINIMAL TESTING, MINIMAL CLUTTER   179

9.9 INDENTING RULE OF IFS   182

CHAPTER SUMMARY   183

THE BOTTOM LINE   185

EXERCISES   185

CHAPTER 10 Loops (IF It's Worth Doing Once, THEN Do It Again)   187

10.1 THE LOOP IS THE LOGIC BASE   188

10.2 THE THREE TYPES OF LOOPS   192

    10.2.1 FOR . . . TO—NEXT   192

    10.2.2 DO UNTIL . . .   193

    10.2.3 IF EOF THEN GOTO   195

10.3 THE MAIN ROUTINE IS A CRITICAL LOOP   196

10.4 THE DANGER OF GOTO   197

CHAPTER SUMMARY   198

THE BOTTOM LINE   198

EXERCISES   199

CHAPTER 11 The Concept of Files (You See and Use Them Every Day)   200

11.1 DEFINITION OF A DATA FILE   201

11.2 EVERYDAY, ORDINARY FILES   201

11.3 DEFINITION OF A RECORD   201

11.4 EVERYDAY, ORDINARY RECORDS   202

11.5 DEFINITION OF A FIELD   202

11.6 EVERYDAY, ORDINARY FIELDS   203

11.7 TYPES OF FILE STRUCTURES   204

11.8 FILE SUBJECT CATEGORIES   208

11.9 FILE LAYOUT   210

CHAPTER SUMMARY   212

THE BOTTOM LINE   212

EXERCISES   213

CHAPTER 12   Random Files (The Only Kind You Really Need)   214

12.1 DEFINITION OF A RANDOM FILE   215

12.2 OPENING A RANDOM FILE   215

12.3 LOCATING THE RIGHT RECORD   217

12.4 READING AND WRITING (GET AND PUT)   219

    12.4.1 GET Statement   219

    12.4.2 PUT Statement   220

12.5 RECORD LAYOUT   222

12.6 PACKING AND UNPACKING   223

12.7 CREATING A RANDOM FILE   225

    12.7.1 Random File Creation Program   225

12.8 DETERMINING THE END OF THE FILE   226

CHAPTER SUMMARY   228

THE BOTTOM LINE   229

EXERCISES   230

CHAPTER 13   Input from the Keyboard (The Key Is to Key in Correctly)   231

13.1 EDITING IS CRITICAL   232

13.2 EDITING LEVELS   232

13.2.1 BASIC Examples for Length, Type, Range, and Specific Value Testing   233

13.3 ERROR MESSAGES   239

13.4 SCREEN NEATNESS TECHNIQUES   244

CHAPTER SUMMARY   247

THE BOTTOM LINE   247

EXERCISES   248

CHAPTER 14   Writing Reusable Edit Procedures (Recycle Your Work)   249

14.1 WRITING REUSABLE EDIT PROCEDURES   249

14.1.1 The Error Routine (It's a Procedure)   250

14.1.2 The Numeric Testing Routine (It's Also a Procedure)   251

14.1.3 The Date Testing Routine (Also a Procedure)   251

14.1.4 Length Test with Editing Routines   253

14.1.5 Numeric Test with Editing Routines   253

14.1.6 Date Test with Editing Routines   254

14.1.7 New Customer Routine   256

14.2 LINE INPUT STATEMENT   262

14.3 LEN FUNCTION   263

14.4 STRING PROCESSING FUNCTIONS   264

14.4.1 ASC Function   264

14.4.2 VAL Function   265

14.4.3 MID$, LEFT$, and RIGHT$ Functions   266

14.4.4 Concatenating Strings   267

14.4.5 Combining These Functions   267

CHAPTER SUMMARY   268

THE BOTTOM LINE   269

EXERCISES   270

CHAPTER 15   Using the Printer (Lay it on the Line)   **271**

    15.1 THE BEGINNING IS THE END   272

    15.2 THE VALUE (AND LACK OF VALUE) IN PRINTED OUTPUT   272

    15.3 DIFFERENT TYPES OF PAGE LAYOUTS   275

    15.4 RULES FOR LAYING OUT A PAGE   275

    15.5 PRINT FORMATS   276

    15.6 FORMAT STATEMENT   276

    15.7 LPRINT, LPRINT USING STATEMENTS   277

    15.8 TAB FUNCTION   279

    15.9 CHR$ FUNCTION   279

    15.10 COMMAS AND SEMICOLONS   280

    15.11 WIDTH STATEMENT   280

    CHAPTER SUMMARY   281

    THE BOTTOM LINE   282

    EXERCISES   283

CHAPTER 16   Displaying to the Screen (It's Your Screen Test)   **284**

    16.1 START AT THE END   286

    16.2 THE VALUE OF SCREEN OUTPUT   286

    16.3 SCREEN LAYOUT TECHNIQUES   287

    16.4 COLOR, UNDERLINING, AND BLINKING   288

    16.5 TEN COMMON SCREEN MISTAKES   289

    16.6 KEEP IT SIMPLE   290

    16.7 PRINT FORMATS   290

    16.8 FORMAT STATEMENTS   290

    16.9 PRINT AND PRINT USING STATEMENTS   291

    16.10 TAB FUNCTION   293

    16.11 COMMAS AND SEMICOLONS   293

16.12 USE OF CHR$ FOR SPACING LINES   293

16.13 CLS STATEMENT   294

16.14 LOCATING A POINT ON THE SCREEN   294

    16.14.1 LOCATE   294

    16.14.2 CSRLIN   295

    16.14.3 POS   295

16.15 THE COLOR STATEMENT   296

16.16 THE ONLY CRITERION   297

CHAPTER SUMMARY   297

THE BOTTOM LINE   298

EXERCISES   299

CHAPTER 17 Calculations (Coming up with the Right Answers)   300

17.1 WHERE CALCULATIONS COME FROM   301

17.2 THE DIFFERENT OPERATORS   302

17.3 LET'S CONCATENATE (COMBINING STRINGS)   302

17.4 DIVISION BY ZERO   303

17.5 WHAT'S CALCULATED FIRST (THE ORDER OF CALCULATION IN A COMPLEX FORMULA)   304

17.6 THE USE OF PARENTHESES   304

    17.6.1 Hints on Parentheses   306

17.7 USE THE RIGHT DATA TYPES   307

17.8 ROUNDING AND PRESENTING THE CORRECT ANSWER   307

17.9 CINT, INT, FIX, AND CLNG FUNCTIONS   309

17.10 MATH FUNCTIONS   312

17.11 THE USE OF STRING FUNCTIONS IN CALCULATIONS   312

17.12 DATE CALCULATIONS   313

CHAPTER SUMMARY   315

THE BOTTOM LINE   316

EXERCISES   317

**CHAPTER 18   Tables (Arrays Subscripted into
the Fourth Dimension)   319**

18.1 FREQUENTLY SEEN ONE-DIMENSIONAL TABLES   320

18.2 FREQUENTLY SEEN TWO-DIMENSIONAL TABLES   320

18.3 AND THREE-DIMENSIONAL TABLES   321

18.4 DEFINING A TABLE (ARRAY)   321

18.5 LOCATING THE ELEMENTS IN A TABLE   324

18.6 SUBSCRIPTS, AND KEEPING THEM STRAIGHT   324

18.7 DIMENSIONING A TABLE   325

18.8 GETTING VALUES INTO ARRAYS   326

18.9 DATA AND READ STATEMENTS   326

18.10 PRINTING OUT A TABLE   327

18.11 A TABLE WITHIN A RANDOM FILE RECORD   328

18.12 A COMPLETE EXAMPLE   328

18.13 COMMON USES OF TABLES IN POWERBASIC   330

18.14 POWERBASIC LIMITATIONS   330

CHAPTER SUMMARY   331

THE BOTTOM LINE   332

EXERCISES   333

CHAPTER 19   The PowerBASIC Debugger (Cleaning up Your Act)   334

19.1 TAKING ONE STEP AT A TIME   335

    19.1.1 Single-Stepping (Trace into)   335

19.2 SKIPPING SOME STEPS   336

19.3 CUT! STOPPING THE ACTION   336

19.3.1 Stopping the Program Manually   336

19.3.2 The Breakpoint Feature   336

19.4 WATCH WHAT YOU'RE DOING!   337

19.4.1 Watch Window   337

19.4.2 Instant Watch   337

19.4.3 Instant Screen (User Screen)   338

19.5 ACTION!   338

19.6 QUICKCHANGE, THEN ACTION   338

19.7 A DETAILED EXAMPLE   339

19.8 HINTS ON USING THE DEBUGGER   343

CHAPTER SUMMARY   344

THE BOTTOM LINE   344

EXERCISES   345

CHAPTER 20   The PowerBASIC Compiler (The Command Performance)   **346**

20.1 THE LAST, SHORTEST, AND EASIEST   346

20.2 STARTING A PROGRAM   347

20.3 STOPPING A PROGRAM   347

20.4 COMPILING A PROGRAM WHEN YOU'RE ALL DONE   347

20.5 A NOTE ON PowerBASIC FEATURES THAT WE SKIPPED   348

THE BOTTOM LINE   349

APPENDIX A PowerBASIC Statement Summary (Selected Statements)   351
APPENDIX B BASIC Reserved Words   355
APPENDIX C Sample Data Dictionary and Naming Rules   357
APPENDIX D Blueprints and Program Structures   360
APPENDIX E Sample Routines   367
APPENDIX F Answers to Exercises   372
INDEX 437

Chapter 1

About BASIC (It's Not as Basic as You Think)

1.1 Learning the Hard Way _____ 1

1.2 Lessons to Learn the Easy Way _____ 2

1.3 How to Use This Book _____ 5

1.4 BASIC and Computer Programming _____ 7

1.5 A Bit About BASIC _____ 9

1.6 Definition of a Program _____ 11

1.1 LEARNING THE HARD WAY

You want to build a storage shed but know nothing about carpentry. So you buy a self-teach book, *How to Build Anything in Wood*. You also buy a thousand dollars' worth of tools.

Shouldn't you start by blueprinting the shed? Naah; you can picture in your head *EXACTLY* what you want. You're itching to get started, so you run down to the building supply store nearby and ask for 50 two-by-fours, 20 sheets of plywood, and a bunch of nails. You haul everything back home, unload it in the basement, and pick up a saw and a tape measure.

Then you check the book.

It says that outdoor buildings need a foundation. Gee, you didn't think about that. So you go back and get some concrete blocks. You set them in rows out by the patio, and then you realize that the ground isn't level. You need a shovel, . . . but that wasn't among the thousand dollars' worth of "essential" tools. So you run out, buy a shovel, and level the site.

Then you check the book.

It says that the floor should be supported by two-by-eight joists, not two-by-fours. So you return to the lumberyard, swap boards, and rush back home to lay them before dark.

In fading daylight, you check the book.

It says the floor should be made of plywood a minimum of 1/2-inch thick. The stuff you bought is one size too thin. Well, it's evening now; you'll have to wait until tomorrow.

The next morning you go back to see the lady at the lumberyard (who is a good friend by now), get the 1/2-inch stuff, and head home to lay the floor.

In the rain, you check the book. . . .

That's how things go for a couple of days. Because of the rain, you end up assembling the walls in the basement. The clouds disappear on day four. As you wrestle an eight-foot-square wall unit up the basement steps, you realize it's too big to fit through the door.

Dumb!

You return to the lumberyard and start checking prices on prefab storage sheds.

1.2 LESSONS TO LEARN THE EASY WAY

Surely, this is not how you would ever start building anything. But when it comes to writing programs, many inexperienced computer users do just as badly.

Where did the carpentry project go wrong? Just about everywhere. But you can save yourself grief in programming by learning some lessons from the storage-shed fiasco.

- **TOOLS.** Sure, you need equipment to do a job properly. But in writing computer programs, you don't have to buy the biggest, fastest, fanciest computer around. And if you have five thousand programming aids, you won't know any of them. Programming demands *COMMON SENSE* more than computer sophistication. Not everyone who blows a fortune on a high-performance, complex car is a great driver—or even a capable one.

(Lesson: Investing in lots of tools won't make you competent. Mastering a few of them will.)

- **TIME.** A book with a title like *How to Program Anything within 24 Hours* is tempting, but the odds are against shortcuts to success. You probably won't be writing smooth-running programs of value in fewer than *24 days.* Computing is more user-friendly than it was a decade ago, but programming is still a mental discipline. Results depend heavily on practice and experience.

(Lesson: Be realistic in your expectations. Did you buy this book figuring to become a programmer by the weekend?)

- **PLANNING.** Should you draw up blueprints or try working from an image in your mind? A mental picture may suffice to choose a door handle or a color scheme. Most professional carpenters are not skilled enough to work from memory. How many can solve problems of angle, distance, support, and fit using only intuition? To use an example from another field, even veteran pilots faithfully consult their manuals and flight plans.

(Lesson: Minutes spent in thoughtful planning—on paper—will save hours once into the job.)

- **PATIENCE.** Itching to write a program and see it work as quickly as possible? That could be a danger signal. If, when you start a project, you're already thinking of how quickly you want to finish, then you'll be working under subconscious pressure to rush or cut corners. Moreover, inexperienced programmers *always* underestimate the scope of a project.

(Lesson: It takes time to learn to program well. Rather than seek shortcuts, set your sights on the end result and then spend the time to achieve it.)

- **FUNDAMENTALS.** How in the world could anyone forget the foundation? Well, new programmers often get sidetracked by what they want the program to look like on screen because of the superbly designed screens in expensive software. But thoughtful program design and sound program structure are behind every fancy screen.

(Lesson: Screens of video-game quality do not make the program good.)

- **WORKING THOUGHTFULLY.** How in the world could you assemble something in the basement that you can't get through the door? There are counterparts in programming. Many programs have undergone tremendous development, only to fail completely because something doesn't "fit." Perhaps there was not enough room to accommodate a growing amount of data. Or sometimes an entire program bombs (just quits) when it encounters a data value that was not anticipated in the design.

   (Lesson: Rules have their place, but they are no substitute for continually thinking about what you're doing related to your plan. There cannot be a rule for every situation.)

Another book might say that as a complete beginner, *YOU, TOO,* can build a three-car garage, alone, in a weekend! Let's be realistic. *PowerBASIC in Plain English* presents a practical approach to computer programming. Together, we will craft *simple, sensible programs that work*—programs free of unneeded complexity and frivolous design.

This book shows you a complete approach to programming, not just a catalog of commands and tricks. We want you to start your "builder's" career with a "storage shed." You'll—

- Design
- Blueprint your design
- Build a firm foundation
- Learn to use the right tools
- Accept experienced guidance
- See results

And eventually, you'll be building castles.

We want to teach you to do a thoughtful job ON YOUR OWN, not stumble through a difficult task following instructions by rote. If you work thoughtfully, you'll gain confidence in tackling larger projects, because you will have learned the fundamentals well.

1.3 HOW TO USE THIS BOOK

There's no such thing as an effective "cookbook" for programming. Programming requires

- An understanding of concepts
- Thought
- Regular practice

But so far as learning how to program can be "taught" or helped along by a book, this approach is the next best thing. Our focus is on understanding the basic idea of everything you do, on thinking about what you're doing (rather than looking up an example every time you want to write a new statement), and on *doing* it, not just reading about it.

When you finish using this book, you'll have a solid start on becoming a successful programmer, but you won't be done at that point. A cookbook is useful to begin learning how to cook, but no one has ever become a chef just by reading good cookbooks. You need to continue practicing this approach to be great.

Here are some suggestions on how you should use *PowerBASIC in Plain English*:

1. As you read this book, take time to look at the sample programs. They're pictures worth a thousand words each. Every minute you invest in thoughtful study of the examples will save you ten when you start writing code yourself.

2. The sample programs, taken in order, illustrate the building-block approach to programming. Our experience has shown this to be the easiest to learn and most efficient in putting out workable programs. The examples will get you off to a good start in your programming career.

3. When you come to an exercise, do it. Don't think it; *write* it. Sure, you've heard such advice before, but we mean it. Some people think programming is done on a keyboard. We're going to show you that the secret of programming is good use of paper and pencil.

4. You're going to wonder why, in a book about the use of PowerBASIC, you won't be working constantly on-screen. You will begin using the software in chapter 3, and you'll use PowerBASIC regularly throughout the book. But in the same way that karate instructors don't make their students begin with doing high kicks and splintering boards, we're going to ease you into actual use of Spectra's product.

   Like all sophisticated software, PowerBASIC can be difficult at the start. We're not giving you a cookbook (as in, "Do this, press that, do this, and don't make a single mistake or the machine will self-destruct!"). Rather, we're going to build your knowledge of PowerBASIC alongside your gradually increasing confidence in program design and structure.

5. You might not understand everything you read at first. Don't panic. Reread it several times; then go on.

   You may not feel ready to use each statement covered. Try using it anyway. Use it until you have a "feel" for how it works.

   There will be times when you won't see the point of an example—or times when you may think you do but will miss a deeper purpose. When this happens, focus on the big picture and ignore the details.

   In each case, do the exercises and go back to the original puzzler. If you still don't understand the item, note it and then go on. When you are through with the next chapter, go back to the original unclear topic and try again. If it's still not clear, go on to the next chapter, finish it, go back to the unclear point, and keep trying.

6. Don't memorize detail. Memorization of particulars gives false security; you need to focus on feeling comfortable with general ideas. No matter how many details you've learned perfectly, you will stumble onto a new problem . . . and then the best way out is to *think*.

Note:

Learning to program is like learning a foreign language. We *expect* that you won't understand everything fully in the beginning. And in a couple of places we *require* that you make some mistakes and then fix them, in order to gain confidence in your own conceptualizing and problem-solving abilities.

7. Don't worry that other people are using constructs, functions, commands, and program statements that you don't find in this book. Rather than explain six ways to do the same thing, the book selects the one or two that make the most sense to us. We find it better to use capably a limited number of tools and do a good job, rather than to decide which of the many tools might work and then look up and try to figure how to use the one that we picked.

8. Don't read what isn't there. It's hard not to project your own ideas onto what is read. But clear your mind each time you pick up the book and then read and understand *WHAT IS THERE.* (Nothing in this book is meant to be implied.)

9. We recommend that you read this book carefully and patiently now, program for several months, and then come back and page through it at your leisure. Many things that seem puzzling the first time through will appear very simple after you've had some experience in programming. Concepts become *real knowledge* after you've had to use them to solve actual problems.

The approach to computer programming in *PowerBASIC in Plain English* is not hard to master. You'll discover that program design is a simple matter once you've gotten the right orientation. You'll marvel at how easily you can write programs that require little correction once you've focused on *understanding the job to be done*, rather than on learning every trick in the programmer's bag. You might chuckle at the scenarios we present in the sample programs, but you'll feel proud of your own accomplishment when we turn things over to you.

1.4 BASIC AND COMPUTER PROGRAMMING

Among the many programming languages available, why is BASIC our language of choice?

1. Because it's everywhere. You and a lot of other people work primarily on personal computers. PCs routinely have BASIC bundled with the hardware—a good reason for the PC user to start with that language.

2. BASIC is better supported than any other programming language, meaning it's the one most frequently developed and most regularly upgraded by software producers.
3. Apart from being common, BASIC is also powerful. This was not always the case, as we'll see shortly. But today's BASICs (and there are several varieties) have plenty of power—meaning flexibility and processing capacity. There's no longer any sacrifice, as there once was, of power in exchange for ease of use.

And why use PowerBASIC, of the several varieties of BASIC around?

- **The environment.** In the PowerBASIC working environment, you never need to get out. You have all the tools you need to do everything right where you are.
- **The building-block process.** It encourages a step-by-step process, as opposed to just writing programs line after line. (As you'll see, PowerBASIC *forces* you to write well-defined routines and tasks as little blocks, which are then linked to form the larger program structure.)
- **The power.** It's one of the most powerful languages we've ever seen.

The environment. With PowerBASIC, you do your program writing, editing, running, and fine-tuning all in one on-screen workspace. This is conducive to working comfortably and productively. You don't have to exit your BASIC program to perform DOS operations, you don't have to go into another program to examine the contents of data files, and so on. Once you're in PowerBASIC, you'll get a lot done.

The building-block approach. The approach you'll learn in this book favors starting with a bare outline or block diagram and then filling in the blocks one at a time. You develop different sections of a program separately, testing all the while. Using this *structured programming method*, you can avoid the biggest source of errors in writing programs: confusion about where you are and what you should be doing.

With *PowerBASIC in Plain English*, you'll learn the wisdom of first defining the overall shape of a program and then filling in the pieces one at a time. You'll test the results of each developed block before going on to the next. This programming concept is far superior to jumping right in and writing program statements as fast as you can. The problem with jumping in and writing is that you're likely to be working in one part of the program when you remember something you'd like to add else-where. You then skip to that part and shoehorn in your modification, . . . but you lose track of what you were doing before that! And you probably also goofed up a routine that was working all right before you "enhanced" it!

The building-block approach gives you the discipline to say, "Let me finish this step in this block and test it, and *then* I'll go to the screen display block and develop that further." Actually, we hope that the approach in this book will make you say, "Never mind the fancy screen—let's get the program *working* and make it *pretty* later!"

One final surprise in our approach to program design: we believe in starting at the end and working backwards. Instead of leaping in and writing program line number one with no design at all, you're going to see the benefits of starting out by designing the *end* of the program—its output. (If you know the answer, you can choose the right questions to lead up to it!) Once the output is designed, the rest of the program can be specified on paper. Only when the program is "blueprinted" completely on paper do we begin the actual program writing. We're sure that after you've used this method a few times, you'll adopt it.

The power. While this book is an introduction to PowerBASIC, we can't begin to describe all of the advanced features that make business programming in PowerBASIC much easier than it is in most other languages. PowerBASIC is an industrial-strength language, easy for a beginner to use but designed for serious applications.

1.5 A BIT ABOUT BASIC

Before we finish this chapter, we need to say a few words about the origins and development of BASIC.

The Beginner's All-purpose Symbolic Instruction Code (B-A-S-I-C) was born at Dartmouth College in the early 1960s. It was designed to be a friendly, easy-to-use method of writing programs and getting results quickly. Previously, students used to keypunch their programs onto cards, submit them to the computer operator, and then wait—usually overnight—to see the results of their work. Often, the program failed to run because a card had been miskeyed (perhaps a single error in keypunching). The student would correct the error by punching a new card, resubmit the program, and wait again. BASIC promised to change all that. It would allow programs to be tested, corrected, and run again almost instantaneously.

Because it was easy to learn and use, BASIC quickly became popular in university settings. Since Dartmouth was using a General Electric computer, GE got interested in this new, "high-level" language. (High-level means that it resembled human language; the programmer could say things like **PRINT,** rather than use numerical or very technical instructions.) BASIC's instant-gratification features made it a hit with GE, and the company soon introduced it to commercial customers. Time-sharing BASIC (in which people at teletype terminals shared the use of a large computer) became a big success.

Thus in universities, business offices, and companies of all kinds, BASIC caught on as a way for nonscientific people to get immediate results with a computer. No more waiting three to six months for a programmer to come in, write a program, send and re-send it to the computer for testing, and eventually turn it over to the people who requested it, to see if the output was useful.

Early BASIC had both hardware and software limitations, though. It could only be used with a teletype keyboard for input and a teletype printer for output. BASIC couldn't "use" disk files as we know them today. It could not test data being keyed in, and it didn't have "nice" printout capabilities.

But hardware capabilities blossomed. As minicomputers were introduced in the early 1970s, they came with BASIC as a standard language— and a powerful one at that. The computer manufacturers and the software development companies rushed to add features to "their" BASICs. BASIC became increasingly popular for writing business programs.

Then came the personal computer. The BASIC that was bundled with a PC was as powerful as any business-oriented language around. By the early 1980s, BASIC programs were being written by millions of people—professional programmers and do-it-yourselfers alike. The Dartmouth language succeeded. Even people with no technical knowledge of computers could make the machine do what they wanted.

BASIC has become the most popular computer language in the world. As we suggested, it's an absolutely natural choice for anyone's beginning programming language.

1.6 DEFINITION OF A PROGRAM

In the spirit of BASIC, here's a simple, nontechnical definition of a program:

> A program is a series of statements (precisely worded instructions) that the computer looks at one at a time and carries out one at a time until it achieves the end result: a "report."

(A "report," as used throughout this book, means any data that is put out [or output] on any medium, such as paper, computer screen, or computer floppy or hard disks.)

CHAPTER SUMMARY

1. Look at the sample programs.
2. Build your knowledge a block at a time.
3. Do the exercises, don't just glance at them.
4. This isn't a cookbook, it's an education in programming.
5. Reread topics and use the examples and exercises to clarify them.
6. Don't memorize detail—grasp the concepts.
7. Don't get confused with a *BIG BAG* of programming tools. We'll build a small tool kit of useful tools.
8. Don't read what isn't there. The author is expressing simple concepts and rules. The hardest part of programming is to think simply. Begin that training in simplicity as you read this book.
9. Reread this book several months from now. You'll get a lot more than you did the first time.

THE BOTTOM LINE

(This is the first in a series of the major points of each chapter. At the end of each chapter, we will repeat the major point of each of the preceding chapters and then add the main message from the one just finished. It's building your knowledge a block at a time and repeating the previous chapters so you don't forget them. Here is your first block.)

1. **BASIC is a personable language, which tells your computer to follow your instructions one at a time until it has produced a desired "report."**

Chapter 2

A BASIC Picture (Is Worth a Few Statements)

2.1 Bikes Peak _____ **14**

2.2 BASIC Programs _____ **15**

2.3 A Note on Conventions _____ **19**

2.4 A Simple Program to Average Three Numbers _____ **22**

2.5 A Note on Reading Programs _____ **23**

2.6 What a Menu Program Does _____ **24**

2.7 Bikes Peak Menu program _____ **25**

Remember the shed example from chapter 1? Take the fiasco one step further.

- Imagine trying to build a shed without ever having seen one.
- Think about a dressmaker trying to make a dress, never having seen it, without a pattern.
- Or imagine putting a jigsaw puzzle together without seeing the picture of it completed.

It would be the same if we were to ask you to write a program, never having seen one. So this chapter briefly explains a couple of programs and shows you what they look like. It also explains the conventions used in this book for keyboard commands, programs, and text.

You'll also meet the folks at Bikes Peak. This imaginary company was started by three entrepreneurs who wanted to make a better mountain bike—and be the best mountain bike company. They're going to need programs to computerize the paperwork in their business. And you're going to work alongside their programmer to write their programs.

2.1 BIKES PEAK

To relate this book to real life, we've made up a company called Bikes Peak, and all the programs in this book will be written for that company.

Art, Barb, and Chuck are three creative thinkers who have designed a better mountain bike: lighter, stronger, faster, sexier. They've set up shop in an old barn (on top of a mountain, naturally), where they assemble custom-crafted components themselves. When a bike's done, they sell it. When a customer has a problem, the three fix it. They love their work, and they make a living at it.

Trouble is, they're not very business-minded (we said they're creative types, right?). So after a couple of years of getting the business off the ground and getting their bikes out to dealers in the area, Art, Barb, and Chuck have discovered that they're *just barely* making a living at it. Like many small businesses founded on a good idea and a good product, Bikes Peak faces some tough decisions.

They need to get their books in order. If they're going to commit Bikes Peak to increased production and a wider dealer (and supplier) network, they've got to systematize the recordkeeping. Inventory is going to get more complicated than, "Oversize down tubes are behind the furnace." Customer lists are going to get more involved than, "Shelly what's-her-name came in after her cousin Phil bought an M3." And it looks as if the payroll is going to get more complex than, "A, B, and C divvy up the proceeds at the end of each month."

They've bought a computer.

That doesn't guarantee anything, of course. (Many an inept businessperson has floundered after buying a computer and using it improperly, or not at all.) But they have seen how friends with small businesses have gotten a better grasp of both their finances and their operations through proper software and conscientious recordkeeping. For creative types, there's something very reassuring about turning the numbers over to a reliable, fast, methodical machine.

What do Art, Barb, and Chuck have for software? Nothing, yet, except Spectra's Power BASIC—and a friend, Donna, who is a free-lance programmer.

2.2 BASIC PROGRAMS

2.2.1 Four Statements We Need for Our First Programs

BASIC programs are made up of statements that instruct the computer to do operations like—

- get data from the keyboard,
- display data on the computer screen,
- print data onto paper,
- perform calculations on data,
- get data from a disk,
- put data onto a disk,
- go to a statement number (other than the next one in line), and so on.

Rather than go into detail on each statement type, we're going to look briefly at the **PRINT, INPUT, GOTO,** and calculation statements. Then we'll put together a small program using these four statements.

Note:

Grasp the general idea of this section. Don't try to understand the detail of the statements, or the programs; we'll cover them thoroughly in later chapters.

2.2.1.1 PRINT

The **PRINT** statement displays data and text labels onto the computer screen. (We'll cover data and data names completely in chapter 5.) For the first example, assume that **price** has a value of 9.95. Then the statement

```
PRINT "The cost will be"; price
```

will display

```
The cost will be 9.95
```

onto the computer screen. In this example, the data is 9.95, and the text label is "The cost will be".

The statement

PRINT "Inventory Report for Bikes Peak"

will display:

Inventory Report for Bikes Peak

onto the computer screen. In this example, there is no data, only the text label "Inventory Report for Bikes Peak".

The statement

PRINT price

will display

9.95

onto the computer screen. In this example, there is no text label, only the data value of 9.95 contained in **price**.

2.2.1.2 INPUT

The **INPUT** statement is used to get data into a computer program using the keyboard. When an **INPUT** statement is executed in a BASIC program, the computer stops and waits for data to be typed in from the keyboard.

The statement

INPUT "Please enter a new retail amount"; price

displays this on the computer screen:

Please enter a new retail amount ?

and waits for the operator to key in a value, which it puts into the data name **price**.

The statement

INPUT price

displays this on the computer screen:

?

and waits for the operator to key in a value, which it puts into the data name **price**.

2.2.1.3 GOTO

The **GOTO** statement tells the computer to go to a statement (other than the next one down) in the program. (Program flow is covered completely in chapter 4. The **GOTO** statement is explained in chapter 7.)
The statement

GOTO calcprice

causes the computer to go to the statement line that has the name **calcprice:** as the first 10 characters in the line.

2.2.1.4 Calculations

Calculations in BASIC are represented in the same way that formulas are shown on paper, with $+$, $-$, $*$, and $/$ representing add, subtract, multiply, and divide, respectively:

c = 10

gives **c** a value of 10,

b = c * 3

results in **b** having a value of 30 (since **c** has a value of 10)

a = b + (c / 5)

gives **a** the value of 32 (when **b** is 30 and **c** is 10)
Now that you have seen a few statement types, we'll go on to statement "labels." A label is either a name or a number that uniquely identifies a line in BASIC. It is always at the beginning of the line.

2.2.2 Numbering the Lines

You have probably seen BASIC programs where each line started with a number:

```
100 INPUT "Enter a value for the cost "; price
110 retailprice = price * 1.5
120 PRINT"Cost is "; price,"Selling price is "; retailprice
130 GOTO 100
```

That's no longer the case. BASIC has improved a lot in a few short years. Every statement line in a program doesn't need to have a unique number in front of it.

However, any statement line that is referred to by any other statement in a program does need to have a label of some kind as the first characters in the line. You have two choices in labeling a statement in BASIC:

1. Give a statement line a *name*. For example,

   ```
   nextcost: INPUT "Enter a value for the cost "; price
   ```

2. Use a *number*. For example,

   ```
   100 INPUT "Enter a value for the cost "; price
   ```

In PowerBASIC you can mix statement line names and numbers at will, provided that all statement labels remain unique. We recommend *naming* lines for readability by the programmer. (Every program actually has two readers: the computer and the programmer.)

In some ways, the computer is pretty smart. It can find statement lines anywhere, easily and quickly, and it can remember where it has found everything. It makes no difference to the computer if you name, or number, statement lines. The task is a breeze, so long as each statement label is unique.

People however, are smart in a different way. Programmers (you included) see, classify, link, and retain information differently from the way computers do. We can figure out that a statement numbered 450 comes somewhere after number 80. We can also guess that statement 450 is roughly halfway through a program whose line numbers run from 10 to 1000. If we look at a lengthy program often enough, we can remember that the routine (a specially defined block in the program) that error-checks keyboard input begins at line 400.

2.2.2.1 Why Use Numbers?

But you, the programmer, won't retain that sort of information for long. If you come back to the program after a lapse of 15 months—or even after one short but busy week—will you remember at what number the error-checking routine begins?

Time and memory aside, lengthy or complex programs are hard to scan. As the programmer, you need to be able to look at a printout of your work and follow the "flow" of the program logic. Yet in almost every program, the logical flow is different from the printed sequence of the statement lines. Control typically jumps back and forth a great deal. So we don't feel that you should use numbers. It is too hard to remember which numbers may represent several dozen routines in a big program. And when you're working with several programs, the number 1700 probably represents something different in each program.

2.2.2.2 Why Use Names?

That's where *names* are useful tools for memorization and comprehension. You can understand that "errorcheck" is a followup routine to the "keyboardinput" routine. You can probably skim even a long printout and spot those names more easily than you can associate the two routines with lines having numbers such as 1100 and 2300. Besides that, you don't have any numbers to keep in order when you reorganize your program, or add a new routine.

As the programmer, the choice between names and numbers is yours. But throughout this book we'll be using line names as labels much more frequently than line numbers, for the reasons we've given above. Later on, as you gain experience, you may consider setting your own rules for using one or the other, or both. Ultimately, the test is whether your choice helps *you* (rather than your computer—it'll work either way) make better sense of your programs.

2.3 A NOTE ON CONVENTIONS

Before we look at some BASIC programs, we need to set six ground rules on how certain words will appear in this book:

- First, we need to show a program line that is too long to fit onto one line in this book.
- We may have to ask you to type in a specific word at the keyboard.
- We have to indicate that the word or words to be typed in will depend on the circumstances of the program.
- Sometimes we have to show that a word in the middle of a sentence is part of a program statement, and not part of the sentence you're reading.
- In our discussions we'll need to distinguish between words the computer always recognizes as "commands" and words that are not "commands."
- Sometimes we simply want to show emphasis on a word in the text.

To do all of this clearly, let's set six conventions on how such words will appear throughout this book.

2.3.1 Conventions in the BASIC Programs in This Book

A PowerBASIC program line can be up to 248 characters long. We can't fit that on one line in this book. So we will end a program line with _ to show that it is continued onto the next line:

```
PRINT custlastnam$; TAB(20); custfirstnam$; TAB(35); custdob; _
TAB(45); custphone#; TAB(60); custlastsale
```

2.3.2 Conventions in the Keyboard Instructions

1. Any time you (or the program user) are asked to press a particular key, the word PRESS will appear capitalized, and the key name is put within angle brackets, like this:

   PRESS ⟨CAPS LOCK⟩
   PRESS ⟨SPACE⟩
   PRESS ⟨TAB⟩⟨TAB⟩⟨TAB⟩⟨TAB⟩ (press TAB 4 times)
   PRESS ⟨RETURN⟩ = PRESS ⟨ENTER⟩
   PRESS ⟨SHIFT + F2⟩ = PRESS ⟨SHIFT⟩ (and hold it as you)
   PRESS ⟨F2⟩

2. Any time you are asked to type in specific word(s), the word TYPE will appear capitalized, and the words to be typed are in bold print, like this:

    TYPE **Good Morning** ⟨ENTER⟩
    TYPE **9.95** ⟨ENTER⟩

3. Normally at the end of each TYPE instruction, you will press the ENTER key (which is the same as the RETURN key). If for any reason you or the program user should *not* press ENTER or RETURN, ⟨ENTER⟩ will not appear at the end of the line. In such a case, the examples above would appear as:

    TYPE **Good Morning**
    TYPE **9.95**

4. To save space and keep the examples clear, we may use TYPE just once to ask you to TYPE several lines:

    TYPE: **Good morning**⟨ENTER⟩
          Good evening⟨ENTER⟩
          Good night⟨ENTER⟩

5. You'll occasionally see the following brackets around words: { }. They will bracket some text, usually a generic term (such as "filename"). Don't type the word or words that actually appear within the brackets; instead, you'll type the *specific values* that are determined by your activity. Here are two sample statements, with an example of how you might type each statement:

    TYPE **{today's date}**

    You type the date, as in:

    010189

    TYPE **GOSUB {name of subroutine}**

    You type the name of a subroutine, such as:

    GOSUB printmenu

2.3.3 Conventions in the Text of This Book

1. The words that the computer always recognizes as "commands" to do something (called "reserved words" in BASIC, since they

are reserved only for BASIC's use, and not yours) will appear capitalized and boldfaced within the sentences, like this:

PRINT
INPUT
IF ... THEN ... ELSE ...
GOTO

A complete list of reserved words in PowerBASIC is found in Appendix B.

2. If the computer does not recognize a word as a "command," it assumes that the word is something whose value can change with the program. These "variable names" (all the words in the program that are not reserved words) will appear in lowercase and boldfaced like this:

price
retailprice
lastname$

3. What's left over to show general emphasis in the text? Simple italics:

Warning! File will be erased!
You must *never* turn off the machine . . .

2.4 A SIMPLE PROGRAM TO AVERAGE THREE NUMBERS

Here are three versions of a program that—

- Asks for three numbers to be input via keyboard,
- Averages them, and
- Displays the answer on the computer screen.

One version has numbered lines, one has named lines, and one has both numbered and named line labels. They all do the exact same thing in the same way. Look at each version, then study the one that's most clear for you, and try to understand how it works. (You'll be typing this program and running it in the next chapter.)

1. With Numbered Lines:

```
100 INPUT"Key in the first number ";num1
110 INPUT"Key in the second number ";num2
120 INPUT"Key in the third number ";num3
140 avg = (num1 + num2 + num3)/3
150 PRINT num1;num2;num3;"***";avg
160 GOTO 100
```

2. With Named Lines:

```
getnext:
INPUT"Key in the first number ";num1
INPUT"Key in the second number ";num2
INPUT"Key in the third number ";num3
avg = (num1 + num2 + num3)/3
PRINT num1;num2;num3;"***";avg
GOTO getnext
```

3. With Both Named and Numbered Lines:

```
getnext:
INPUT"Key in the first number ";num1
110 INPUT"Key in the second number ";num2
120 INPUT"Key in the third number ";num3
140 avg = (num1 + num2 + num3)/3
150 PRINT num1;num2;num3;"***";avg
160 GOTO getnext
```

2.5 A NOTE ON READING PROGRAMS

A first look at any large, unfamiliar program is like looking at the cockpit of a 747. How do you make sense of it all?

Don't Panic.
Break it up into small, manageable pieces.
Look at the **REM** statements.
Remember that every program has only three functions.

1. Take it slowly. Take a few breaths, get a cup of coffee, get up and walk to another office. Relax, and convince yourself that you can do it; because you can. After 26 years of programming, the initial reaction is always the same to me, and this first step is always necessary.

2. Using a pencil, draw blocks around what seem to be the sections or logic groups (statements that seem to belong together because they are the same kind of statement, because they comprise an identifiable routine, or because they are all indented the same). Very simply (in a few simple words), try to identify what each block does.

3. Look at the **REM** statements, which are really comments, or **REM**arks, to help the programmer understand how the program works.

4. Remember that every program

   a. Brings data in,
   b. Processes it, and
   c. Puts out some kind of report (on screen, to the printer, or onto disk).

2.6 WHAT A MENU PROGRAM DOES

The next program that you're going to see is called a "menu" program. It's known as a menu program because its purpose is to display a "menu" of choices onto the screen, from which the computer user (operator) picks one selection. In our case, we're going to ask the operator which program he or she wants to run.

A menu program does three things:

Step 1
Displays the menu—Displays on the computer screen several possible selections from which to choose.

Step 2

Prompts for selection—Asks for and accepts input from the keyboard that determines which item (in our case, program) is selected.

Step 3

Runs the selection—Runs the selected program.

2.7 BIKES PEAK MENU PROGRAM

Here are three versions of the Bikes Peak Menu Program, which displays the program menu choices, prompts you to enter a selection, and then runs that selection. One version has numbered lines, one has named lines, and one has both numbered and named lines. They all function in exactly the same way. Look at each version, then study the one that's most clear for you, and try to understand how it works. (You'll also be typing this program and running it in the next chapter.)

1. With numbered lines:

```
  10   REM -- program "firsmenu.bas" -- created 010189
 500   GOSUB 1000 : REM -- perform the print routine
 520   INPUT "Number from menu"; menuselect$ : REM -- Step #2 Asks for the selection
 530   program$ = "bikes" + menuselect$ :REM -- form the program name
 540   PRINT "Selecting program "; program$
 550   CHAIN program$ : REM -- Step #3-runs that program
 990   END
1000   REM -- printmenu (Step #1- displays the menu)
1010      CLS : REM -- clear the screen
1020      PRINT "* * * * * BIKES PEAK * * * * * *"
1030      PRINT "* * * * * PROGRAMS * * * * * *"
1040      FOR c = 1 TO 5: PRINT: NEXT c : REM -- space 5 lines
1050      PRINT "1 Inventory"
1060      PRINT "2 Customers"
1070      PRINT "3 Mail List"
1080      PRINT "4 Order Processing"
```

```
1090     PRINT "5 Monthlies"
1100     FOR c = 1 TO 4: PRINT: NEXT c : REM -- space 4 lines
1120     RETURN
```

2. Lines with numbers, and others with names:

```
10   REM -- program "firsmenu.bas" -- created 010189
500   GOSUB printmenu : REM -- perform the print routine
520   INPUT "Number from menu"; menuselect$ : REM -- Step #2 Asks for the selection
530   program$ = "bikes" + menuselect$ :REM -- form the program name
540   PRINT "Selecting program "; program$
550   CHAIN program$ : REM -- Step #3-runs that program
990   END
printmenu:
   REM -- (Step #1- displays the menu)
   CLS : REM -- clear the screen
   PRINT "* * * * * BIKES PEAK * * * * * *"
   PRINT "* * * * * PROGRAMS * * * * * *"
   FOR c = 1 TO 5: PRINT: NEXT c : REM -- space 5 lines
   PRINT "1 Inventory"
   PRINT "2 Customers"
   PRINT "3 Mail List"
   PRINT "4 Order Processing"
   PRINT "5 Monthlies"
   FOR c = 1 TO 4: PRINT: NEXT c : REM -- space 4 lines
RETURN
```

3. Without line numbers:

```
REM -- program "firsmenu.bas" -- created 010189
   GOSUB printmenu : REM -- perform the print routine
   INPUT "Number from menu"; menuselect$ : REM -- Step #2 Asks for the selection
   program$ = "bikes" + menuselect$ :REM -- form the program name
   PRINT "Selecting program "; program$
   CHAIN program$ : REM -- Step #3-runs that program
   END
printmenu:
   REM -- (Step #1- displays the menu)
   CLS : REM -- clear the screen
   PRINT "* * * * * BIKES PEAK * * * * * *"
   PRINT "* * * * * PROGRAMS * * * * * *"
```

```
FOR c = 1 TO 5: PRINT: NEXT c : REM -- space 5 lines
PRINT "1 Inventory"
PRINT "2 Customers"
PRINT "3 Mail List"
PRINT "4 Order Processing"
PRINT "5 Monthlies"
FOR c = 1 TO 4: PRINT: NEXT c : REM -- space 4 lines
RETURN
```

This program has two main sections (or three, if you broke it up that far):

- The **printmenu** section, which displayed the menu
- The prompt for and running of the selection.

Recall what we said in chapter 1 about not instantly understanding everything you read in this book. You don't have to worry about what goes on in each statement line; that's not the purpose of the examples. What we want you to understand is that the three versions above are functionally identical. The statements are correct, the logic is valid, and the computer will perform the **printmenu** routine exactly the same way in all three cases.

By the way, if you have a "feel" for how the Menu program works, great!! Go back for an even closer look and try to figure out more of the detail.

If you have no "feel" for the Menu program, clear your mind of the program and go on. You'll have the feel by the end of the next chapter.

CHAPTER SUMMARY

1. Use names for line labels.
2. When looking at a program for the first time:
   - Don't panic.
   - Draw blocks around the apparent sections. Identify what each block does.
   - Look at the REM statements.

3. A menu program is a way to set a group of programs up so that a computer user can easily run the program that he or she wants.

THE BOTTOM LINE

---

1. BASIC is a personable language, which tells your computer to follow your instructions one at a time until it has produced a desired "report."

2. **When you look at a BASIC program, break it up into sections, using the block-line method. Then look at each block, one at a time, to figure out what each does.**

EXERCISES

1. On a piece of paper, rewrite the first program in this chapter to average six numbers, rather than three, and print out the results.

2. Rewrite the Menu program (on paper) to print three additional program selections:

6	Special Sales
7	Service Bulletins
8	Forecasting

Chapter 3

PowerBASIC (Your First Workout)

3.1 Starting PowerBASIC (and Bailing Out) _____ **31**

3.2 Typing in a Program _____ **33**

3.3 Saving a Program _____ **38**

3.4 Opening an Existing Program _____ **40**

3.5 Testing a Program by Running It _____ **42**

3.6 The PowerBASIC Environment _____ **45**

3.7 Setting PowerBASIC Options _____ **45**

Ever try to work on your car, lawn mower, or washing machine without having all the right tools at your fingertips? You figure out what the problem is and start the tedious, complex procedure to fix it (about 74 steps), when you find that you need a tool that isn't there.

So you go off to find where your spouse, kid, or sibling put the tool the last time he or she used it. After wasting only 45 minutes, you've got it. Now you go back to your repair job, and—you've forgotten at what stage you were. So you start at the beginning, checking each little detail to see where you left off. You find where you are, get a little further, and need a washer.

You stop work, get the washer, and repeat the previous step of checking your work. . . . In this situation, you find that you waste more time than you spend actually working.

Programming is a lot like a complex repair task. There are thousands of detailed steps, and you must always be aware at what stage you are. But PowerBASIC provides you with the tools and the working environment to accomplish your programming task without wasting time and searching for tools. Once you begin programming in PowerBASIC, you never need to leave it until you take a break or finish. It also gives you good methods of checking your work. We'll start using it in this chapter.

This morning, we're working with Donna to write the menu program, which you've already seen. From this opening menu all of Bikes Peak's other programs will be selected.

As a graduate of our Super Programmer Institute, she knows the approach. For each programming task, she starts at the end, asks herself a series of questions, and works backwards:

Q: What is the purpose of the menu program?
A: To produce a menu listing all of Bikes Peak's programs, from which one program can be selected to run. It will "chain" (pass program control) to whatever program the user selects from the menu, thus automatically starting that new program. (This and other operations will be covered later; for this chapter, we'll pay attention to just the on-screen menu)
Q: What are the end results or output report(s) produced?
A: A menu of programs on screen.
Q: What input does she need to write this report?
A: The name of each program selectable by the computer user—for now:

- Inventory
- Customers
- Mail List
- Order Processing
- Monthly Reports

(As the Bikes Peak system grows, she'll add new names to the menu.)

Again, because Donna wants you to ease into writing BASIC, she's proposed that we do the menu in a quick-and-simple version to get the flavor of how it's done. It will only take a few minutes to do so, and you'll see quickly that it runs and works. Then she and you will return to the program in future chapters to make the actual opening menu for Bikes Peak.

We'd like you to follow along, on your own computer, as Donna writes the sample opening menu program for Bikes Peak. (Once again, don't worry about understanding everything you do. And if you run into trouble, don't panic. We'll show you right away how to exit and restart, so you can always back up and try again.)

3.1 STARTING POWERBASIC (AND BAILING OUT)

A directory on a computer disk is similar to a chapter in a book. Directories are normally set up to separate different kinds of programs, just as chapters in a book cover different topics. We assume you've set up PowerBASIC in its own directory. (If you followed the instructions in chapter 1 of the PowerBASIC manual it will be in directory *pb*.) Now, get into the PowerBASIC directory and type "pb". For example,

> TYPE **cd\pb**⟨ENTER⟩ (get into the PowerBASIC directory)
> **pb**⟨ENTER⟩ (run PowerBASIC)

(If you have any problem getting PowerBASIC started, check file directories to locate the correct directory; consult your DOS and PowerBASIC reference manuals if necessary.)

Once PowerBASIC has started up, the screen you see is the workspace of PowerBASIC. The large opening is the window in which you'll write and edit your programs. There's nothing in the working (editing) window right now, so it's labeled **noname.bas.** At the bottom of the screen is a smaller opening, labeled *Watch.* You'll learn more about it in chapter 8.

You now have at your fingertips a lot of PowerBASIC commands. To make it easier to list and select from the possible choices, they've been combined into several general groups. The names of the groups are listed across the top of the screen (see Figure 3.1).

The group labels across the top of the screen are your *alternatives* in choosing what you'll be doing with PowerBASIC. Hence, they are always accessed by means of the ALT key. (If you use a mouse, you just point to the label of the alternative you want to select and click.)

For your first exercise in using PowerBASIC, we want to achieve four important goals:

1. Show you how to get out of PowerBASIC
2. Get you back into PowerBASIC so you can create a new program file
3. Save the program
4. Run the program

Getting into and out of PowerBASIC means getting into and out of some program file. So our first alternative selection is the *File* group. *File* is reverse-highlighted. PowerBASIC is ready to perform whatever *File*

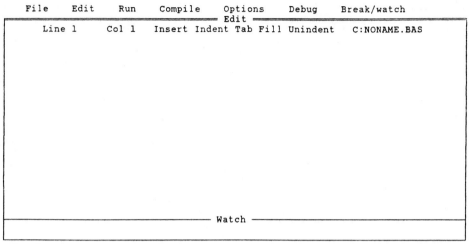

Figure 3.1

operation you and Donna select from the *File* menu. To confirm that *File* is your chosen alternative,

PRESS ⟨ENTER⟩

The third entry on the menu of *File* operations, *New*, is eventually what Donna wants to do. But first, we want to show you how to get out

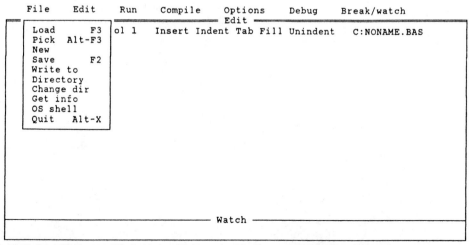

Figure 3.2

of PowerBASIC. Notice that the last entry on the File menu is *Quit*. One easy way to get out of PowerBASIC is to type the first letter, which is highlighted in the word ***Q****uit*.

TYPE **q**⟨ENTER⟩

And you're out! Another way that you can exit PowerBASIC at any time, without using the *File* menu, is

PRESS ⟨ALT + **x**⟩

So remember, in the beginning, if you become confused and want to start typing the program all over, you have a ready alternative. That is, from within PowerBASIC, you can press ALT and then type x (for *E*xit), and you're out.

3.2 TYPING IN A PROGRAM

Now, let's reenter PowerBASIC:

TYPE **pb**

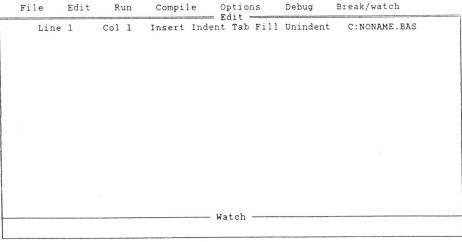

```
     File    Edit    Run    Compile    Options    Debug    Break/watch
    ═══════════════════════════════════════ Edit ═══════════════════════════
        Line 1      Col 1    Insert Indent Tab Fill Unindent    C:NONAME.BAS




















                                  ─ Watch ─
    ─────────────────────────────────────────────────────────────────────────
    F1-Help  F5-Zoom  F6-Switch  F7-Trace  F8-Step  F9-Compile F10-Menu
```

Figure 3.3

To clear the work area for a new program file, pull down the *File* menu:

PRESS ⟨ENTER⟩

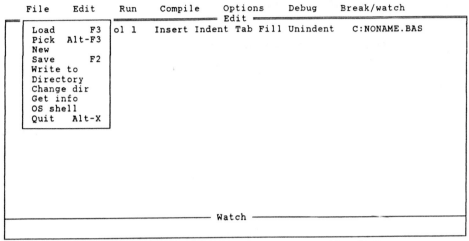

```
     File    Edit    Run    Compile   Options   Debug   Break/watch
 ┌─────────────────────────── Edit ═════════════════════════════════┐
 ╔═════════════╗ ol 1   Insert Indent Tab Fill Unindent   C:NONAME.BAS
 ║ Load     F3 ║
 ║ Pick Alt-F3 ║
 ║ New         ║
 ║ Save     F2 ║
 ║ Write to    ║
 ║ Directory   ║
 ║ Change dir  ║
 ║ Get info    ║
 ║ OS shell    ║
 ║ Quit  Alt-X ║
 ╚═════════════╝
 │
 │
 │
 │                           ──── Watch ────
 └───────────────────────────────────────────────────────────────────┘
  F1-Help  F5-Zoom  F6-Switch  F7-Trace  F8-Step  F9-Compile F10-Menu
```

Figure 3.4

Move down to the third selection, the one Donna wants, and press ENTER:

PRESS ⟨ENTER⟩

```
     File    Edit    Run    Compile   Options   Debug   Break/watch
 ┌─────────────────────────── Edit ═════════════════════════════════┐
      Line 1      Col 1    Insert Indent Tab Fill Unindent   C:NONAME.BAS




 │
 │
 │
 │
 │
 │                           ──── Watch ────
 └───────────────────────────────────────────────────────────────────┘
  F1-Help  F5-Zoom  F6-Switch  F7-Trace  F8-Step  F9-Compile F10-Menu
```

Figure 3.5

Now,

⟨RIGHT ARROW⟩

to move to the *Edit* selection, and

PRESS ⟨ENTER⟩

At the top right of the screen, it says you're now working on a program called **noname.bas.** The cursor is in the top left corner of PowerBASIC's working (editing) window, ready for you to begin typing the program you'll be creating. Donna has a certain convention she always follows in writing the first line of a newly created program; you should use it, too.

TYPE **rem -- program "firsmenu.bas"** {**today's date**}⟨ENTER⟩

A **REM**ark statement of this form, which includes the program name and the date of creation, will be the first line of every program.
OK. Let's type the statement lines that follow the **REM** statement.

3.2.1 Guidelines for Typing in PowerBASIC Programs

As you type in program statements, keep a few guidelines in mind:

1. *Save yourself grief and time: carefully read the text below and type the statements exactly.* Watch your spacing and punctuation. A colon (:) looks a lot like a semicolon (;), but if you substitute one for the other PowerBASIC will be quick to point it out.

2. You can always correct a mistake before seeing an error message by using the ARROW keys, BACKSPACE, and/or DELETE.

Now you're going to see how easily the building-block approach of PowerBASIC works. The first statement of your program will signal that you'll be calling a block (routine) from within the main block.

TYPE **call printmenu**⟨ENTER⟩

3.2.2 Writing a Routine within a Program

Now,

> PRESS ⟨ENTER⟩

to leave a blank line before typing the routine. Then

> TYPE **sub printmenu**⟨ENTER⟩

You now should type in your routine and then go back and finish writing the main program.
On screen you now have the following information:

```
        File     Edit     Run     Compile     Options     Debug     Break/watch
                                            ═ Edit ═
        Line 4       Col 14   Insert Indent Tab Fill Unindent * C:NONAME.BAS
rem -- program "firsmenu.bas" 10190
call printmenu

sub printmenu




                                    ─ Watch ─

  Fl-Help  F5-Zoom  F6-Switch  F7-Trace  F8-Step  F9-Compile Fl0-Menu
```
Figure 3.6

Go ahead and type in the following statements of the routine (beginning right at the present cursor position, just below the line **sub printmenu**):

> TYPE: **cls**⟨ENTER⟩
>   **print "* * * * * BIKES PEAK * * * * * *"**⟨ENTER⟩
>   **print "* * * * * PROGRAMS * * * * * *"**⟨ENTER⟩
>   **print**⟨ENTER⟩

print "1 Inventory"⟨ENTER⟩
print "2 Customers"⟨ENTER⟩
print "3 Mail List"⟨ENTER⟩
print "4 Sales"⟨ENTER⟩
print "5 Monthly Reports"⟨ENTER⟩
end sub⟨ENTER⟩

You've just typed your first routine in PowerBASIC! You should now see the following statements on screen:

```
  File    Edit    Run    Compile    Options    Debug    Break/watch
══════════════════════════════════════ Edit ══════════════════════
      Line 12    Col 1    Insert Indent Tab Fill Unindent    C:NONAME.BAS
rem -- program "firsmenu.bas" 10190
call printmenu

sub printmenu
cls
print"* * * * *   BIKES PEAK    * * * * * *"
print"* * * * *    PROGRAMS     * * * * * *"
for c = 1 to 5: print: next c
print "1 Inventory"
print "2 Customers"
print "3 Mail List"
print "4 Sales"
print "5 Monthlies"
end sub



─────────────────────────── Watch ───────────────────────────


F1-Help  F5-Zoom  F6-Switch  F7-Trace  F8-Step  F9-Compile F10-Menu
```

Figure 3.7

Now that the routine is complete (and hopefully error-free), we want to go back and finish writing the main part of the program, which has called the routine. First, we're going to type in the rest of **firsmenu.bas.** We need to move the cursor back up to the beginning of the first blank line below the **call printmenu** line by using the arrow keys. Now enter the following:

TYPE **print**⟨ENTER⟩
input "Enter Number from Menu";menuselect$⟨ENTER⟩
program$ = "bikes"+menuselect$⟨ENTER⟩
print "Selecting program ";program$⟨ENTER⟩
chain program$⟨ENTER⟩
END⟨ENTER⟩

In order to see the whole program clearly, we'll

PRESS⟨F5⟩

to zoom the edit window. The program should look like this:

```
    File    Edit    Run    Compile    Options    Debug    Break/watch
       Line 9     Col 1    Insert Indent Tab Fill Unindent * C:NONAME.BAS
rem -- program "firsmenu.bas" 10190
call printmenu
print:print:print:print
input"Enter Number from Menu";menuselect$
program$ = "bikes" + menuselect$
print"Selecting program ";program$
chain program$
END

sub printmenu
cls
print"* * * * *  BIKES PEAK   * * * * *"
print"* * * * *   PROGRAMS    * * * * *"
for c = 1 to 5: print: next c
print "1 Inventory"
print "2 Customers"
print "3 Mail List"
print "4 Sales"
print "5 Monthlies"
end sub


  F1-Help  F5-Zoom  F6-Switch  F7-Trace  F8-Step  F9-Compile F10-Menu
```

Figure 3.8

3.3 SAVING A PROGRAM

Now Donna saves the program. She knows that Murphy's Law applies especially to computer programming, so she always saves a program *before* running it. (Any number of things can cause a program to hang up, losing all the programming work done up to that point, and you'll have to start over.) Before we save the program, let's change its name. Move the cursor to the first line of the program and replace **firsmenu.bas** with

TYPE **bikemenu.bas 010189**⟨ENTER⟩

The screen now should look like this:

```
        File    Edit    Run    Compile   Options   Debug   Break/watch
        Line 1      Col 1    Insert Indent Tab Fill Unindent  C:BIKEMENU.BAS
rem -- program "bikemenu.bas" 10190
call printmenu
print:print:print:print
input"Enter Number from Menu";menuselect$
program$ = "bikes" + menuselect$
print"Selecting program ";program$
chain program$
END

sub printmenu
cls
print"* * * * *  BIKES PEAK   * * * * * *"
print"* * * * *   PROGRAMS    * * * * * *"
for c = 1 to 5: print: next c
print "1 Inventory"
print "2 Customers"
print "3 Mail List"
print "4 Sales"
print "5 Monthlies"
end sub


    F1-Help  F5-Zoom  F6-Switch  F7-Trace  F8-Step  F9-Compile F10-Menu
```

Figure 3.9

Now go to the *File* menu:

PRESS ⟨ALT + **f**⟩
PRESS ⟨ENTER⟩

You now see the *File* menu, which offers two ways of saving a program to a file. The first time you save a program, select the second one, ***Write to***:

TYPE **w**
(OR PRESS ⟨DOWN ARROW⟩ 4 TIMES, then PRESS ⟨ENTER⟩)

The *Write to* box pops up.
The cursor is now inside a *New Name* box, waiting for you to type in the file name to be saved. Let's use **bikemenu** as the file name.

TYPE **bikemenu**⟨ENTER⟩

PowerBASIC saves this starter menu program under that name. It also changes the title of the program you've created, as you can see at the top right of the editing window.

```
     File     Edit     Run    Compile    Options    Debug    Break/watch
                              1 21  Insert Indent Tab Fill Unindent  *  C:NONAME.BAS
rem  Load      F3    emenu.bas"  10190
cal  Pick   Alt-F3
pri  New                rint
inp  Save      F2    from Menu";menuselect$
pro  Write to         + menuselect$
pri               ———————— New Name ————————
cha      NONAME
END
                                                             │
     OS shell
sub  Quit   Alt-X
cls └────────┘
print"* * * * *  BIKES PEAK    * * * * * *"
print"* * * * *    PROGRAMS    * * * * * *"
for c = 1 to 5: print: next c
print "1 Inventory"
print "2 Customers"
print "3 Mail List"
print "4 Sales"
print "5 Monthlies"
end sub
```

```
   F1-Help  F5-Zoom  F6-Switch  F7-Trace  F8-Step  F9-Compile F10-Menu
```
Figure 3.10

Now, exit PowerBASIC.

PRESS ⟨ALT + **x**⟩

(We just wanted to give you some practice in the exit route.)

3.4 OPENING AN EXISTING PROGRAM

Now let's go back in and run **bikemenu.bas**, to see if it works. Reenter PowerBASIC:

TYPE **pb**⟨ENTER⟩

Open the *File* menu:

> PRESS ⟨ALT + **f**⟩
> PRESS ⟨ENTER⟩

The first time you entered the *File* menu, you wanted to type in a new program. This time, you want to *load* a program that *already exists*. So, to select that menu option, you can either

> TYPE L⟨ENTER⟩ (for **L**oad Program)

or

> PRESS ⟨ENTER⟩

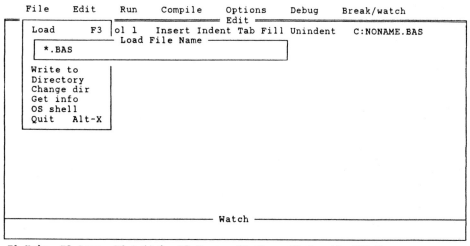

```
     File    Edit    Run    Compile    Options   Debug    Break/watch
  ┌──────────────────────────────── Edit ══════════════════════════════┐
  │  Load       F3 │ol 1   Insert Indent Tab Fill Unindent    C:NONAME.BAS│
  │  ┌─────────────── Load File Name ───────────────────────┐           │
  │  │ *.BAS                                                 │           │
  │  ├────────────┐                                                      │
  │  │Write to    │                                                      │
  │  │Directory   │                                                      │
  │  │Change dir  │                                                      │
  │  │Get info    │                                                      │
  │  │OS shell    │                                                      │
  │  │Quit   Alt-X│                                                      │
  │  └────────────┘                                                      │
  │                                                                      │
  │                                                                      │
  │                                                                      │
  │                                                                      │
  │                                                                      │
  │                                ── Watch ──                           │
  └──────────────────────────────────────────────────────────────────────┘
  F1-Help  F5-Zoom  F6-Switch  F7-Trace  F8-Step  F9-Compile F10-Menu
```

Figure 3.11

The cursor is in the *Load File Name* box, waiting for you to type the name of the file you want to open. You type

> TYPE **bikemenu**⟨ENTER⟩

and there's your program.

3.5 TESTING A PROGRAM BY RUNNING IT

Your first program is ready to run. Let's see what happens.

PRESS ⟨ALT + **r**⟩
PRESS ⟨ENTER⟩

If everything has been typed in correctly, this is what you should see on your computer screen:

```
       * * * * *   BIKES PEAK   * * * * * *
       * * * * *    PROGRAMS    * * * * * *



       1 Inventory
       2 Customers
       3 Mail List
       4 Sales
       5 Monthlies



       Enter Number from Menu?
```
Figure 3.12

(You may not like the spacing or the layout. Leave it for now; in future chapters we're going to show you how to format things more attractively.)

Pick a number from the menu and then press ENTER.

TYPE {**a number, 1 to 5**}⟨ENTER⟩

You've just run your first PowerBASIC program. If you see the program listing and, superimposed upon it, the error box below, then that's *good* news: it runs correctly!

- If that's the case (you have the following error box), then skip to the section below called, "IT RUNS!"
- If you got an error message other than the following box, or if the program didn't run satisfactorily, skip to the section below called, "IF IT DOESN'T RUN . . .".

The boxed error message you should see is:

```
   File    Edit    Run    Compile   Options   Debug    Break/watch
=============================================== Edit ===============
    Line 1      Col 1    Insert Indent Tab Fill Unindent   C:BIKEMENU.BAS
rem -- program "bikemenu.bas" 10190
call printmenu
print:print:print:print
input"Enter Number from Menu";menuselect$
program$ = "bikes" + menuselect$
print"Selecting program ";program$
chain program$
END                    ============= Error =============
                       | CHAIN/RUN from .EXE file only.  Press ESC. |
sub printmenu          ===================================
cls
print"* * * * *   BIKES PEAK    * * * * *"
print"* * * * *    PROGRAMS     * * * * *"
for c = 1 to 5: print: next c
print "1 Inventory"
print "2 Customers"
print "3 Mail List"
print "4 Sales"
                          ============= Watch =============
```

F1-Help Esc-Abort

Figure 3.13

The ".EXE file" referred to is the compiled version of this program. There's no problem; you simply haven't yet compiled it onto disk, so the .EXE file doesn't yet exist. You can clear the error box by pressing the ESC key.

3.5.1 It Runs!

Congratulations. You've keyed in your work carefully, and you've followed directions. Pat yourself on the back and skip to the "SUMMARY" section below.

3.5.2 If It Doesn't Run . . .

There could be one of a number of reasons. The usual problem is that something was not keyed in quite correctly.

PRESS ⟨F5⟩

to zoom the program listing. You should now see your main program listing on screen. Do a two-step comparison:

1. Compare your main program carefully with the listing below for **bikemenu.bas.** Correct any errors, as explained previously.
2. Compare the lines you typed for the procedure **printmenu.** Correct any errors. Then save the file once again:

PRESS ⟨ALT + **f**⟩
PRESS ⟨ENTER⟩
TYPE **s**

When you've saved the corrected file, try running it again as explained before (section 3.5). If you don't have any luck in fixing the program to give the results described above *within 20 minutes*, then save the file on disk. We'll be coming back to it in future chapters.

The program should look exactly like the one below. Compare it one last time and then exit PowerBASIC:

PRESS ⟨ALT + **x**⟩

```
REM -- program "bikemenu" 010189
CALL printmenu
PRINT
INPUT "Enter Number from menu"; menuselect$
program$ = "bikes" + menuselect$
PRINT "Selecting program "; program$
CHAIN program$
END

{procedure "printmenu}
SUB printmenu
CLS
PRINT "* * * * * * BIKES PEAK * * * * * *"
PRINT "* * * * * * PROGRAMS * * * * * *"
PRINT
PRINT "1 Inventory"
PRINT "2 Customers"
PRINT "3 Mail List"
PRINT "4 Sales"
PRINT "5 Monthly Reports"
END SUB
```

3.6 THE POWERBASIC ENVIRONMENT

The real beauty of PowerBASIC is its ease of use. It helps you do every programming task without leaving the PowerBASIC environment. It lets you be as productive as you want to be. PowerBASIC is a working environment in which a programmer can

1. Write a program
2. Test a program
3. Change a program
4. Get a program to change or test
5. Save (to disk) a program you've changed or written
6. Run a program with real data for actual results
7. Merge part or all of a program or routine with another
8. Bring in pieces from several programs and then quickly and easily cut and paste selected statements and routines into a working program
9. Build and test routines that will be used later in hundreds of programs
10. Easily correct errors
11. Print a program

3.7 SETTING POWERBASIC OPTIONS

Before you become totally immersed in the PowerBASIC environment, we need to set some options to suit your computer and our way of working. To set the PowerBASIC options, get into PowerBASIC:

TYPE **cd\pb**⟨ENTER⟩
TYPE **pb**⟨ENTER⟩

The main screen will come up,

PRESS ⟨ALT + **o**⟩

```
   File     Edit     Run    Compile    Options    Debug    Break/watch
 ┌──────────────────────────────────────┬─────────────────┬────────────────┐
 │      Line 1    Col 1   Insert Inde│ Compiler        │ C:NONAME.BAS   │
 │                                        │ Linker          │                │
 │                                        │ Environment     │                │
 │                                        │ Directories     │                │
 │                                        │ Parameters      │                │
 │                                        │ Save options    │                │
 │                                        │ Retrieve options│                │
 │                                        └─────────────────┘                │
 │                                                                           │
 │                                                                           │
 │                                                                           │
 │                                                                           │
 │                                                                           │
 │                              ──── Watch ────                              │
 ├───────────────────────────────────────────────────────────────────────────┤
 └───────────────────────────────────────────────────────────────────────────┘
 F1-Help  F5-Zoom  F6-Switch  F7-Trace  F8-Step  F9-Compile F10-Menu
```

Figure 3.14

and the *Options* menu will come up. If it doesn't,

    PRESS ⟨ESCAPE⟩ several times

and then start again.

    Once you get the *Options* menu, select the *Compiler* and

    PRESS ⟨ENTER⟩.

Now select the *Generated code* option and

    PRESS ⟨ENTER⟩

Then, select the type of computer that you are using (or the computer that the programs you are writing will be run on). If the computer is an XT type, then select the *8086/8088* and

    PRESS ⟨ENTER⟩

Otherwise, for computers in the 80286 (AT), 80386, and 80486 categories, select the *80286* and

    PRESS ⟨ENTER⟩

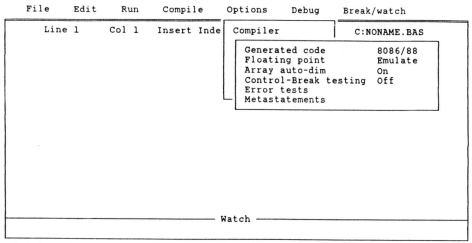

Figure 3.15

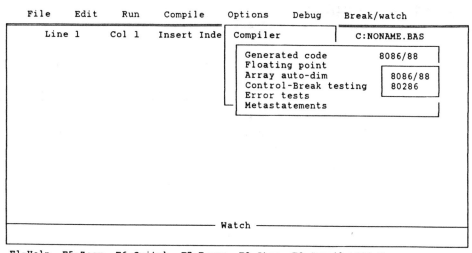

Figure 3.16

Then,

PRESS ⟨ESC⟩⟨ESC⟩

to get back to the main *Options* menu.

Last, select the *Save options* choice and

PRESS ⟨ENTER⟩

to save your choices.

PRESS ⟨ESC⟩ to leave the *Options* menu.

Then exit PowerBASIC. The options are set.

PRESS ⟨ALT + **x**⟩

You're done.

CHAPTER SUMMARY

1. A menu program is a way to set the system up so that a program user can easily run the program that he or she wants.
2. Separate your procedures (smaller routines) with a blank line.
3. Read the book carefully. Type accurately, not quickly.
4. Errors are easy to correct in PowerBASIC. Don't get upset when you make them.
5. Save your programs BEFORE you run them.

THE BOTTOM LINE

1. BASIC is a personable language, which tells your computer to follow your instructions one at a time until it has produced a desired "report."

2. When you look at a BASIC program, break it up into sections, using the block-line method. Then look at each block, one at a time, to figure out what each does.

3. **PowerBASIC gives you a complete working environment, which encourages writing programs in building-block fashion.**

EXERCISES

1. Take Exercise 1 from chapter 2,
   - get into PowerBASIC,
   - type in the program,
   - save it, and
   - then run the program.

2. Do the same for Exercise 2 in chapter 2.

Chapter 4

Programming Logic and Diagrams (Errors Are Usually in Thinking, Not in Programming)

4.1 Program "Flow" and Logic ——————————————— 51

4.2 The Nature of Programming ——————————————— 58

4.3 Precision of the BASIC Language ——————————— 59

4.4 Three Secrets of Good Programming ——————————— 60

4.5 The Program Blueprint ——————————————————— 61

4.6 Bikes Peak Programs ——————————————————— 66

4.7 PowerBASIC—Skimming the Menus ——————————— 67

We hope you enjoyed your first taste of PowerBASIC in chapter 2. There's plenty more ahead, but first we turn to an important discussion.

The biggest mistake people make is in starting to program without understanding the problem and completely defining the solution.

Just as you should look before you leap and think before you speak, you should understand the logic of your program *before* you write one single statement.

In chapters 2 and 3, we asked you to read, type, and run a fully operational program (**bikemenu**). Hopefully, there were few troubles, since Donna at Bikes Peak had already worked out the design of that program. Now it's time for *you* to roll up your sleeves and begin solving problems through designing (as opposed to just typing) programs.

4.1 PROGRAM "FLOW" AND LOGIC

Water always flows in one direction—downward, following the path of least resistance to its ultimate destination, the sea. There may be changes of speed or direction; in whitewater you might swear the flow has reversed! The force behind the constant, irreversible flow of water is gravity. (See Figure 4.1). It may be mysterious, but there's no denying its absolute power. In computer programming, there's a similar force. Gravity is to water flow as *logic* is to program flow.

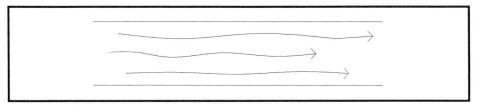

Figure 4.1

Like gravity, you may find logic hard to pin down. But you'll know its action when you see it, and you can count on its inevitability when you design things. If you understand what program logic is and how it works, then you can control your programs.

As with water, so with program flow: it's not usually a straight course.

4.1.1 Rocks and Routines

A rock diverts the flow of a stream, but once the water is past the rock it joins the main flow once more. An island is simply a bigger diversion. (See Figure 4.2).

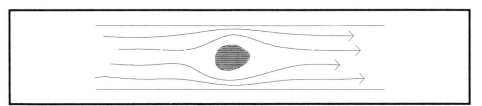

Figure 4.2

A program *routine* is like a rock or an island. It diverts the program flow for a while, but the program always returns to the main flow. (See Figure 4.3).

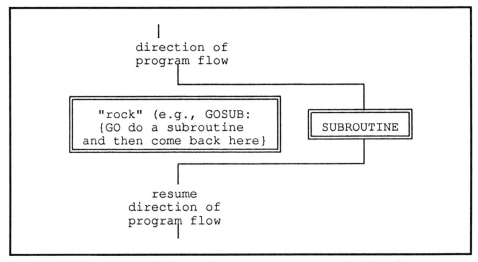

Figure 4.3

4.1.2 Watergates and IF...THENs

A watergate uses the flow of water to do some work. If the gate is closed, water follows the path of the river. If the gate is open, it admits (diverts) water to do some form of work, like turn the waterwheel at that old mill. Once the work is done, the water rejoins the main flow (See Figure 4.4).

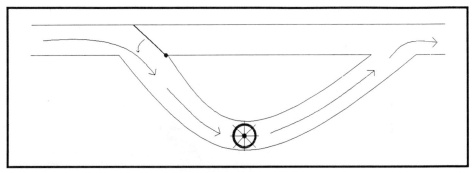

Figure 4.4

The programming counterpart to a watergate is a statement of the **IF . . . THEN** type (there are several forms). It's used to test the truthfulness of a condition: **IF...** {a condition is true} **THEN** {perform some work}. (Chapter 9 discusses **IF** statements.) See Figure 4.5.

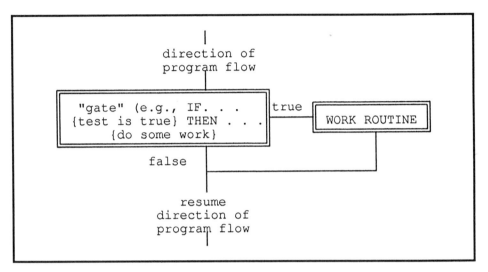

Figure 4.5

4.1.3 Pumps and Loops

You've probably been wondering about a "reversal" of gravity. Don't machines such as pumps and fountains *raise* water? In a fountain (or any pumping system), an external force of some kind temporarily overrides the force of gravity. (See Figure 4.6). Without that unnatural force, the water cannot possibly "reverse" itself.

A fountain is like a *loop* in a program. Here, a loop statement forces the program to go back and repeat some process (Figure 4.7). There are several members of the "loop" family, but they all operate in the same way.

Thus, apart from temporary obstructions and diversions,

- gravity moves water down to its destination, the sea, and
- programming logic moves data down the program to the end result, the report.

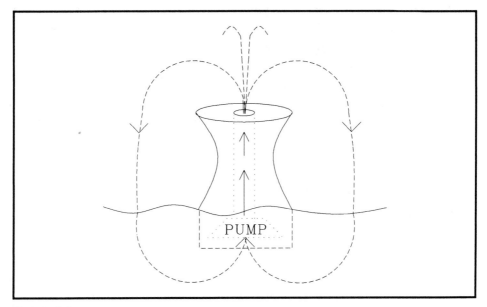

Figure 4.6

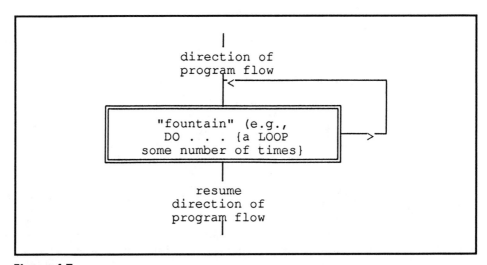

Figure 4.7

With the flow analogy in mind, look again at the definition of a computer program, which we presented in the first chapter.

A program is a series of statements (precisely worded instructions), that the computer looks at one at a time and carries out one at a time, until it reaches the end result: a report.

(Keep in mind that a report can appear on screen, at the printer, or as a disk file.)

We said in chapter 2 that a computer is pretty smart. In another way, it's also pretty dumb; it can do only one thing at a time. True, it can do thousands of instructions per second. But it reads instructions, acts on them, and performs a task to its logical conclusion one step at a time.

The computer starts at the first statement. It reads the instruction and performs it. Then it looks at the next statement in sequence and performs that. And so on, down the program, processing all statements sequentially (statement 2 after statement 1, statement 3 after statement 2, and so on.). The only exception is when it's told to go elsewhere in the program. Once it goes to that part of the program, it will process the first statement found there, then the next, and so forth, until it's told to **GO** . . . somewhere else (perhaps back to where it was before the initial **GO** . . .).

So what is program logic? It's the *actual sequence* of your BASIC program statements, in the order in which they're seen by the computer. Since you control the sequence of statements (you're writing the program), *your logic* controls the computer.

Good logic ensures a smooth flow:

Good logic: (Figure 4.8)
Smooth water path: (Figure 4.9)

Bad logic, like whitewater, can sink you.

Bad logic: (Figure 4.10)
Whitewater: (Figure 4.11)

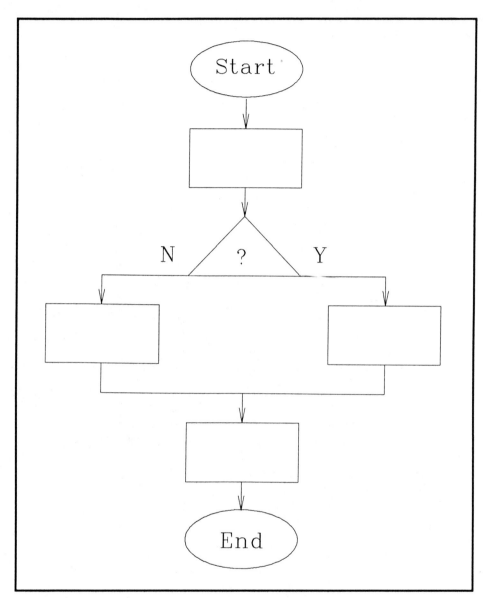

Figure 4.8

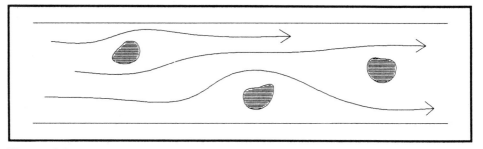

Figure 4.9

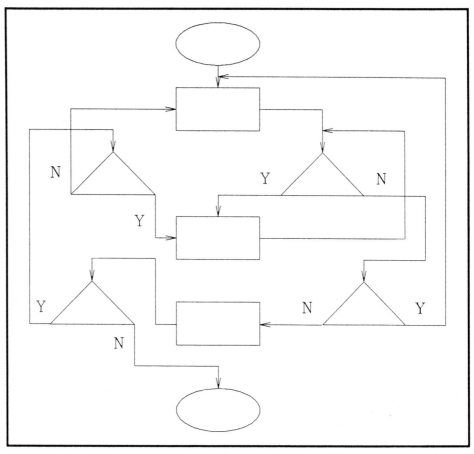

Figure 4.10

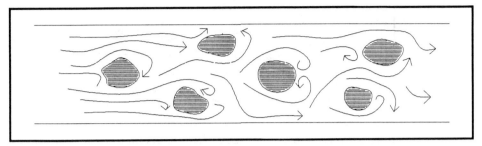

Figure 4.11

4.2 THE NATURE OF PROGRAMMING

Programming is simply the translation of human ideas into language that a computer can follow. This fact presents you with three challenges:

1. The structure of the program *must be simple.*

    This is for *your* benefit, not the computer's. There are three reasons why a program (in running form and in printed form) must be clear and simple:

    a. That marvel of engineering, the all-powerful computer, will NOT magically clarify a design that is a little obscure. A vaguely defined program is likely not to work at all.

    b. You, or some other programmer, will read your program in the future. If it's not clear enough for *you* to remember what you wrote a few months or some years previously, how will a total stranger make sense of the program listing?

    c. An error of logic is the worst kind of programming error you can make, because it's the hardest to identify. The computer won't find it for you (as it will a mistake in a name or in the structure or use of a statement). You can only find an error in logic by tearing your program down into little routines and testing each separately. It can be a long process—especially when there's a combination of errors. Therefore,

    M A K E   Y O U R   L O G I C   P R E C I S E !

    As we said before, the biggest mistake people make is in starting to program without understanding the problem and without completely defining the solution. Before you begin writing a program in BASIC, the logic must be completely clear to you. In other words, you don't write the program before you totally understand

- what the program is supposed to do and
- how the program is supposed to do it.

2. **The detailed logic presented** *must be perfect.*

A computer can execute only simple statements, such as **PRINT, READ, GOTO,** and so on. It can't determine that your calculation is adding when it should be subtracting, or that your program has gotten into an endless loop (where your logic causes a computer to repeat a loop forever—or until you turn off the machine). In other words, it can't guess what you meant to say, only what you actually tell it. Therefore,

K E E P   Y O U R   T H O U G H T S   P R E C I S E !!

When the computer reads a program, it can't figure out your *intended* logic. To the computer, the actual sequence of program statements *is* your logic. It'll do exactly what it is told (even if the instruction is totally wrong), with no criticism at all. It does what you say, absolutely. Unlike a person, a computer can't say "I know what you mean" to something you don't express clearly.

3. The language must be *exactly* correct.

Computers are dumb. They can't figure things out imaginatively, guess at something spelled incorrectly, reinterpret a sentence that is structured improperly, or fill in words that have been left out. Your "sentences" must adhere to all the rules of BASIC. (The rules for writing different kinds of statements will be explained in later chapters.) Which leads to...

4.3 PRECISION OF THE BASIC LANGUAGE

While a computer can't check your logic, it does check each statement for syntactic correctness (according to BASIC's rules of grammar). The computer does so by reading one word at a time and anticipating what permissible words might follow. If it finds something wrong, it'll stop.

This is important to you in two ways:

1. Every word (or symbol) in a statement is considered to be either a *reserved word* or a *variable name*. Reserved words are the action verbs (**PRINT**, **READ**, **LINE INPUT**) or special functions (**DATE$**, **COLOR**) that BASIC understands as commands to do something. The variable names that you choose for data items are the nouns, which are acted upon by the verbs (reserved words). To the computer, *everything* other than a reserved word is a variable name. Don't use a reserved word as a variable name by mistake, or you'll have a mess.

   Give a computer a word it doesn't understand, and it'll either stop dead or consider the word to be the variable name for a new, undefined data item. And when it "finds" an undefined piece of data, it gives the data a starting value of zero. You lose either way.

2. BASIC statements are like simple English sentences. Our language has a great deal of flexibility, but the computer's does not. BASIC can work only with a few very simple, direct statement types in a restricted word order.

   Have you ever been approached by someone who couldn't speak much English? Think about the simple vocabulary and sentences you had to use to get the person to understand your response. Well, to your computer, English is a foreign language. Keep it simple.

As you can see, BASIC restricts how you can present ideas to a computer. Which brings us to . . .

4.4 THREE SECRETS OF GOOD PROGRAMMING

Everything we've just said about program logic affects the quality of your program design. Let's summarize with three valuable secrets:

1. **STATE IT SIMPLY.** Use the simplest of BASIC's many statements. Although BASIC often has several ways of accomplishing a task, you should keep in mind what makes good, clear technical writing: you never use a big word when you can use a small one; you never use a complex sentence when you can use a simple one; you avoid unnecessary words; and you keep paragraphs short.

Rather than memorize 150 statements (including those not available in other, less advanced BASICs), why not learn and use repeatedly the simple ones that get the job done best? That's much easier than looking up and relearning the more powerful and complex statements that you haven't used for a while. You'll make fewer mistakes and waste less time.

2. **NAME IT SIMPLY.** Choose variable names that identify the data being named. The city in your customer file could be **custcity**, the state **custstate**, the zip **custzip**, and so on. Name the retail price in the "item" file **itemretlpric**, the wholesale price **itemwholpric**, the cost **itemcost**. Also, avoid using unnecessarily long names. (We'll explain variable names in chapter 5.)

3. **STRUCTURE IT SIMPLY.** Good logic is clear and simple. If your design doesn't meet that test, you'll probably never be able to get your program to run properly.

Much better to have good logic from the start! To help you start correctly, we're introducing the blueprint, a tool you'll use recurrently throughout this book.

4.5 THE PROGRAM BLUEPRINT

The actual writing, typing, and running should be the simplest and quickest part of programming. It's much more difficult to understand the problem, define it, and lay out the logic of the solution. Let's call this thinking process "blueprinting."

The steps in blueprinting a program are to understand and define—

1. the PURPOSE(s) of the program;
2. the end results (OUTPUT) of the program, usually a report in the form of a screen display, printed page, or file on disk;
3. the source (INPUT) of the data necessary to fill in the report or produce the OUTPUT;
4. the source of the hidden data ("HIDPUT") found in the formulas that produce the OUTPUT; and
5. the block diagramming (LOGIC) required to produce the OUTPUT.

Now we'll go into detail on how to blueprint. (By the way, you probably don't know exactly how to do any of this yet, since we don't describe these processes until later in the book. For now, just grasp the concept; you'll be doing a lot of practicing. We'll run an example through the blueprint process when we're finished detailing it.)

Step 1
PURPOSE. State in a single, simple sentence (no ands, ors, ifs, or commas) what the *single* major purpose of your program is. Then, break the sentence down to list the major tasks that this program is supposed to accomplish—again, each task in a single, simple sentence. If the program is so simple that there's only one task, then one sentence is enough.

Step 2
End Result (OUTPUT). On a piece of paper, lay out each page that will be displayed on the screen or printed by the printer. If a file of data is to be saved onto disk as a result of this program, then draw on paper what the disk file contents will look like.

Step 3
Necessary Data (INPUT). Look at the OUTPUT data (in Step 2) that must be present in order to accomplish the end result and determine its source (where it comes from—another file, a calculation, or keyboard input). As you're doing this, give meaningful names to the OUTPUT data to be created by this program.

Step 4
Hidden Data (HIDPUT). If a calculation (formula) is involved, then determine the source of all the data contained in the formula. The source could be another file, another calculation, or keyboard input. Keep on doing this until every piece of data has a source within the program. This can be tough, especially for beginning programmers, but it's important that you find each source. Whole systems have been programmed that didn't work because one piece of data had no source within one program and thus had a value of zero, making all reports useless.

Step 5
LOGIC. A good way to look at your logic is to put it into simple block diagrams. Each block diagram should fit onto a single 8½ by 11 sheet of paper; if it doesn't fit, then the logic is probably too complex. (Remember that secret of good programming: make it simple.) If you can't fit all

the functions or procedures on one sheet of paper, then put the major logic onto one sheet and the other (sublogic) routines on other sheets. In any case, *force* yourself to be constrained—that's the purpose of using a single 8½ by 11 sheet for block diagramming the logic. Fitting the logic onto one sheet forces simplicity.

The rules of block diagramming are simple: put each step within a block and connect the blocks with arrows to show program flow direction. The two sample program blueprints that follow will give you a good picture; we'll be block diagramming all our programs from here on. Read until the end, and you'll be a block-diagramming expert!

Note:

Take your time. The time you spend blueprinting, to understand and define the problem and solution, will pay you back *tenfold* at the programming stage. Conversely, every minute you think you save by not defining the problem will cost you ten or more at the programming stage. Five minutes or so now will save you an hour later.

4.5.1 Sample Blueprint #1

Chuck and Art of Bikes Peak decide to make up a mailing file of potential customers. So they buy a mailing list from a cycling magazine and get ready to key in the list. Here's their program to enter the names, shown in a program blueprint.

PROGRAM NAME: **mailkey1**
PURPOSE: To key the magazine mailing list into our computer.
OUTPUT RESULT: File on disk, containing 20,000 names and
  addresses. The name of the file is "mail". The description is . . .

Data Name	Description	Location in File (Position)	Maximum Length
mailname	prospect's name	1–30	30
mailaddr1	1st line of address	31–60	30
mailaddr2	2nd line of address	6–90	30
mailcity	city	91–110	20
mailstate	state	111–112	2
mailzip	zip	113–121	9

INPUT (data sources): Source for all data is keyboard input. The operator of the program keys in all the information on each person and saves it onto the disk.

Data	Source
mailname	key entry
mailaddr1	key entry
mailaddr2	key entry
mailcity	key entry
mailstate	key entry
mailzip	key entry

HIDPUT (data in formulas): None.

LOGIC (block diagram):

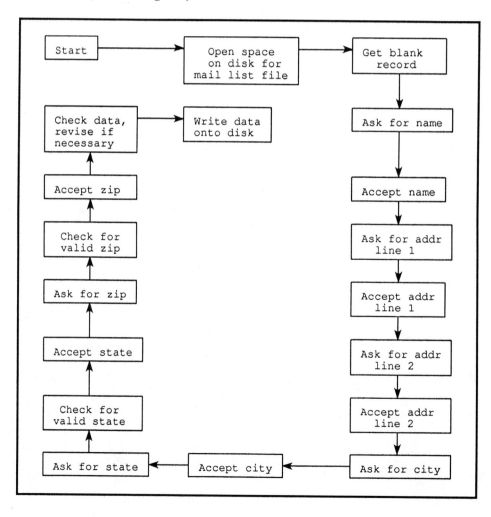

4.5.2 Sample Blueprint #2

This is the blueprint of the program Chuck and Art are using to print out mailing labels to their potential customers.

PROGRAM NAME: **maillabl**
PURPOSE: To print mailing labels for all the people in our MAIL file.
OUTPUT RESULT: One mailing label for each person.

```
CHUCK BUTKUS
1675 ROUTE 9
CLIFTON PARK  NY  12065
```

INPUT (data sources): All the data for the label is found in the file called MAIL, which is on our computer disk.

Data	Description	Source
lablname	prospect name	"mail" file
labladdr1	1st addr line	"mail" file
labladdr2	2nd addr line	"mail" file
lablcity	city	"mail" file
lablstate	state	"mail" file
lablzip	zip	"mail" file

HIDPUT (data in formulas): none.
LOGIC (block diagram):

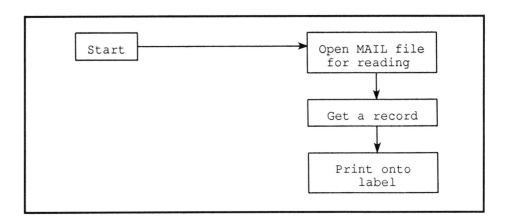

4.5.3 Sample Blueprint #3 Through . . .

We'll be using blueprints for every program in this book, so you'll get plenty of practice. The program blueprint is a flexible tool for good programming. It's a reliable way to ensure that the data names, statements, and program logic are all clear and simple. If you produce a clear program blueprint, your programming tasks become easy. A cloudy blueprint means a stormy programming session.

4.6 BIKES PEAK PROGRAMS

Here's the list of programs and systems that the folks at Bikes Peak would like Donna to write for them. (A system is simply two or more programs, closely related to one another, that use data from many of the same files.)

List of Possible Programs for Bikes Peak
MAILING LIST

- Key in potential customers.
- Print mailing labels for potential customers.

CUSTOMER LIST

- Enter new customer data.
- Change customer data.
- Look up customers.
- Special-events invitations mailing.
- Service bulletins.
- Special sales.

INVENTORY

- Enter new inventory data.
- Change inventory data.
- Lookup inventory data.
- Enter sales.
- Reorder report.

- Print inventory value.
- Price list (giving retail and wholesale prices).
- Sales by month (No accounts receivable; cash only).
- Sales forecasting.

You will not write all of these programs in the course of this book. Sometimes we'll just ask you to think about adding future programs as you design current programs.

The list is far from complete, but it should give you some idea of the amount of programming that goes into the setup of systems for a small business. Most businesses would have a payroll system, an accounts payable system, a general ledger system, and a complex order processing system. Bikes Peak doesn't need these yet; they do everything on a cash basis. With that big picture in mind, you'll be more aware of how programs serve one another and how a common pool of data (in a small number of files) can serve many programs.

At the end of this chapter, we'll ask you to think about and then design a Bikes Peak program. Then you'll write it and go on to modify it in the following chapters.

4.7 POWERBASIC—SKIMMING THE MENUS

Now we'll switch from design for a little while and explore the tool kit that PowerBASIC gives you.

4.7.1 The File Menu

PRESS ⟨ALT + **f**⟩

The *File* menu appears. If it doesn't, keep trying until it does.

The *File* menu is really misnamed. It really is a program menu, which is used to manipulate entire programs or blocks of programs that are already on disk or are currently in the *Editor*. Each line of the menu gives you a different operation that can be performed with a program or routine.

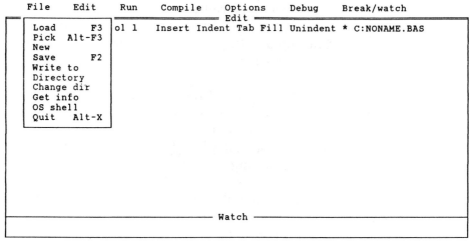

Figure 4.12

To select an operation, just

PRESS 〈DOWN ARROW〉

until the line you want is highlighted. Then

PRESS 〈ENTER〉

When you first enter PowerBASIC (like right now), the *Editor* has nothing in it. That's why **NONAME.BAS** appears on the second line of the screen. When you bring a program into the *Editor*, the program name will appear on the second line. The *File* menu is your means of moving programs to and from the *Editor* and the disk. It will be covered in detail in chapter 6.

4.7.2 The Edit Selection

If you are still in the *File* menu, then

PRESS 〈RIGHT ARROW〉〈ENTER〉

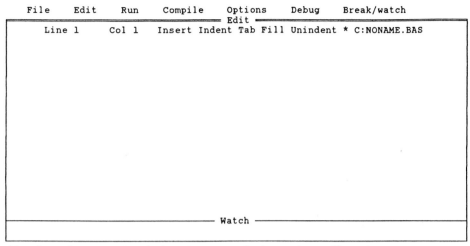

```
    File    Edit    Run    Compile    Options    Debug    Break/watch
                                   Edit
    Line 1      Col 1    Insert Indent Tab Fill Unindent * C:NONAME.BAS
```
```
                                   Watch
```
```
Fl-Help  F5-Zoom  F6-Switch  F7-Trace  F8-Step  F9-Compile Fl0-Menu NUM
```

Figure 4.13

and you're back in the *Editor*. You can now add, delete, or change any part of your program. The *Editor* is explained in chapter 8.

4.7.3 The Run Selection

If you're in the *Editor*, then

PRESS ⟨ALT + **r**⟩

to Run a program
If you're in one of the menus at the top of the screen,

PRESS ⟨ESC⟩

until you're out of that menu, and

PRESS ⟨ALT + **r**⟩

to Run a program.

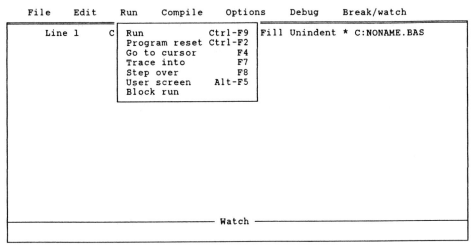

Figure 4.14

4.7.4 The Compile Selection

If you're in the *Editor, then*

PRESS ⟨ALT + **c**⟩

to *Compile* a program.
    If you're in one of the menus at the top of the screen,

PRESS ⟨ESC⟩

until you're out of that menu and

PRESS ⟨ALT + **c**⟩

to *Compile* a program.

4.7.5 The Options Menu

(We've covered this in chapter 3.) To get into the *Options* menu
if you're in the *Editor,*

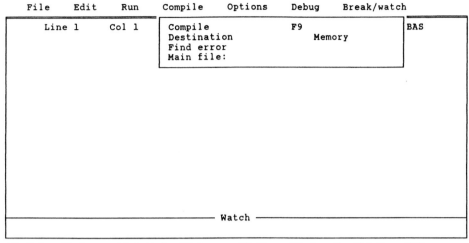

Figure 4.15

PRESS ⟨ALT + **o**⟩

If you're in one of the meus at the top of the screen,

PRESS ⟨ESC⟩

until you're out of that menu, and

PRESS ⟨ALT + **o**⟩

for the *Options* menu.

4.7.6 The Debug Menu

If you're in one of the menus at the top of the screen,

PRESS ⟨ESC⟩

until you're out of that menu, and

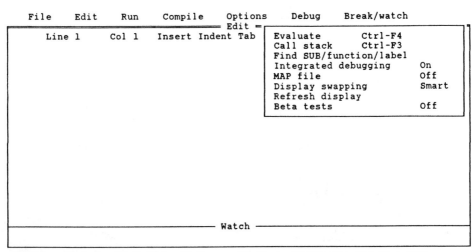

```
 File     Edit     Run     Compile     Options     Debug     Break/watch
┌─────────────────────────────────────────────┬────────────────────────────┐
│    Line 1     Col 1     Insert Inde│Compiler          │ * C:NONAME.BAS     │
│                                    │Linker            │                    │
│                                    │Environment       │                    │
│                                    │Directories       │                    │
│                                    │Parameters        │                    │
│                                    │Save options      │                    │
│                                    │Retrieve options  │                    │
│                                    └──────────────────┘                    │
│                                                                            │
│                                                                            │
│                                                                            │
│                                                                            │
│                                                                            │
│                                                                            │
│                                                                            │
│                            ──── Watch ────                                 │
└────────────────────────────────────────────────────────────────────────────┘
 F1-Help  F5-Zoom  F6-Switch  F7-Trace  F8-Step  F9-Compile F10-Menu NUM
```

Figure 4.16

PRESS⟨ALT + **d**⟩

for the *Debug* menu.
If you're back in the *Editor*,

PRESS ⟨ALT + **d**⟩

```
 File     Edit     Run     Compile     Options     Debug     Break/watch
┌───────────────────────────────── Edit ═══┬──────────────────────────────┐
│    Line 1     Col 1     Insert Indent Tab│Evaluate        Ctrl-F4       │
│                                          │Call stack      Ctrl-F3       │
│                                          │Find SUB/function/label       │
│                                          │Integrated debugging    On    │
│                                          │MAP file                Off   │
│                                          │Display swapping        Smart │
│                                          │Refresh display               │
│                                          │Beta tests              Off   │
│                                          └──────────────────────────────┘
│                                                                            │
│                                                                            │
│                                                                            │
│                                                                            │
│                            ──── Watch ────                                 │
└────────────────────────────────────────────────────────────────────────────┘
 F1-Help  F5-Zoom  F6-Switch  F7-Trace  F8-Step  F9-Compile F10-Menu NUM
```

Figure 4.17

and you are in the *Debug* menu. This menu is used to trace the history of your program logic. Chapter 19 will explain the *Debug* menu in more detail.

4.7.7 The Break/Watch Menu

If you're in one of the menus at the top of the screen,

PRESS ⟨ESC⟩

until you're out of that menu, and

PRESS ⟨ALT + **b**⟩

for the *Break/watch* menu.
    If you're back in the *Editor*,

PRESS ⟨ALT + **b**⟩

and you're in the *Break/watch menu.*

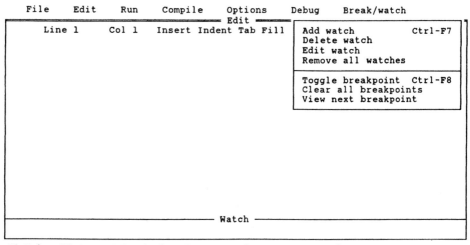

Figure 4.18

This menu is used to trace the logic and calculations of your program. Chapter 19 will explain the *Break/watch* menu in more detail.

Notes on Moving Directly to a Menu

In this section, we could have started with the *file* menu and then pressed the RIGHT ARROW to move through the menus. Normally, however, to get into one of the PowerBASIC selections, just

PRESS⟨ALT⟩

Then type the first letter of the selection you need. It will place you directly in that selection.

CHAPTER SUMMARY

1. The nature of programming demands that you present perfect logic in perfect fashion (using exactly correct language).

2. BASIC restricts you to using just reserved words and variable names, in a limited number of statements. While it may seem to be a pain to have to work with these limitations, they do force simplicity.

3. The secret of good programming is to use the simplest program statements, with meaningful variable names, in programs written with good logic.

4. Make sure that your logic is correct. It's the worst error to find and fix.

5. Always use a program blueprint (to make one thing—your logic—perfectly clear).
    a. State your major PURPOSE in a single, simple sentence. If the major purpose is comprised of several subpurposes, state them in one sentence each.

b. Specify the end result of your program. List each data item that is OUTPUT.

c. Determine the source (INPUT) of each data item in your OUTPUT.

d. Find the source for all your HIDPUT, the data items in the formulas that define your OUTPUT.

e. Put your LOGIC into a block diagram that displays your program steps.

THE BOTTOM LINE

1. BASIC is a personable language, which tells your computer to follow your instructions one at a time until it has produced a desired "report."

2. When you look at a BASIC program, break it up into sections, using the block-line method. Then look at each block, one at a time, to figure out what each does.

3. PowerBASIC gives you a complete working environment, which encourages writing programs in building-block fashion.

4. **Blueprint your program before you write *ONE LINE* of code.**

EXERCISES

1. Art and Barb want to set up their first program, the one that lets them key new customer data into the Bikes Peak customer file. Besides new customer information (similar to the mail list data), they eventually want to have other information on the file, such as:

   Sales last year
   Sales year-to-date

Date last mailing
Date last purchase
Number of K1, K2, and K3 (three bike models) purchases
Dollar value of K1, K2, and K3 purchases

Jump in and try your first blueprint. You'll find it a novel experience, and you'll be amazed at how close you come to the one we've put together. Please, work at this until you are completely satisfied with your blueprint, or until you have spent at least two hours puzzling over it. Blueprints take time, even for accomplished professionals, and the kind of thinking required is not done every day. Use the blueprint for **mailkeyone,** as an example. (Our blueprint is in Appendix F.)

2. Blueprint the program that looks up the customer data and displays it on the computer screen. Use the blueprint for **maillabl** as an example. See Appendix F for our blueprint.

Chapter 5

Types of Data and Names (Stick to the Rules, or There's Chaos)

5.1 What Data Is, and Why It's Needed _____ **79**

5.2 The Need for Data Names _____ **81**

5.3 Different Data Types _____ **84**

5.4 PowerBASIC and Naming Data _____ **86**

5.5 Rules for Data Names _____ **87**

5.6 The Data Dictionary _____ **89**

5.7 The REMark Statement _____ **92**

5.8 A Little Help on PowerBASIC Help _____ **94**

Figure 5.1 is a map of part of downtown Mazeville. You want to locate 4147z Chucker Street.

If you're having a problem, good. That's what we had hoped. Just go on to the next paragraph.

Now picture yourself driving into a city that we'll call Gridlook, USA (Figure 5.2). You're looking for 123 East 100th Street. Could you find it?

Getting a sense of direction is a lot easier in Gridlook than in Mazeville (for most people) because you can reason where a street or number is likely to be. The streets and avenues are laid out systematically: streets run east-west, and avenues run north-south. The numbers, too, are predictable: low numbers are at Avenue D and increase the further east or west you go from that benchmark. Unlike in Mazeville, in

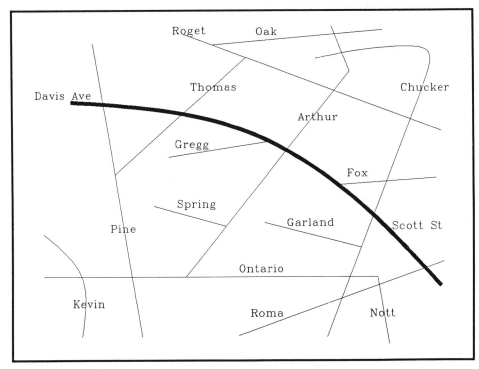

Figure 5.1

	90th	100th	110th		120th	130th
Avenue A						
Avenue B			west			
Avenue C						
Avenue D					north ->	
Avenue E						
Avenue F			east			

Figure 5.2

Gridlook you can start anywhere and then quickly and confidently redirect your search, based on the predictability of the layout and the names.

Finding your way around a city can be easy or infuriating, depending on the *layout* and the *naming* of the streets. Finding your way around a program printout can also be either a snap or a pain, depending on two things:

- How well organized is the program structure? (chapters 4 and 6)
- How well is the data named? (this chapter)

Picking up a printout of someone else's program is like opening a map of an unfamiliar city. With a few minutes of study, you should get a sense of the overall layout—the program organization. Then comes the question of making sense of variable names. (Recall from chapter 4 that everything in the program other than BASIC's reserved words is a variable or a comment.) In fact, even looking at your own programs after a month or so away from them can make you wonder why you used the variable names you did when you wrote them. Can you remember, a year after writing a program, what **w%** represents? Or **totnum?** "Total number," probably, but of what?

It's simpler to understand and modify a program with meaningful data names but no documentation (explanatory notes) than to do so with a well-documented program with data names that are unsystematic. (You'll be seeing examples of good and bad names later.)

Good data names are not just important; they're *critical*.

5.1 WHAT DATA IS, AND WHY IT'S NEEDED

Data is the collection of ingredients that your computer uses to cook up the finished product that you see as a report on paper or on screen. Data items are the raw materials that computer programs combine and present in different forms on screen, on disk, or at the printer. Data items are the particulars from which averages, percentages, and counts are derived for reports. The major function of any program is the processing; without data, programs would have *nothing to process*.

Here's a simple example of what data is and what can be done with it. Your consulting firm came in and did a job for Bikes Peak, for which you'll calculate how much they owe you and send them a bill:

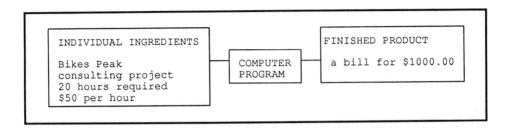

How does the bill get made from the raw ingredients? The data (four items, in our example above) is first put into your computer by way of a program that accepts keyboard input. (In some cases, data can be input by some type of scanner, such as a bar-code reader.) The data is then stored on disk for later processing by other programs you've written. Eventually, your computer will use the stored data to produce a report (the bill) by running one of several programs.

The flow of data into and through a computer, and its eventual transformation into reports, looks like this:

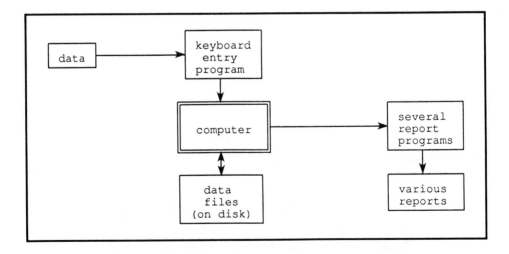

How well this system works depends, in part, on how well you name and lay out your data. Let's see why names make a difference.

5.2 THE NEED FOR DATA NAMES

Your computer's memory is really a grid of *locations*. Like the map of Gridlook, the memory locations are identified systematically, so that the computer is precise in storing and retrieving information. No matter how large the memory (and it could contain several million locations), the computer can keep track of what is where—everything in every location.

Before placing a data item in a memory storage location, the computer requires your program to assign a variable name to the location. Thereafter, the data item becomes the occupant of a location that the computer remembers as being such-and-such a *variable*. Thus, a data item can be recalled from its memory location by having the computer look for a particular variable name.

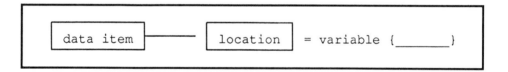

There's a technical term for a memory location: a *field*. A variable name corresponds to a physical location, but, more importantly, it identifies whatever value (data item) is occupying that location (*field*).

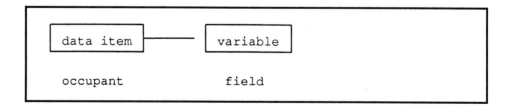

Let's take a look at a portion of a "neighborhood" in memory and see what's there.

There's a program running in the computer right now, and this small area of memory (four fields out of thousands) has some activity. Three of the four fields have been assigned variable names; the current program is not now using the fourth location. (It is not being used as a field for any data.)

Let's look at the contents of the three fields being used by the program.

Thirty seconds later, the computer operator has entered data for another company. Now the fields could look like this:

```
 L_____
 |                      |
 _____
| Dirty Diapers, Inc   |        location/field "company name"
 _____
|                      |        location (empty)
 _____
| Lower Body Drive     |        location/field "street address"
 _____
| 091889               |        location/field "date"
 _____
 |                      |
 r_____
```

Just as the occupants of a building can change with time, so the values residing within the fields can also change. Inside a computer, these values change often, and very quickly. For a given program, the field names remain the same, while the occupants (specific values) can change every fraction of a second.

```
 _____
| 110889               |        location/field "date" at time 1
 _____
 |                      |
 r_____


 _____
| 091889               |        location/field "date" an instant
 _____                        later
 |                      |
 r_____
```

Since all processing of data is performed within computer memory, the computer must know where all the data resides in memory. It must be able to find, process, and store back any single data item at any time. Before the development of high-level languages like PowerBASIC, programmers used a binary number (a series of ones and zeros) to tell the computer where to find a data address (location) in memory. It was difficult to write and modify programs with cumbersome forms of that sort.

Using PowerBASIC, all you have to do to define a field is give it a name. The computer will find and remember the location every time you use the name in your program. (Actually, in making your definition (name) you also have to give the field a data type; we'll turn to this feature of data naming next.)

5.3 DIFFERENT DATA TYPES

The programmer's life would be easy if all data could use the same format (data type). That's not the case. BASIC has several different numeric data types and one other data type for text data.

PowerBASIC distinguishes between two major data types:

- numeric (number characters)
- alphanumeric (letters, numbers, and/or symbols)

Take note that the alphanumeric (also called the *string*) data type contains all the numbers, but includes other characters as well.

The alphanumeric, or string, data type will not work for calculations in PowerBASIC. It also takes up a lot of space in memory or on a disk file for each data item that contains only numbers. For that reason, Power-BASIC has numeric formats (data types), which take up less space and are quicker to manipulate in calculations.

There are four numeric formats, making five the total number of data types you'll use in your programming. The five data types are:

1. short integers
2. long integers
3. single-precision numbers
4. double-precision numbers
5. strings (alphanumeric)

Before we talk about each data type in detail (including the distinctions between the four numeric types), let's look at a table giving essential information about each type.

Data type	Sample values	Name format	Sample names	Typical statement assigning value to a field
Short Integers	33 -30000	[name]%	**paycode%** **numcust%**	**paycode% = 3** **numcust% = 10000**
Long Integers	1234567890 81184	[name]&	**uspop&** **numitems&**	**uspop& = 220000000** **numitems& = 583714**
Single-precision numbers	5.23 -407.513 .951743	[name]! or [name]	**payrate!** **listprice**	**payrate! = 16.50** **listprice = 16.95**
Double-precision numbers	.1456824656 7320085.314 -66.834913	[name]#	**ytdpay** **cubft#**	**ytdpay# = 27593.34** **cubft# = 8248199.6**
Strings (alpha-numeric)	"Mary" "14 2nd St." "tel.no."	[name]$	**firstname$** **strname$** **telnum$**	**firstname$ = "Ted"** **strname$ = "DESIRE"** **telnum$ = "4480300"**

Detailed Explanation:

1. **Short integers.** Short integers are small whole numbers (no decimals). The permissible range of numbers is:

   0 to 32767 (positive numbers)
   0 to -32768 (negative numbers)

   Integers are typically used

   - for counting in programs (e.g., how many times a loop has been run)
   - for any small number that will never have decimal places (e.g., age, number of dependents, or some code)

   You should try to use integers as much as possible, because—

   - they take up less space than other numbers (the same space as two alphabetic characters, or two bytes)
   - calculations with integers can be performed very quickly

2. **Long integers.** Long integers are large, whole numbers (no decimals) that can have a value from:

   0 to 2,147,483,647 (positive numbers)
   0 to −2,147,483,648 (negative numbers)

Long integers are used for

- calculations involving large whole numbers
- special calculations (beyond the scope of this book)

3. **Single-precision numbers.** Single-precision numbers are small numbers (up to six digits, either positive or negative), that can have decimal places. While they can also be whole numbers, they need not be. This data type is used for most calculations, since programmers usually need fewer than six digits of decimal accuracy (the maximum possible for this data type).

4. **Double-precision numbers.** Double-precision numbers are large numbers (up to eighteen digits, either positive or negative), that can have decimal places. They can be whole numbers, but need not be. This data type is used for calculations where high accuracy is important in calculations.

5. **Strings.** A string is any alphabetic ("purchase"), alphabetic-and-numeric ("K2"), numeric ("300"), and/or special character or characters (see below).

    Strings cannot be used in calculations; however, PowerBASIC does provide a number of modifying or "massaging" operations with string variables. In addition to the numbers 0 through 9 and the letters of the alphabet, the following symbols are permissible in strings:

    ! @ # $ % & * ( ) __ + = \ |

    Strings can be any length from 0 to 255 characters long. You'll see them enclosed in quotation marks in BASIC.

5.4 POWERBASIC AND NAMING DATA

PowerBASIC has its own "hands-off" data dictionary of words with special meanings. As we mentioned in chapter 2, these words have been reserved mainly to denote action verbs; they cannot be used for data names. If you used a reserved word in the wrong place syntactically, PowerBASIC would become confused. It would either process your program incorrectly or stop in error.

Some of PowerBASIC's reserved words are:

BEEP	**ELSE**	**GET**	**MID$**	**REM**
CLEAR	**END**	**GOSUB**	**NAME**	**RESTORE**
CLOSE	**EOF**	**GOTO**	**NEXT**	**RETURN**
COMMON	**ERR**	**IF**	**OFF**	**SCREEN**
DIM	**EXIT**	**INPUT**	**ON**	**STRING**
DO	**FOR**	**LOG**	**POS**	**VAL**

Not all the reserved words are actual, full words, but most of them do resemble English words. You'll find a complete list of PowerBASIC's reserved words in Appendix B.

Apart from the reserved words, there are a few special words that also cannot be used as data names. Two such words are

- **DATE$**
- **TIME$**

Unlike data names, where you assign a name to a value, these two special words return a value to you (or the computer user) when you insert them into a statement. For example, the following statement line will produce the output shown (assume that the program is run at 04:25 on October 27, 1989):

PRINT "Last modified on "; DATE$; " at "; TIME$

Last modified on 10/27/89 at 04:25

Finally, there's a special word, **REM**, you'll be using frequently, as section 5.7 will show.

5.5 RULES FOR DATA NAMES

If there's a single golden rule in naming data items, it is to maintain uniqueness. The problems you want to avoid are—

- using the same data name for two different data items
- using a data name that you will not understand when you read it later

The first problem, redundancy, is likely to occur if data names are short. In particular, you may use a name in one routine of a program and then forget and use the same name elsewhere (which mixes up the values of your variables).

The second problem, obscurity, is likely to occur if you use an abbreviated data name that seems clear at the time you write the program but that, you see later, is too abbreviated.

There's a flip-side problem, too. You might figure that long data names with lots of specific information would avoid both of the problems above. But too-long names are easy to misspell and take up a lot of space on a PowerBASIC line (which can't be more than 248 characters).

With these warnings in mind, we'd like to propose six rules for data names, which will steer you safely through these critical waters:

Rule		**Examples**
1. Names should be meaningful to you, the programmer. (Remember, the data type also helps explain what kind of data occupies the field name).	Not good:	**fn personsfirstna**
	Good:	**fnam yr%**
	Better:	**firstname purchy**
2. Names should be short; we recommend not more than 12 characters.	Not good:	**stad streetaddres**
	Good:	**stradd**
	Better:	**street**
3. Names should be consistent.		
a. All data items from the same file should use the file name as the first part (prefix). Thus, we recommend using short filenames (up to 4 characters).	Not good:	**cusomeraddr name prtlstprc**
	Good:	**custadd custnam partlstprc**
	Better:	**custstreet custlastname partlistpric**
b. The same data item seen in several files should	Not good:	**cno pnum**
	Good:	**cusno prtno**

have the same suffix in each name.	Better:	**custnum parnum**
c. All items that are dates should have the same abbreviated suffix, e.g., **dt,** **dat,** or **date.**	Not good: Good: Better:	**pdt hirdt bald** **paydt hiredt baldt** **paydate hiredate** **balancedate**
d. All numbers that identify things (such as "customer number," "part number," "Social Security Number," etc.) should have the same abbreviated suffix, e.g., **no** or **num.**	Not good: Good: Better:	**cusnmb** **prt#socialsn** **cusno prtno ssno** **custnum partnum** **ssnum**
4. Names should not be cryptic. Use vowels when necessary for clarity.	Not good: Good: Better:	**cutot dtsnt** **currunpdtot dtsent** **totunpaid datesent**

5. Make yourself a *data dictionary* with all data names for each program. Place it at the very beginning of every program. (See the next section.)

Finally, the golden rule of data naming:

6. Make data names unique. Include enough characters to make them clear, but no more.

5.6 THE DATA DICTIONARY

The best way to explain what a data dictionary is and what it's for is to see one. Let's look at a sample here, say for data on customer purchases:

```
REM -- Data Dictionary
REM -- baseprice            base price of bike
REM -- city$
REM -- custbirthdat$        customer's birthdate
REM -- custfirstnam$        customer's first name
```

```
REM -- custlastname$        customer's last name
REM -- custstreet1$         customer's street address, line 1
REM -- custstreet2$         customer's street address, line 2
REM -- disc                 discount from base price (percent)
REM -- model$               model of bike purchased
REM -- purchtot             purchase price total
REM -- purchyr%             year of purchase
REM -- salestax
REM -- st$                  state
REM -- zip%                 zip code
REM -- Work Variables:
REM -- accesstot            total price of accessories
REM -- c                    loop counter
REM -- subtot               subtotal
```

The data dictionary includes all the data names (variables) encountered in the program. We recommend putting them in two major groupings:

- data names that are saved in files, followed by
- "work variables" (those used in the program but not saved)

Within each grouping, list the data names in alphabetical order.

In this sample, we've illustrated what makes a good data dictionary:

1. Each entry in the dictionary gives the data name and then an expanded definition of what the data name means. Note the recommended limit of 50 characters; there's no need to write full sentences to expand on a data name.

2. Data names should include the character suffix that defines the data type (as we explained in "DIFFERENT DATA TYPES" above). The dictionary entry **zip%** makes it clear that the zip code is to be a short integer (instead of a long 9-digit integer).

3. Where there can be no confusion about what data item a name represents, it's safe to omit the expanded definition in the dictionary. See **city$** and **salestax** above. However, we do advise definitions where there might be confusion, as with three similar data names based on the letters "s" and "t": **salestax**, **st$**, and **subtot**. How might a data name of just **st** be read a year later?

4. The "work variables" are simple data names for the "little" variables used in standard routines, as well as the results of calculations typically performed within **PROCESS, SUBCALC,** and **MASSAGE** routines (as you'll see in the next chapter). Since they tend to serve a workhorse function, being used again and again in your programs, it's less critical to give them uniquely readable names. For example, you might decide by yourself that **c** will always be a loop counter, in all your programs, year in and year out. (Loops are covered later on.)

A data dictionary may take up hundreds of **REM** statement lines in your program. Even so, it's worth the work and space because a good dictionary will save you, the programmer, hours in the long run.

A final word of advice: consistency throughout all your programs is the key to proper use of data names. Here's a tip learned from experience:

Make a Master Data Dictionary, tape it to the wall by your computer, and use it forever.

As you set up the data dictionary for your first program, start yourself a Master Data Dictionary, on a separate piece of paper, of the data names (which you might use again in future programs, whether in the Bikes Peak system or some other programming project). Don't precede the names with "bike"; instead, use "cust" "part", or "invn" (or something you like that applies to a class of files), where appropriate, as the first four characters of the name. That way, the name will be more general and able to be used elsewhere. But give each a name that works for you.

Then tape the Master Data Dictionary on the wall beside your computer so that it's available for reference and for adding to whenever you write programs. This way, your data names will be consistent not only within one system of programs but throughout all the programs and routines you'll ever write. It sounds simple, but in the course of a year this little trick will save you *weeks* of work! Take the word of someone who learned this the hard way.

Refer to Appendix C for help in making a Master Data Dictionary of often-used data names.

5.7 THE REMARK STATEMENT

The **REM**ark statement, or **REM**, is solely for the benefit of the programmer. The *user*, the person who is running the program, never sees the statement. **REM** statements are English-text explanations of names, calculations, routines, and so on. It's important for the programmer to understand what data names mean and what each routine and calculation does. It's even more important for someone (other than the original programmer) who is looking at your program for the first time.

The syntax is very simple:

REM {any amount of text up to 250 characters}

We suggest inserting a space, two hyphens, and a space after the word **REM** and before the message of the statement. Our experience has shown that this helps make **REM** statements stand out on the printed page.

PRINT custlastname$, custfirstname$, custaddress1$, custcity$,
REM--get string data
RESTORE
RANDOMIZE
RETURN
REM begin routine calcsalestax

If you didn't notice *both* **REM** statements, then our point has been emphasized.

Where should you use **REM**s? A series of them should appear right at the beginning of every program. This opening group of **REM**s will contain the program name, date created, a message indicating its purpose, and the complete data dictionary. Thereafter in the program, **REM** statements should be used sparingly. Usually, a single line at the beginning of every major routine will make even a long program more legible.

REM statements should be concise. There's little reason to say anything more than what is needed to serve two purposes:

1. Aiding a person who is scanning your program—perhaps looking to see where routines are located.

2. Aiding a programmer who needs to understand a statement, a routine, a calculation, and so forth, that is not self-explanatory. Think of helping a programmer who has your level of knowledge of BASIC but who is not familiar with your particular program.

One last thing: it is permissible to put a **REM** statement on the same line as another statement. To do so, separate the **REM** from the end of the other statement with a colon (:). This signals to PowerBASIC to ignore everything after the **REM** in that statement line. (The program can safely ignore the entire **REM** statement, since its contents are only messages to the programmer, not to the program itself.)

Notice the formats we suggest for the various **REM**arks in the following program excerpt:

```
REM -- program "maillist.bas" -- 11/01/90
REM -- purpose: to print mailing list
REM -- data dictionary (may be more than 100 REM statements)
REM -- contains data item names and brief explanation of each
REM -- custlastname$      customer last name
REM -- custstreet1$       customer street address, first line
REM -- custstreet2$       customer street address, second line
REM -- etc.
REM -- program chains to "maillabl.bas"
GOSUB -- fileopen: REM -- open routine
GOSUB -- main: REM -- main control
GOSUB -- [etc.]
  .
  .
  .

REM -- begin main control
main:
    .
    .
    .
```

5.8 A LITTLE HELP ON POWERBASIC HELP

We recommend this method of getting on-screen help.

1. PRESS ⟨F1⟩⟨F1⟩ for general *Help*.

   PRESS ⟨ESC⟩ to exit *Help*

2. When you need information on a specific topic, like an error, a keyword, or even part of a PowerBASIC menu, just move the cursor to the word or text that you would like help for. Then,

   PRESS ⟨F1⟩

   Help specific to that topic will appear.

   PRESS ⟨ESC⟩

   to clear the *Help*.

When you are in the *Editor* (writing a program), you can

PRESS⟨CTL⟩⟨F1⟩ for BASIC language help.

To get to the *Help Index*,

PRESS ⟨F1⟩⟨F1⟩

A screen of topics will appear. Move the cursor around the help box, place it onto a topic, then

PRESS ⟨ENTER⟩

and you get information on that topic. Then

PRESS ⟨F1⟩

The screen of topics will reappear. Browse through the topics, selecting several in the same fashion; then return to the *Contents* until you are comfortable with this section of *Help*.

You now should be able to use PowerBASIC *Help* at any time. If you still are not comfortable with using *Help*, go back and browse through it again until it's almost second nature. Then relax for thirty minutes and come back to this chapter to do the exercises.

CHAPTER SUMMARY

1. Data is essential. Without it, there's no need for computers.

2. PowerBASIC needs data names to identify where data is located in computer memory.

3. PowerBASIC has two major data types, numeric and alphanumeric. Numeric is further broken down into four types, giving a total of five:
   - short integers (values between -32768 and 32767)
   - long integers (values between -2147483648 and 2147483647)
   - single-precision numbers (up to 6 digits, including decimals)
   - double-precision numbers (up to 18 digits, including decimals)
   - strings (alphanumeric characters)

4. Some names and words are reserved for use by PowerBASIC. The complete list is found in Appendix B.

5. Make up a data dictionary with meaningful data names for each program as you write it. Combine parts of the dictionaries of all your programs into a Master Data Dictionary, which you will keep by your computer.

6. Data names should be:
   - meaningful
   - short
   - consistent
   - clear, not cryptic

7. Use **REM**ark statements to make up your data dictionary and to make your program readable and understandable in the future.

8. You can get into *Help* at any time by

PRESS⟨F1⟩ (the function key)

for general help, or place the cursor on the topic that you want help for, and

PRESS⟨CTL + F1⟩

to get advice on a specific topic (the one that the cursor is on).

THE BOTTOM LINE

1. BASIC is a personable language, which tells your computer to follow your instructions one at a time until it has produced a desired "report."

2. When you look at a BASIC program, break it up into sections using the block-line method. Then look at each block, one at a time, to figure out what each does.

3. PowerBASIC gives you a complete working environment, which encourages writing programs in building-block fashion.

4. Blueprint your program before you write one line of code.

5. **Data names should be meaningful, short (but not cryptic), consistent, and clear.**

EXERCISES

1. Check the names that you've made up for the Bikes Peak customer file in Exercise 1 of chapter 4 against the rules in this chapter. Make any necessary changes.

2. Blueprint a program to key in new inventory items. Besides a part number and a description, you should allow for

two prices,
a cost,
sales for 12 months,
an on-hand quantity,
total sales last year, and
a last count date,

among other things. Give meaningful data names to each item. Use Exercise 1 from chapter 4 as an example. (Check Appendix F when you're done to see what we've suggested as a blueprint.)

3. Blueprint a program to look up the inventory information and display it on the computer screen. Use Exercise 2 from chapter 4 as an example, and check your results with Appendix F.

Chapter 6

Organizing the Program (It's a Routine Process)

6.1 The Role of the Routine _____ **98**

6.2 Organizing a Program _____ **99**

6.3 The Ten-Part Classic Program _____ **104**

6.4 Routines From Now On _____ **110**

6.5 From Blueprint to Routines _____ **111**

6.6 File Commands—Back to the PowerBASIC Environment ____ **113**

Remember the storage shed in chapter 1? Skip this chapter, and the counterpart could happen in your programming. Understand it thoroughly (this one may take several readings), and you're on your way to programming glory! This approach is part of a self-developed technique that we find invaluable.

6.1 THE ROLE OF THE ROUTINE

Chapter 4 showed you how to *blueprint* a program. Before you begin *writing* it, there's an intermediate process that helps produce a well-organized program. Using the blueprint, you should then block out and design the *routines* of the program.

You'd think that the millions of computer programs ever written would have little in common. However, there *are* some things that are generic, and they exist at this intermediate level between blueprint design and writing the statements.

- There are certain routines that occur in most programs. In other words, most programs have a predictable structure.
- The routines fit together, feed one another, and follow from each other in a predictable way.

A new program is not a blank piece of paper onto which any number of statements and data names can be written in infinite combinations. Instead, the key to organizing your program is to build it up as a series of routines (individually defined tasks, whether large or small).

As we saw in chapter 4, before you begin writing a program, you need to ask yourself two questions:

1. What is the program supposed to do? (Purpose and Output)
2. How is it supposed to do it? (Input, Hidput, and Logic)

You answered these questions in the program blueprint. If you did a good job, your design will be a simple, logical one.

The next step is to determine the structure of the program. This building-block plan of the routines in a BASIC program does two things:

1. It shows you the program as a series of tasks to be done. ("What's this program supposed to do?")

2. It tells you which kinds of statements—sometimes even which particular BASIC statements—need to be written to do those tasks. ("How's the program supposed to do it?")

The result is a well-defined program that is easy to write.

6.2 ORGANIZING A PROGRAM

Logic gives your program *sense*. Organization gives your program shape, or *structure*.

Every program needs a solid structure to build upon, something substantial to attach statements to. As with the storage shed, you can't put a program together on the fly. To give you a starting point, we're going to propose a common structure for all programs, a sort of classic program. (Some sections of the program, in certain cases, may not be used.)

To begin, let's look at the basics of every program that has ever been written, or ever will be.

Every program

1. brings data in,
2. processes it, and then
3. puts out some kind of report (on screen, to the printer, or onto disk).

Consequently, there will be three major routines in every program.

6.2.1 The Major Routines

- IN
- PROCESS
- OUT

These three major routines are under the control of one master routine, which we'll call **MAIN CONTROL.** Our classic program organization looks like this:

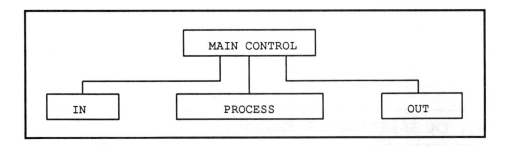

Now let's start expanding this basic structure.

If the computer is going to work with any existing data (as opposed to having the user type in everything), then it needs to read what has already been stored on disk in files. This gives us a standard **FILEREAD** routine.

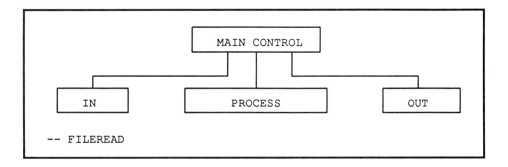

Some programs need only one **PROCESS** routine. Others require a lot of small processing routines, all fed and controlled by the major **PROCESS** routine. We'll call these smaller subcalculation routines **SUBCALC.**

A program typically has a few small, commonplace routines that need to be done: error checking, error handling, getting keyboard input, editing keyboard input, and data formatting. All routines of this sort take data and manipulate ("massage") it in some way to make it easier to use. So we'll put these into a program section called **MASSAGE** routines.

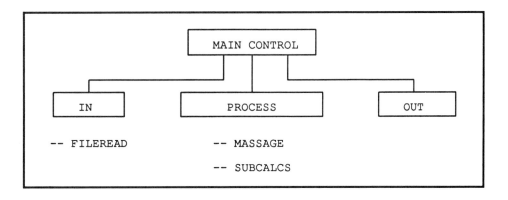

Recall that in chapter 1, we defined a report as output that can be directed to the screen, to the printer, or onto a disk. In our classic program structure, we need to differentiate these report types. This gives us three separate subsections for the **OUT** part of our program:

- **SCREENOUT** (for the screen)
- **PRINTOUT** (for the printer)
- **FILEOUT** (for disk file output)

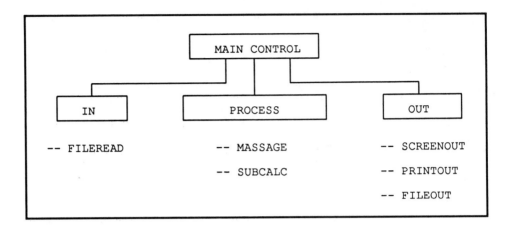

6.2.2 The STUB

Finally, we need a **STUB,** which is a small group of statements at the beginning of the program required to get the program started.

Typically, the **STUB**

1. enables the **DATE** routine,
2. commands the program to **OPEN** the files that are going to be read, and
3. turns things over to the **MAIN CONTROL** routine.
4. After **MAIN CONTROL** supervises all the processing of data, it returns control to the **STUB,** which
5. closes all files and then ends the program.

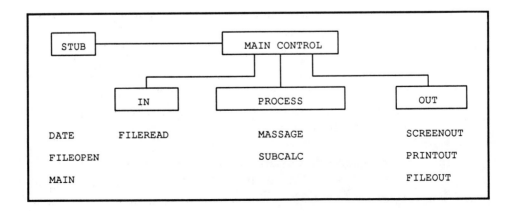

6.2.3 The END

The actual end of a program is in the **STUB.** A well-designed BASIC program will almost never have an **END** statement as the last statement of the program listing, since the **STUB** is at the beginning of the program and all the routines are listed *after* the **STUB.** Instead, the **END** statement (the conclusion of the program) normally appears as the last statement of the **STUB** section.

```
Program Listing
┌──────────────────────┐
│  ┌────────────────┐  │
│  │ Stub           │  │
│  │                │  │
│  │ END            │  │
│  ├────────────────┤  │
│  │ Routine        │  │
│  ├────────────────┤  │
│  │ Routine        │  │
│  │                │  │
│  ├────────────────┤  │
│  │ Routine        │  │
│  ├────────────────┤  │
│  │ Routine        │  │
│  │                │  │
│  │                │  │
│  ├────────────────┤  │
│  │ Routine        │  │
│  │                │  │
│  └────────────────┘  │
└──────────────────────┘
```

As we'll see in a moment, the program does all of its work before the **END** statement is reached. The **STUB** periodically passes control of the program to one of the several routines (all listed in the large second part of the program), back again to the **STUB,** on to the next routine, and so on. Finally, control returns to the **STUB,** reads the **END** statement, and finishes.

An alternative to using an **END** is a **CHAIN** statement. Instead of just ending the program, the **CHAIN** first ends the program that has the **CHAIN** statement, then runs an entirely new program. You've already seen an example of the **CHAIN** statement: you used it to conclude the program in chapters 2 and 3, **bikemenu**. You'll be using **CHAIN** in all the programs that are selected and run from a menu.

6.3 THE TEN-PART CLASSIC PROGRAM

We can now list the ten parts of the classic program structure:

1. **STUB**

   - Directs program flow to:
   - **DATE** routine
   - **FILEOPEN** routine
   - **MAIN** routine
   - Includes **CLOSE** statement
   - Includes **END** statement (More commonly, **CHAIN**s to another program)

2. **FILEOPEN** routine

   - Opens all files
   - Establishes the layout of each file

3. **MAIN CONTROL** routine

   - Calls **FILEREAD, MASSAGE, CALC/SUBCALC,** and **OUT** routines

4. **FILEREAD** routine

   - Reads files
   - Unpacks information

5. **MASSAGE** routines

   - Any commonplace tasks that format or handle data —e.g., errors, input, date, and so forth.

6. **CALC** routine

- Changes data
- Produces value to be saved or displayed
- (Optionally) calls **SUBCALC** routines

7. **SUBCALC** routines

- Detailed calculations

8. **SCREENOUT** routine

- Outputs information to screen

9. **PRINTOUT** routine

- Outputs information to printer

10. **FILEOUT** routine

- Outputs changed data back to files

Keep in mind that the names of these routines will not appear in PowerBASIC. We've made up these names to illustrate program organization.

Before we look more closely at each section of the classic program organization, let's compare

1. their frequency within a program and
2. the routines that each enables:

Routine	Number of occurrences	Routines that will be enabled
1 **STUB**	One	All others
—**CLOSE**		
—**END/CHAIN**		
2 **FILEOPEN**	One	None
3 **MAIN CONTROL**	One	**FILEREAD, PROCESS, SUBCALC, 3 OUTPUT**
4 **FILEREAD**	One for each file	None
5 **CALC**	None to several	**SUBCALC, MASSAGE**
6 **SUBCALC**	None to dozens	None
7 **MASSAGE**	6 or more	Other **MASSAGE**
8 **SCREENOUT**	None to dozens	None
9 **PRINTOUT**	None to dozens	None
10 **FILEOUT**	One per file out	None

Now let's see what each section of this classic program organization looks like.

Look at this as an outline or survey of the statements and concepts that will be covered in this book. Take your best GUESS at the new terms and statements that appear. DON'T WORRY about not understanding the detail of each statement. We'll explain them to you in later chapters.

1. **The STUB.** This is a group of statements that typically look like this:

```
REM -- program "xxxxxxxx.bas" -- created [date]
REM -- data dictionary
REM -- contains data item names and brief explanation of each
REM -- data dictionary could be more than 100 REM statements!
REM --
GOSUB getdate: REM -- enables date setting routine
GOSUB dimarrays: REM -- enables routine that sets the sizes of tables
GOSUB openfiles: REM -- enables routine that opens the files
GOSUB main: REM -- enables main control routine
CLOSE: REM -- closes all files
END: REM -- stops the program
```

Every program you write should begin with a **STUB** of this form. There are three reasons why:

a. It puts all descriptive information (program name and date, names and explanations of all data items) at the very beginning, where you can skim it at a glance even if this program listing is one of many printouts filed in a binder.

b. It starts your program with a building-block structure, as is shown by the series of **GOSUB** statements in the **STUB**. The arrangement of the blocks is clearly visible at the top of the program listing.

c. You can use the **STUB** to build your program one block at a time:

   • write one new routine (block)
   • test-run it
   • correct any errors before going on to the next block

The **STUB** is *not* **MAIN CONTROL.** It only enables **MAIN CONTROL.** It actually does little work and contains no logic (it makes no decisions). **MAIN CONTROL** is a separate major routine, which controls file input, processing, and output. Think of the **STUB** as an outline of the chapters of a book. It just points to the chapters.

A classic **STUB** is on the previous page. We recommend that you use it at the beginning of each new program, taking out any statements that aren't needed. (You should never need to add any.)

2. **FILEOPEN routine.** Three types of statements typically appear in a **FILEOPEN** routine:

   - **OPEN**, for all files to be used by the program
   - **DIM**, to define the size of a table of data items found in the file
   - **FIELD**, to define the location of data items within a file

   The **FILEOPEN** routine places the descriptions or definitions of all file data in one place in your program structure.

3. **The MAIN CONTROL routine.** This is the "traffic cop" for the **IN, PROCESS,** and **OUT** routines. In fact, the **MAIN** routine has control over everything except the **STUB, getdate, dimarrays,** and **openfiles.**

   The bulk of the **MAIN CONTROL** routine will be a loop that enables **FILEREAD, SUBCALC, MASSAGE,** and the three **OUT** routines. It enables these other routines over and over again, until all the data has been processed and sent to one of the **OUT** routines.

   Because the **MAIN CONTROL** is the center of your program, it's essential to check and double-check the blueprint and the design of this routine. It seems, from our experience, that **MAIN CONTROL** is the routine where the more catastrophic errors are commonly found. An error of logic can also be more difficult to find in **MAIN CONTROL** than anywhere else in a program. So take the time to design **MAIN CONTROL** thoughtfully.

   MAIN CONTROL contains the following statements:

   - **GOSUB**, to enable a subroutine
   - **CALL**, to enable a procedure
   - **GOTO**, to redirect the program to a specific line within the **MAIN CONTROL** routine

- **IF...THEN**, to test if a condition is true, then do something
- Statements that "assign" values, such as

```
numlines% = 0
custnum% = 1
```

4. **The FILEREAD routine.** Once a file is open, its contents can be read. However, a random-access file has its numeric data "packed" in, to reduce storage space on disk. So the **FILEREAD** routine has to "unpack" the numeric data before it can be used.

   Two statement types will appear in a typical **FILEREAD** routine:

   - **GET** (to go get a record from a random-access file)
   - the "unpack" statements (which you'll learn about later on)

5. and 6. **The CALC and SUBCALC routines.** These are the routines that perform math or data manipulation (move data around). **MAIN CONTROL** calls the **CALC** routines, which in turn normally call **SUBCALC** routines for complex processing.

   Once again, it is best to group routines of this type in one part of the program, for readability and ease of modification.

   Here are the statement types that appear in **CALC** or **SUBCALC** routines:

   - **CALL**, to enable a procedure (a minor and repeated routine)
   - **GOTO**, to redirect program flow to another place within the CALCULATION or SUBCALC routine
   - **IF...THEN {calculate}/CALL/GOTO**, to do the indicated operation only if a condition is true
   - "Assign" statements and other statements that manipulate, calculate, or move data (see examples of "assign" statements just above)

   and sometimes,

   - **LSET**
   - the "pack" family of statements (**MKI\$, MKS\$, MKD\$,** and **MKL\$**), which pack data to go into random files.

7. **Frequent MASSAGE routines.** There can be any number of these small, data-manipulating, convenience routines. When you find yourself needing a short or simple routine that will be repeated

during a program, put it with other **MASSAGE** routines. These small routines can all be assembled in one clear, easy-to-read group rather than scattered throughout the program.

That way, you'll always know where to go looking for any **MASSAGE** routine you need to modify. And you'll always know where you can put a new one to find it later.

Some **MASSAGE** routines, their purposes, and examples:

- **NUMERIC EDIT,** to make sure a number is valid
  (Is 12201B a valid number?)
- **DATE EDIT,** to make sure a date is valid
  (Is 023089 a valid date?)
- **DATE COMPARISON,** to find the earlier of two dates
  (Which is earlier, 043089 or 053188?)
- **DAYS ELAPSED,** to calculate the number of days between two dates
  (How many days elapse between 04/30/89 and 11/03/90?)
- **DATE SWAP,** to change a valid date into a standard format for use in date calculations
  (Swap your standard format MMDDYY, into YYMMDD, e.g., 11789 into 890117)
- **ROUNDING,** to round off for dollars and cents to two decimals
  (0.60508 dollars per [currency unit] = $0.61)

Appendix E contains a number of sample **MASSAGE** routines, ready for you to use in your programs with little or no modification.

The **MASSAGE** routines can use all statement types, with the following exceptions:

- no file **GET**s and **PUT**s
- no **GOSUB**s (**CALL** is okay)
- no **CLOSE**
- no **END**

8. **The SCREENOUT routine.** Sends data to the screen only. The statement types that are found in the **SCREENOUT** routine are:

- **PRINT** and **PRINT USING**
- the "string" family of statements (**CHR$**, **STR$**, **MID$**, and so on.)
- **LOCATE** (locates the blinking cursor on the screen)
- **CLS** (clears the screen)
- **COLOR** (lets you use different colors on the screen)

- **CSRLIN** (tells the program what line the cursor is on)
- **POS** (tells the program what column the cursor is on)
- **TAB** (positions the cursor at a specific column on the screen)
- "format" statements that are used along with **PRINT USING**

9. **The PRINTOUT routine.** Sends data to the printer only. Statements used in the **PRINTOUT** routine are:

- **LPRINT** and **LPRINT USING**
- the "string" family of statements (see above)
- TAB
- "format" statements

10. **The FILEOUT routine.** Sends data to a disk file only. The **FILEOUT** statements are:

- **PUT**
- **LSET**
- the "pack" family of statements (**MKI$**, **MKS$**, **MKD$**, and **MKL$**), which pack data destined for random files.

Chapter 12 covers random files and outputting of data to them.

6.4 ROUTINES FROM NOW ON

Our use of the word "routine" so far has been as a general term of program organization. From now on, we'll be using the word as the formal term for the building blocks of a program.

In fact, that's what a program is: a **STUB** and all its ROUTINES!

We work with two types of routines in PowerBASIC, the *subroutine* and the *procedure*. In this chapter, we've introduced you to the concept of routines as a family. We'll explain *subroutines* and *procedures* in detail in the next chapter. And because they are fundamental parts of the building-block approach, almost every chapter in this book will give you practice with them in the programming exercises.

Here's the basic difference between the two types of routines:

- Subroutines are generally the major routines that control processing logic.

● Procedures are usually minor routines that accomplish a single task (usually one that is repeated) with some data, rather than control anything else.

With this in mind, look again at the relationships of the major routines of the classic program and the choice between making each one a subroutine or a procedure:

Routine	Number of occurrences	Routines that will be enabled	Subroutine or procedure?
1 **STUB**	1	All others	—
2 **FILEOPEN**	1	None	Subroutine
3 **FILEREAD**	1 per file	None	Subroutine
4 **MAIN CNTRL**	1	**FILEREAD, PROCESS. SUBCALC, 3 OUTPUT**	Subroutine
5 **CALC**	0 to dozens	**SUBCALC, MASSAGE**	Subroutine
6 **SUBCALC**	0 to dozens	None	Either
7 **MASSAGE**	6 or more	Other MASSAGE	Procedure
8 **SCREENOUT**	0 to dozens	None	Either
9 **PRINTOUT**	0 to dozens	None	Either
10 **FILEOUT**	1 per file	None	Subroutine

More on this distinction in the next chapter. Just remember: program organization is a *routine process*.

6.5 FROM BLUEPRINT TO ROUTINES

The blueprint format that you learned in chapter 4 is pretty close to a block diagram of your program. All we have to do is to link the steps in the blueprint with specific program routines (subroutines and procedures).

The Rules Are:

1. Always use the standard **STUB**. The **STUB** is the same for every program. No new control statements go into it. ONLY THE DATA DICTIONARY DEFINITIONS OF THE VARIABLE NAMES

SHOULD EVER BE ADDED. If there are no tables (an unusual program), the **GOSUB** to **dimarrays** should have a **REM** in front of it. OTHER THAN THAT, THE **STUB** SHOULD NEVER CHANGE.

2. Every program should contain exactly ONE **FILEOPEN** routine, whether there are a dozen files in the program or none. ALL **OPEN**S SHOULD BE IN THIS ROUTINE. If no files are to be opened, then leave the subroutine itself with only a blank **REM**ark and a **RETURN** statement.

3. Each file that is read should have ITS OWN **FILEREAD** ROUTINE. This routine gets and unpacks one record each time it is summoned. If you have six files, then have six **FILEREAD** routines.

4. The **MAIN CONTROL** DOES NO WORK ITSELF. It just serves as the major loop, which controls getting data, processing it, and outputting it. Its function is to control all the **READ**s, **CALC**s, and **WRITE**s (or **PRINT**s). Therefore, no tasks from your blueprint are assigned to **MAIN CONTROL.**

5. All PRINT tasks go to **PRINTOUT** routines. All SCREEN tasks go to **SCREENOUT** routines. Usually, one master routine for each different screen layout or printed page layout is a good idea. Each of the master routines may or may not have several other routines that it controls.

6. Each file written should have its own FILEOUT routine, with several minor routines if needed.

7. The **CALC** routine controls calculations and the movement of data. It is called from **MAIN CONTROL. SUBCALC,** which do the actual calculations, are controlled by either the **CALC** routine or the **OUT** routines **(SCREENOUT, PRINTOUT, or FILEOUT),** whichever works more easily in your program. Assign calculation and data movement tasks to the **SUBCALC** and don't worry about what controls the **SUBCALC** until the very end. Do what works most easily in your program.

8. **MASSAGE** routines are almost always procedures that do some specific operation (massaging) on a certain type of data. They can

be used many times in the same program and usually are worth saving for use in other programs. Most programmers build up a library of routines that they use over and over in different programs. Because the work they do is so detailed, you probably won't assign any of the tasks from your blueprint to one of them. Your tasks will usually be broader in scope than would be served by a MASSAGE routine.

Steps in converting a blueprint into a routine:

1. Write each step of your blueprint down the left side of a piece of paper.

2. Using rules 1–8 above, assign each task to a routine.

3. You know you'll always have one **STUB,** one **FILEOPEN,** one **FILEREAD** for each file read, one **FILEOUT** for each file written, and one **MAIN CONTROL,** so...

4. Get another sheet of paper and group the tasks by each type of **SUBCALC** and **OUT** routines.

5. When you are done, decide how many routines of each type you want, or whether you want to group several tasks into one routine.

6. Decide if you want the **SUBCALC** controlled by one major **CALC** or by the **OUT** routines.

7. You now have a program structure.

6.6 FILE COMMANDS—(BACK TO THE POWERBASIC ENVIRONMENT)

(Relax for fifteen to twenty minutes before beginning this section—set the book down and get your mind off of it for a few minutes.)

The *File* menu is used to get and save programs. We need to define a few words (special definitions, only as related to the *File* menu) before we go futher with the discussion.

1. The *Environment* is the PowerBASIC on-screen environment that is used to write, modify, and test programs.

2. A *Module* is any self-contained program, or part of a program, that is usually added to another program in PowerBASIC. (It has its own name and is changed or corrected separately from other programs. It is saved separately from the rest of the program.)

3. A *Program Block* is any section of program statements in a program, subroutine, or procedure.

Now We'll Browse Through the *File* menu:

1. The *Load Program* command gets an existing program from the disk and brings it into the PowerBASIC environment. It clears the entire environment of any programs before bringing in the requested program.

2. The *Pick* command gives you a faster way of loading and working with several programs, one right after the other. Since we aren't covering advanced topics, we'll skip this feature. A professional programmer would find it very handy.

3. A *New* (program) is one that you start fresh. This command clears any previously loaded program statements so that you can start typing in a completely *New* program on a blank screen.

4. The *Save* command saves the current module onto the disk. The curent module is the one that is being displayed on the screen at the time the *Save* command is invoked.

   If the current module was orginally loaded from the disk, it is saved under that name, and the original one is replaced on disk.

   If the current module doesn't yet have a name (it is a new program freshly typed in), then PowerBASIC will ask you for the name. If a module with that SAME name already exists on the disk, the *Save* command will replace the existing one.

5. The *Write to* command saves the current module onto the disk, but it lets you key in the name. As with the *Save* command, if another module is on the disk with the same name, it will be replaced.

   This command is used to save programs with different versions under different names. In this way, the original version is not replaced on the disk. It's also useful for something that programmers rarely talk about. In many cases, a program that needs to be written is similar to one already written. Using PowerBASIC, the programmer can get a program close to what is needed into the environment, make several changes, and then save it as an entirely new program.

6. The *Directory* command lets you look at the contents of the current PowerBASIC directory.

7. The *Change dir* command lets you change the directory in which PowerBASIC is working.

8. The *Get Info* command provides technical information about the program currently in the PowerBASIC enviornment. We won't get technical enough to use this in this book. To an advanced programmer, however, the information could be invaluable.

9. The *Os shell* command lets you leave PowerBASIC temporarily to do something in DOS. You can return to PowerBASIC at any time by

   TYPE **exit**⟨ENTER⟩

10. The *Quit* command leaves PowerBASIC completely.

CHAPTER SUMMARY

1. Program structure makes writing simpler because it breaks up the logic into small, manageable blocks. You can work on one block at a time and ignore the rest of the program. This approach makes testing quicker and easier.

2. Every program contains three major sections:
   - IN
   - PROCESS
   - OUT

3. The classic program structure contains a **STUB** and nine (or fewer) other routine types.
   - **FILEOPEN**
   - **MAIN CONTROL**
   - **FILEREAD**
   - **CALC**
   - **SUBCALC**
   - **MASSAGE**
   - **SCREENOUT**
   - **PRINTOUT**
   - **FILEOUT**

4. Routines are the building blocks of program organization. You should think of program structure in terms of tasks to be done and assign each task to a routine.

5. Subroutines control program input, output, and major logic decisions.

6. Procedures perform small and/or frequently repeated tasks, usually on data.

7. Transform your blueprint into routines before you begin programming.

8. The commands of the *File* menu are:
   - Load Program (one already existing on disk)
   - Pick (among several previously used programs)
   - New Program (you are keying it in for the first time)
   - Save (the current module onto disk)
   - Write to (save the current module under another name)
   - Directory (look at the current one)
   - Change dir (to another directory)
   - Get info (about the current program)
   - Os Shell (temporarily exit to the operating system)
   - Quit (leave PowerBasic completely)

THE BOTTOM LINE

1. BASIC is a personable language, which tells your computer to follow your instructions one at a time until it has produced a desired "report."

2. When you look at a BASIC program, break it up into sections using the block-line method. Then look at each block, one at a time, to figure out what each does.

3. PowerBASIC gives you a complete working environment, which encourages writing programs in building-block fashion.

4. Blueprint your program before you write one line of code.

5. Data names should be meaningful, short (but not cryptic), consistent, and clear.

6. **Program organization is not fluff. Organize your thoughts, assign the tasks to routines, and then program each routine.**

EXERCISES

1. Take the blueprint of program **mailkey1** and, using the seven steps, form the program structure.

2. Take the blueprints of the program exercises at the end of chapter 4 and formulate the program structure.

3. Enter PowerBASIC and write the actual lines of the **STUB** from this chapter; save it as a routine called "STUB."

4. Take the blueprints from chapter 5 and set up the program structure, using the seven-step process.

Chapter 7

Control of Routines (Getting Data in and out of the "Windows")

7.1	Routines	121
7.2	Subroutines (Major Flow Diversions)	121
7.3	Procedures (Minor Repeated Tasks)	125
7.4	The Routine-Selection Test	128
7.5	An Arbitrary Decision	129
7.6	Global and Local Data	130
7.7	Data into and out of Subroutines	131
7.8	Data into and out of Procedures	132
7.9	The GOTO "Problem"	135
7.10	Notes on Using the Menus	137
7.11	File Menu Details	138

Picture an "open" office environment, where people walk freely into and out of any office (Figure 7.1). When you go somewhere to get a file folder, you can carry the folder back to your own workspace. It's easy to get information. But the system requires careful management, or else no one will know where any of the file folders are. Anyone in any office can use, abuse, or lose an original document. Recovery from misuse of files could be lengthy or impossible.

Now envision a "closed" environment, where people can only get and use file folders within their own offices. Here, glass windows

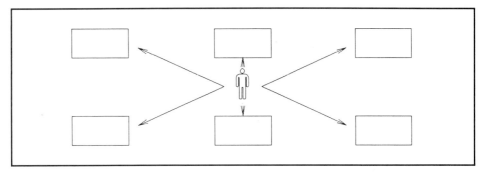

Figure 7.1

separate one office from another. (We mean regular glass windows; no connection to "windowing" computer software.) You exchange information in the files through a system of copying:

1. You jot your question on a piece of paper and hold it up to the window.
2. Someone in the next office reads what you're asking for and gets the necessary file.
3. The person looks up the information you want.
4. He or she responds to you by jotting back a reply and holding it up to the glass for you to see.

No one is allowed to carry the physical data out of an office. It takes more effort and time to exchange information between offices, but everyone knows where every file folder is at all times. It's much easier to control what belongs in your own office—and nobody else is going to mess up or lose any of your original documents (Figure 7.2).

In terms of getting a job done, each of these environments has advantages and disadvantages over the other.

- Open favors wide distribution and sharing of tasks (e.g., if several offices must develop a specific document).
- Open doesn't work well in keeping original data intact.
- Closed works fine for processing small amounts of information, especially for frequently enabled small tasks.
- Closed makes transfer of information into and out of offices less flexible.

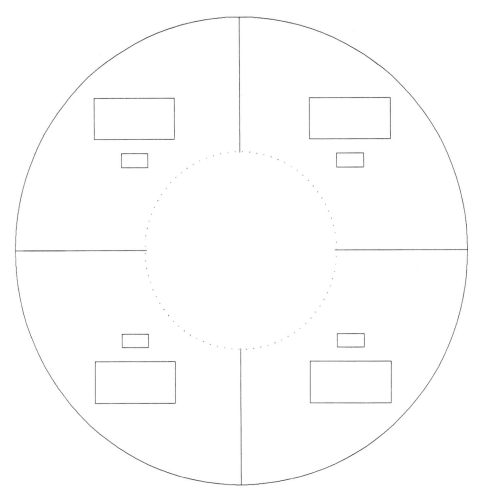

Figure 7.2

Most real-life offices have both shared documents and non-shared documents. A business will find that each office type offers something to the design of a work system that solves the staff's needs.

Handling data in a program is like distributing and processing documents in an office where there are a lot of different tasks to do. BASIC deals with open and closed access by offering you two ways of processing information (the two types of routines that we've mentioned several times). In this chapter, you'll look closely at *subroutines* and *procedures*. You'll also learn exactly how information (data) moves into and out of the routines in your programs.

7.1 ROUTINES

We suggested in chapter 6 that you can think of a program as being simply a **STUB** and all its routines. It's not a bad way to think of program organization, because it suggests that *everything* should be considered part of a task, part of one routine or another.

A statement is a single sentence in BASIC that accomplishes one simple task. (Refer back to chapters 2 and 3, the sample programs, for a look at some statements, or chapter 6 for brief explanations of some statements.) A routine is *a group of program lines* treated as if they were all one gigantic statement. You name each routine, and that name defines the entire routine "statement" (which could easily include a hundred individual statements). You'll recall from chapter 6, "The END," that the routines don't appear physically next to the statement that enables them. At some earlier point in the program, a statement line will *enable* the routine, meaning that program control flows to the routine.

We work with two types of routines in PowerBASIC, the *subroutine* and the *procedure*. The basic difference, once again, is that

- Subroutines are generally the major routines that control processing logic.
- Procedures are usually minor routines that accomplish a single task (usually a repeated one) rather than control anything else.

7.2 SUBROUTINES (MAJOR FLOW DIVERSIONS)

By "control processing logic," we mean that subroutines are the blocks of the program that the *main* flow of program logic enters and exits. Just as you can drive along an interstate highway and exit occasionally to see a point of interest without really leaving the principal route, so can the program follow its main logic while permitting detours for specific purposes. Whenever main flow moves out of the **STUB,** it goes to a subroutine.

So we can say that *a subroutine is a significant subsection of the main program flow.* In a moment, we'll look at the details. First, let's see what happens when we enable a subroutine (which is done with the **GOSUB** statement):

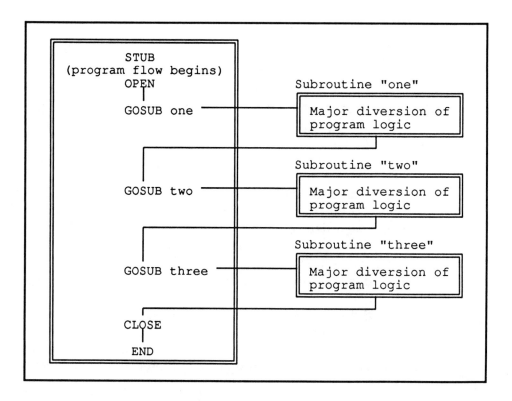

As a true *subsection* of the program in which it occurs, a subroutine cannot stand on its own (unlike a procedure). Therefore, you should think of a subroutine as a major rerouting of your program logic to accomplish an integral, major task.

Subroutine **one** in the diagram above is effectively one big statement made up of individual statement lines. It may be performed once in the running of the program or many times, depending on how often a **GOSUB one** statement is encountered. At every occurrence of a **GOSUB one**, the program branches directly to the routine named **one** and begins reading the statements there as if they were the next ones in the program listing. (All of this holds true for subroutines **two** and **three** as well.)

The syntax of the **GOSUB** and of the subroutine it enables are:

GOSUB {name of subroutine}

.

{intervening lines of program}

.

{name of subroutine}:

.

.

.

RETURN

Note that the lines of the subroutine do not directly follow the **GO-SUB** in the program listing. One or more lines separate the **GOSUB** and the line starting with the subroutine name with which that **GOSUB** is associated. This is intentional: a program should not be able to "wander" into a routine in the normal downward progression of program flow. The routine must be enabled only by the proper statement.

Now take a look at how flow moves into, out of, and around the **GOSUB** statement and the parts of the subroutine. The numbers in parentheses at the right link each line to the steps of the flow process as explained below:

{program begins}

.

.

GOSUB {name of subroutine}	(1)
{statement following GOSUB {point of RETURN}	(5)

.

.

{any statement to prevent reading the following line, e.g.,	
END}	(6)
{name of subroutine}:	(2)
. {routine commences}	(3)

.

RETURN	(4)

Here's how it works:

1. The program flow reaches the **GOSUB** statement line, where the program reads in the name of the subroutine being enabled.

2. The logic then jumps to the line beginning with that subroutine name. (A colon follows the subroutine name.)

3. There, the subroutine begins. (Remember, a routine is treated as if it's one long statement. The indenting of the entire routine suggests that.)

4. Its statements are executed sequentially up to the **RETURN** statement, at which time the program flow goes back to *the line immediately following* the **GOSUB.**

5. Program flow resumes at the line after the **GOSUB.**

6. As we've pointed out, just before the first line of the subroutine there must be a statement of some kind—such as **END** or **RETURN**—that will prevent the program from entering the subroutine via the normal downward flow of logic.

A subroutine must *only* be entered (enabled) by way of the **GOSUB** statement.

Now let's try it with the menu program for Bikes Peak, using the same numbers in parentheses at the right to refer to the steps above:

```
REM -- program "firsmenu.bas" -- created 010189
    GOSUB printmenu : REM -- perform the print routine                      (1)
    INPUT "Number from menu"; menuselect$ : REM -- Step #2 Asks for the selection   (5)
    program$ = "bikes" + menuselect$ :REM -- form the program name
    PRINT "Selecting program"; program$
    CHAIN program$ : REM -- Step #3-runs that program
    END                                                                     (6)
printmenu:                                                                  (2)
    REM -- (Step #1- displays the menu)                                     (3)
    CLS : REM -- clear the screen
    PRINT "* * * * * * BIKES PEAK * * * * * *"
    PRINT "* * * * * * PROGRAMS * * * * * *"
    FOR c = 1 TO 5: PRINT: NEXT c : REM -- space 5 lines
    PRINT "1 Inventory"
    PRINT "2 Customers"
```

```
PRINT "3 Mail List"
PRINT "4 Order Processing"
PRINT "5 Monthlies"
FOR c = 1 TO 4: PRINT: NEXT c : REM -- space 4 lines
RETURN                                                        (4)
```

7.3 PROCEDURES (MINOR REPEATED TASKS)

Like side trips in traveling, small tasks are common in a program. But there's no need to create a separate routine for *every* small task to be done. Sometimes you can just write a line or two of code right within the subroutine.

When a small task is done repeatedly, though, you should consider the *procedure*. And if a task is to repeat the same manipulation or calculation at different points of the program with different values each time, then the *procedure* is a natural choice.

To help you decide whether to use a procedure or a subroutine, let's start with two *very general* guidelines.

1. **Is it a minor task?** Does it perform a series of calculations relating to one end result? Or does it transform one number or string into the format in which it's printed? If so, consider it a minor task, or procedure. But if it makes any major processing decisions (decides which of many other routines to enable), then the task is major and should be a subroutine.

2. **Is it a repeated task?** Is it enabled by several other routines within the same program? Can it be used with different kinds of data? The procedure was designed for these needs.

The key is to ask yourself if the task is *repetitive* as well as unrelated to control of program flow.

Procedures are incidental to main program flow. In fact, procedures are not even integral parts of the programs in which you happen to write them while working in PowerBASIC. A procedure can be saved outside the program that uses it and then later used in any other programs.

> A procedure can stand alone, independently of data names. It can be plugged into other programs with ease.

This is the real value of the procedure. If there's a *small task* to be done, one which might apply to *similar kinds of data with different names*—even to *data in different programs*, then do the task with a procedure. (We'll see some examples in a moment.) The **CALL** statement enables a procedure.

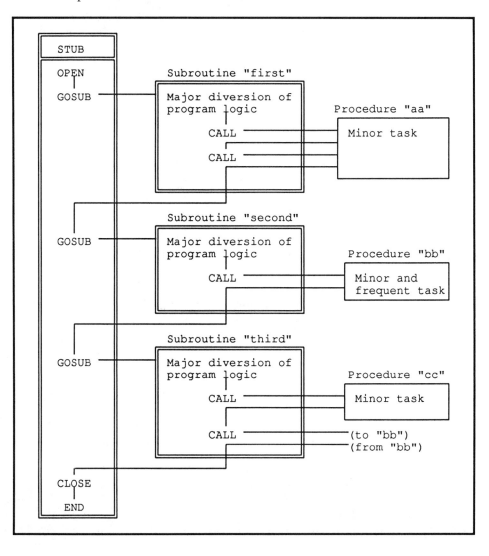

The diagram shown on 126 includes two points regarding the use of procedures.

1. One procedure, **aa,** is **CALL**ed twice by the same subroutine to do a task (perhaps with two different sets of data). Another procedure, **bb,** is **CALL**ed twice from two (or more) different subroutines of the program. In your programs, you'll create procedures that need to be repeated many times, possibly hundreds.

2. We have not included any **CALL**s in the **STUB.** It is all right to do so, but it's not common. One reason is that we don't find repeated tasks in the **STUB** itself. The **STUB** is a one-time summoning of major routines. That is, program logic passes through the **STUB** only once.

The **CALL** statement and the procedure have the following syntax:

```
CALL {name of subroutine (data)}
             .
{intervening lines of program}
             .
SUB {name of procedure (data)}
             .
             .
             .
END SUB
```

Let's look at it in a program:

```
REM—program "bikemenu.bas" 010189
CALL printmenu
PRINT : PRINT : PRINT : PRINT
INPUT "Number from menu"; menuselect$
program$ = "bikes" + menuselect$
PRINT "Selecting program"; program$
CHAIN program$
END

{procedure "printmenu"}
SUB printmenu
CLS
```

```
PRINT "* * * * * * BIKES PEAK * * * * * *"
PRINT "* * * * * * PROGRAMS * * * * * *"
FOR c = 1 to 5: PRINT: NEXT c
PRINT "1 Inventory"
PRINT "2 Customers"
PRINT "3 Mail List"
PRINT "4 Sales"
PRINT "5 Monthlies"
END SUB
```

You can see that the procedure has a syntax very similar to that of the subroutine. And it should also never be entered as a result of the natural downward flow of logic.

> A procedure *must* only be entered (enabled) by a **CALL** statement.

7.4 THE ROUTINE-SELECTION TEST

Recall the classic program structure from chapter 6. There are three routines, that can be either subroutines or procedures. How do you decide whether a particular **SUBCALC**, **SCREENOUT**, or **PRINTOUT** routine should be a subroutine or procedure?

These are sometimes questions of judgment rather than of fixed rules. And in many cases, either choice would work. So we'd like to propose a simple test to help you in judging whether a new block of programming statements should be formatted as a subroutine or as a procedure. (Your judgment will get better as you gain more experience in designing and writing programs.)

Read this test like a program: make your yes-or-no choice at each step and then follow the indicated flow to either the next question or the exit.

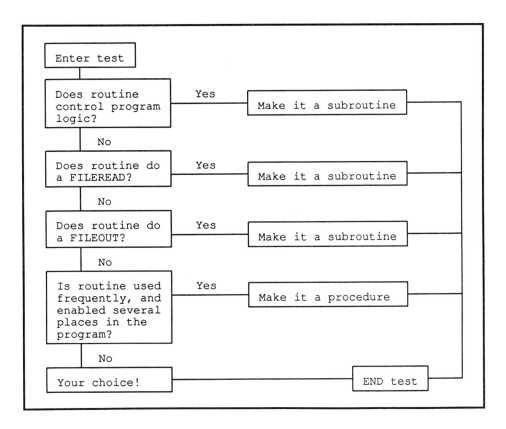

7.5 AN ARBITRARY DECISION

The routine-selection test will quickly tell you which routine type to use for a **FILEOUT** routine. But what about a **SCREENOUT** or **PRINTOUT** routine? **SCREENOUT** and **PRINTOUT** seem to be similar to **FILEOUT** in function. But there are differences:

- **SCREENOUT** may be very frequent, such as for user prompts.
- **SCREENOUT** is often used for small or transitory tasks (unlike the "major" task of saving data to a disk file).
- **SCREENOUT** usually involves printing diverse data items in similar formats.

- **PRINTOUT** lies somewhere between **FILEOUT** and **SCREENOUT** in these particulars.

We prefer to leave the choice for **SCREENOUT** and **PRINTOUT** open to the programmer. You should decide whether the routine you're creating "feels" like a major or a minor routine. (Your choice will probably depend on how data is to be handled, as we'll see shortly.)

Even if you decide to change your mind after having written the routine, the similarity of subroutine and procedure means that there should not be much work involved in switching over. The differences in syntax are slight, apart from adding (or removing) the "window" through which data moves. Before we look at the data window of the procedure, let's look at data program-wide.

7.6 GLOBAL AND LOCAL DATA

Remember the rule in chapter 5 that each data name must be unique? That's because data names are generally "global" throughout an entire program (including all the subroutines). Whenever a variable name is given a value, the value is carried for that name throughout all the subroutines. When a statement reassigns another value to the variable name, that new value is given to the variable name throughout the program. The value is always carried into a subroutine, and it is always carried out from the subroutine. The value of any data name in any subroutine can be changed by any other subroutine.

Within a *procedure* it's easier to prevent accidental changes to the values of data names (variables) in the larger program because the procedure is "blind" to the rest of the program. The procedure is not aware that other data names or other values even exist. Variable names within a procedure are "local;" they don't get values from outside the procedure, and they don't carry a value out to the program.

> Inside a *procedure*, data names are *local*. Only the data names passed to the procedure can be changed (more on this later).

Before we look at data handling in both types of routines, we want to emphasize one more time the danger of careless data naming. So here are *three rules for global vs. local data names*:

1. Global—Inside the **STUB** and all subroutines, *be sure* to use unique, meaningful names.

2. Local—In procedures, you *can* use simpler, shorter data names such as **a**, **b**, **x$**, **y%**, and so on (especially since procedures usually perform a common function to many different kinds of data, rather than to a specific dataname).

3. The safe bet is to avoid *all* duplication of local and global data names in a program if possible.

Creating a data dictionary for your programs is the best way to check your work; that's the time when you're most likely to spot any duplications. Even the local variables used within procedures deserve a **REM** statement in the data dictionary, just to be sure there will be no trouble. A duplicate name is an expensive time-waster to find later on.

7.7 DATA INTO AND OUT OF SUBROUTINES

Subroutines and procedures are similar but *not* equivalent. The central issue is how each handles data. Actually, only the *procedure* requires special treatment of its data input. For a subroutine, you can simply assume that

> Any data name anywhere in the program can be altered by any subroutine.

Like the first office at the beginning of this chapter, the subroutine is completely "open" to information exchange. A subroutine shares data indiscriminately with the entire program. If the subroutine reads in or assigns any value to a data name, then the changed value will be retained upon returning from the subroutine. *Everything that happens inside the subroutine gets carried outside.*

7.8 DATA INTO AND OUT OF PROCEDURES

A procedure is *not* an integral part of the program. It's connected to the rest of the program by a "window." Remember the closed office at the beginning of this chapter? People in one office had to show pieces of paper at windows to request information from another office. That's how the procedure works, too.

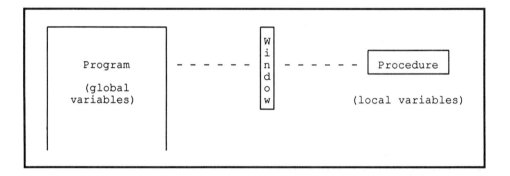

The format for writing the line that enables a procedure is:

CALL {procedure name (global variables)}

The procedure itself (which does not immediately follow the **CALL** statement in the program code) has this syntax:

SUB {procedure name (local variables)}
  .
  .
  .

  .
END SUB

The window process (the conversion of global variables into local variables) is different, but not complicated. Let's look.

7.8.1 The Data "Window"

Suppose you're writing a program that will contain a procedure called **custdiscount**. Within the routine, you're going to calculate a discount for purchases by good customers.

1. Select the variables to be brought in from the program:

   totalsale
   custrating%

   totalsale is the single-precison dollar total of the purchase being transacted. **custrating%** is an integer value ranging from 0 to 3. The higher the number, the better the customer.
   Because they come from the program "world" outside of the calculating procedure, **totalsale** and **custrating%** are *global* data names. The **CALL** statement will pass the value of the data names **totalsale** and **custrating%** in through the data window of the procedure:

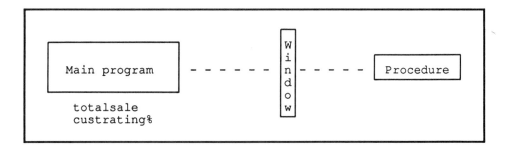

The **CALL** statement would be

CALL custdiscount (totalsale, custrating%)

2. Now add the variables that will be sent back to the program from the procedure. Let's include another single-precision global data name, **discount**. The value stored in this data name will be the end result of the procedure's discounting calculation. It will be the *output* of the procedure whenever a discount is given. So three global variables will be passed through the data window:

CALL custdiscount (total sale, custrating%, discount)

3. Create an *exactly equal number* of *local* variables, using unique and meaningful names *different* from the global variables:

amount
rating%
discamt

amount becomes the data name that the procedure will use for the total amount of the sale (before discounting). **rating%** is the value we'll test to see if the customer qualifies for a discount. (Assume 2 or higher is "good.") **discamt** will be the figure resulting from the discount calculation.

Now our data window will use six variables:

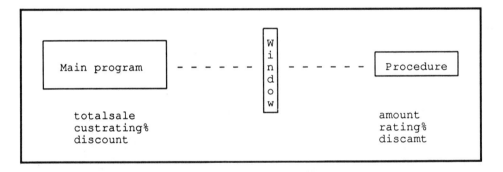

The statements defining the procedure itself look like this:

SUB custdiscount (amount, rating%, discamt)

.

.

END SUB

4. The procedure creates a *one-to-one correspondence* for all data names *in the order given* in the two sets of parentheses:

- first-listed global (**totalsale**) is linked to first-listed local (**amount**).
- the second pair is linked (**custrating%** and **rating%**).
- third-listed global (**discount**) is linked to third local (**discamt**).
- (and so on for other data names).

Note that the local variables must agree *in type* with the corresponding global variables—as in the case of the two integer variables and four single-precison variables above.

In other words, the procedure equates:

amount = **totalsale** (meaning, "Inside the procedure treat **amount** as if it were **totalsale**.")

rating% = **custrating%** (meaning, "Inside the procedure, treat **rating%** as if it were **custrating%**.")

discamt = **discount** (meaning, "Inside the procedure, treat **discamt** as if it were **discount**.")

Meanwhile, what's happening outside the procedure? There is only one connection between the procedure and the program, the data window (the names in parentheses in the **CALL** and **SUB** statements). Only those data names in the window can be modified by the procedure. All other variables in the program are left untouched.

So that's the data window. Here's what the statements will be:

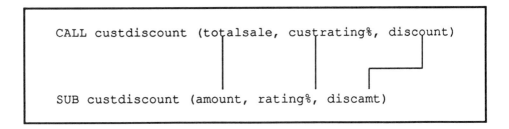

7.9 THE GOTO "PROBLEM"

Program logic is normally redirected by a **GOSUB** statement for major tasks and by a **CALL** statement for minor tasks. There's one other statement that does roughly the same thing—but with one important difference from **GOSUB** and **CALL**.

The **GOTO** is tempting because it's the easiest of the three flow-redirecting statements to grasp and use. Here's the syntax:

GOTO {line name or number}

That's it. Pretty simple. And what happens when flow moves to the line name or number that follows the **GOTO**? The program carries on at that point. The important difference here is that, with the **GOTO**, the program flow *does not* return to the line immediately following the enabling statement (as it does with both **GOSUB ... RETURN** and **CALL ... END SUB**). The program moves to a new section and stays there, until it's redirected again—if ever. In other words, will the program ever come back to the statement(s) following the **GOTO**? That's the potential problem. Look at this program excerpt. When will the program print "Back to here"?

```
REM--program underway
.
.
GOTO newplace
PRINT "Back to here"
CLOSE
END
.
.
newplace:
PRINT "Now at new place in program"
REM--program continues from here on downward
.
.
```

The answer is, "Back to here" will never be printed unless some statement redirects flow to the line following the **GOTO**. (A **GOSUB ... RETURN** or **CALL ... END SUB** would do so automatically.) Neither will the program ever reach the **CLOSE** and **END** statements!

Some years ago, some "experts" decided that the **GOTO** statement was a bad one. They felt that programmers abuse the **GOTO** and make a mess of their programs by jumping around and losing track of what was going on. As a result, even some capable programmers have avoided the **GOTO**.

We feel that **GOTO**s simplify certain situations, such as redirecting program flow WITHIN A ROUTINE based on the outcome of some simple decision or condition. Prohibiting the **GOTO** means the programmer has to fabricate several (or many) statements of the **IF ... THEN** family for each simple "flow around" statement. But these **IF**s can get very complex—sometimes 30 or 40 program lines for a single statement! At that point, the program becomes unreadable.

We believe that the **GOTO**, properly used (it can only reference statements within the same routine), makes it easier to read statements that would otherwise be too complex. The **GOTO** can clarify the logic of the program. We encourage *careful* use of **GOTO**s, especially when combined with **IF ... THEN** statements WITHIN THE SAME ROUTINE.

Thus, there are three statements that control redirecting of program logic:

- **GOSUB** enables a subroutine elsewhere in the program.
- **CALL** enables a procedure elsewhere in the program.
- **GOTO** redirects program execution to a new statement elsewhere in the *SAME ROUTINE. Caution:* Remember that program control will *not* automatically return to the program line following the **GOTO** statement.

Here is our ABSOLUTE "**GOTO** rule":

Use **GOTO** only to go somewhere else within the same routine.

Now, back to using the PowerBASIC environment:

7.10 NOTES ON USING THE MENUS

1. Once you have selected a menu, BE VERY CAREFUL. A wrong move could destroy a perfectly good module on the disk. Take it slowly; check three times before you actually choose a command.
2. Once you select a line item or command on a menu, BE EVEN MORE CAREFUL! Use the arrow keys, if necessary, to move around within the command box then, either key in the requested text or PRESS ⟨ENTER⟩ to make the selection.

7.11 FILE MENU DETAILS

The commands most used on the *File* menu are

- *Load*
- *New*
- *Save*
- *Write to*

We will now get into, and then out of, each of these commands.

7.11.1 Load

PRESS ⟨ALT + **f**⟩
PRESS ⟨ENTER⟩

and you get the *Load* program block. It prompts you for a file name. But there is a lot of flexibility in this command. It works in this fashion:

TYPE *.**bas**⟨ENTER⟩

and you will be given a list of all BASIC programs in the PowerBASIC directory. You can then move the cursor to the program you want to bring in and

PRESS ⟨ENTER⟩

to load the program.

TYPE **a:***.**bas**⟨ENTER⟩

and you will be given a list of all BASIC programs in the **a:** disk (the first floppy disk). Again, you can then move the cursor to the program you want to bring in and

PRESS ⟨ENTER⟩

to load the program.

> TYPE {**some directory name**}*.bas ⟨ENTER⟩

and you will be given a list of all the BASIC programs in that directory.

> TYPE {**the program you want to bring into PowerBASIC**} ⟨ENTER⟩

The previous programs will be cleared, and the specified program will be brought in.

> PRESS ⟨ESC⟩

to leave this command.

7.11.2 New

> PRESS ⟨ALT + **f**⟩

and you are in the *File* menu. Now, move the cursor down to *New*,

> PRESS ⟨ENTER⟩

and the edit window is cleared. Now, you are placed in the PowerBASIC environment, ready to type in a new program.

7.11.3 Save

> PRESS ⟨ALT + **f**⟩

> Move the cursor down to the *Save*.

> PRESS ⟨ENTER⟩

to save (in this case a blank screen) with the name **noname.bas**

7.11.4 Write To

PRESS ⟨ALT + **f**⟩

Move the cursor down to *Write to,*

PRESS ⟨ENTER⟩

and you have the *Write to* block. It works similarly to the *Save* command above except that it asks for a name to give the saved program.

TYPE **xyz**
PRESS ⟨ENTER⟩

Use this command the very first time that you save a new program, to give it the name that you want it saved as on the disk.

CHAPTER SUMMARY

1. Subroutines control program input, output, and logic.

2. Procedures perform minor, repeated tasks.

3. **GOSUB** and **CALL** statements enable subroutines and procedures respectively.

4. Global and local variables give you flexibility in making changes universally or within a single procedure.

5. The data "window" of the procedure passes changes made to only those data names (variables) explicitly listed in the **CALL** and **SUB** statements, and no others.

6. The **GOTO** statement serves a definite purpose but should be used with caution only to go somewhere within the same routine. It is *not* a simple substitute for (or equivalent to) either **GOSUB** or **CALL**.

7. The commands of the *File* menu which you will use the most are:

   - Load Program (one already existing on disk)
   - New (you are keying it in for the first time)
   - Save (the current module onto disk)
   - Write to (save the current module under another name)
   - Quit (leave PowerBASIC completely)

8. Once you have selected a menu, BE VERY CAREFUL selecting the command that you want. Be even more careful after you've picked the command and are picking the parameters in the command screen. The accidental pressing of the ⟨SPACE⟩ could cause a change or erasure that might take hours to reconstruct.

THE BOTTOM LINE

1. BASIC is a personable language, which tells your computer to follow your instructions one at a time until it has produced a desired "report."

2. When you look at a BASIC program, break it up into sections, using the block-line method. Then look at each block, one at a time, to figure out what each does.

3. PowerBASIC gives you a complete working environment, which encourages writing programs in building-block fashion.

4. Blueprint your program before you write one line of code.

5. Data names should be meaningful, short (but not cryptic), consistent, and clear.

6. Program organization is not fluff. Organize your thoughts, assign the tasks to routines, and then program each routine.

7. **Break your program up into subroutines and procedures; then use GOSUB and CALL. Use GOTO only to go somewhere else within the same routine.**

EXERCISES

1. Define each routine from the blueprint in chapter 4, Exercise 1, as either a subroutine or a procedure. Define any variable names that are passed to the procedures.

2. Define each routine from the blueprint in chapter 5, Exercise 1 (the program to enter new inventory data) as either a subroutine or a procedure. Define which variable names are passed to the procedures.

3. Blueprint and write a small program with two procedures on paper. Write one procedure as some formula or calculation(s) that you would like to program (Example—average three numbers) and one procedure to print out the results of that calculation. Save the paper—you'll be trying the program in the next chapter.

Chapter 8

The PowerBASIC Editor (You've Got a Friend)

8.1 Why You Need an Editor _____ **144**

8.2 Using the Editing Keys _____ **144**

8.3 FIND _____ **147**

8.4 FIND AND REPLACE (CHANGE) _____ **148**

8.5 CUT and PASTE _____ **149**

8.6 PRINTING Program Blocks _____ **151**

8.7 READING AND WRITING Program Blocks _____ **151**

8.8 Syntax Checking _____ **152**

8.9 Example of Using the Editor _____ **153**

Art tried his hand at programming—he decided to write a marketing report (marketing is his bag) that summarized how customers first heard about Bikes Peak. He was able to come up with a report, but, unfortunately it wasn't very readable. So he asked Donna to "clean up" the program and make the report more understandable.

Normally, Donna wouldn't take on such a job—but she has Power-BASIC, and she knows that with its powerful Editor, she can make short work out of this job.

Imagine a word processing typewriter that allows you to insert, delete, move, search for words, search and replace automatically, and cut and paste sections of text. That's basically what the PowerBASIC Editor does for you in programming.

8.1 WHY YOU NEED AN EDITOR

For the past seven chapters, you've been doing things with just the DEL and the ARROW keys. Now you'll really appreciate the time and grief that the Editor will save you.

You need an editor to—

- Correct mistakes.
- Insert additional program lines.
- Delete program lines.
- Change a variable name throughout the entire program.
- Move a routine or part of a routine to another part of the program.
- Find everywhere that a variable is used (or changed) throughout the program.
- Copy a piece of code to another part of the program and then change a small portion of it.

8.2 USING THE EDITING KEYS

There are so many keys for editing that remembering them all can give you a headache. So we just don't fiddle with all the keys; instead we master a few of them. The keys we recommend are:

HOME key—brings cursor to first position in a program line
END key—moves cursor to the last position in a program line
TAB key—moves cursor eight spaces to the right
ARROW keys—move cursor one line up or down, or one position left or right
BACKSPACE key—deletes the character to the left of the cursor
DELete key—deletes the character at the cursor
INSert key—never press the key by itself—it will put the Editor into Typeover mode, and you may write over good lines of code. The top middle of the Edit window states whether the Editor is in Insert or in Typeover mode. If you strike the INSert key by mistake, and the Editor is in Typeover mode, just press INSert to put the Editor back into Insert mode.
PAGE UP, PAGE DOWN—move cursor one screen up or down

F1—calls for PowerBASIC *Help*

F2—saves the program that you're working on

F3—loads a new program

F5—zooms the window (enlarges it to take up the whole screen)

F6—moves to another window (seldom used)

CTRL + **kb**—marks the start of a block (which will later be moved, copied, or erased)

CTRL + **kk**—marks the end of a block (which will later be moved, copied, or erased)

CTRL + **kh** keys—deselects, or unmarks, the marked block

CTRL + **ky** keys—deletes selected block from the program

CTRL + **kv** keys—moves selected block into the program at this cursor location

CTRL + **kc** keys—copies selected block into the program at this cursor location

CTRL + **kr** keys—reads a block from the disk and puts it into the program at this cursor location

CTRL + **kw** keys—writes the marked block onto the disk

CTRL + **kp** keys—prints the marked block onto the printer. (If no block is marked, then it prints the entire program.)

CTRL + **qf** keys—finds a string of up to 30 characters in your program

CTRL + **qa** keys—finds and replaces a string of up to 30 characters in your program with another string

The HOME key, whenever it is pressed, will bring the cursor to the first position of the line that the cursor is on.

The END key, when pressed, brings the cursor to the last position of the line that the cursor is on.

The TAB key moves the cursor eight spaces to the right. It remains on the same line. Since we always work with the Insert mode on, this has the effect of putting in eight spaces and moving everything (to the right of the cursor) over four positions.

The ARROW keys move the cursor all through the program, without disturbing any of the program text. The LEFT ARROW moves the cursor one position to the left each time it is pressed. The RIGHT ARROW moves the cursor one position to the right each time it is pressed. The UP ARROW moves the cursor up one line each time it's pressed, and the DOWN ARROW moves the cursor down one line each time it's pressed.

The BACKSPACE key deletes the character to the left of the cursor each time it is pressed. If the cursor is at the beginning of a line, pressing the BACKSPACE key will join that line to the end of the one above it.

The DELete key will delete the character at the cursor each time it is pressed. If the cursor is at the end of a line when the DELete key is pressed, the line below is attached to the end of that current line.

The INSert key should never be pressed (by itself) unless you don't see the *Insert* at the top right of the Edit window. Then press it once. The missing *Insert* indicates Typeover mode—when you key in, you write over the top of the existing text. (You could write over several lines of good original code by mistake.) The *Insert* shows that you are in Insert mode, which is the standard mode of PowerBASIC. This means that, as you type, all text to the right of the cursor is moved over. It makes adding variable names, program lines, commas, and semicolons (the normal additions and changes in programming) very easy. We *always* work in Insert mode, to keep things simple. When we make mistakes in spelling, we just use the DELete key to remove characters and then type it again, rather than worry about the Insert/Typeover mode. It's one fewer thing to remember, and we believe in keeping things as simple as possible.

The PAGE UP (PGUP) key displays the next screenful of statements above the current screen. The PAGE DOWN (PGDN) key displays the next screenful of statements below the current screen.

Press the F1 key twice whenever you're in the Editor, and you'll be in the *Help Index*. You can then select a topic to review; then PRESS ESC to put yourself back into Editor.

The F2 key saves the program that you are working on. We encourage you to press F2 often as you're working on your program. It safeguards against loss of power, a flaky computer, and clearing out lines of code by mistake.

The F3 key loads a new program from the disk. Make sure that you save the old program if you've changed it.

Use the F5 key to enlarge the Edit window so that it takes up the entire screen. Whenever you lose your place, are generally confused, or just can't find something because you can't see enough of the program, just press F5, and you'll get the full picture. Then use your ARROW keys or PGUP and PGDN keys to get your bearing. Press F5 again whenever you want to go back to the regular window size.

Whenever you want to move, copy, delete, or save program line or group of lines (a program block), the size of the block must be defined, or MARKED. Mark the beginning of a block by moving the cursor to the start of the block and press CTRL + **kb**; then move to the end of the block and press CTRL + **kk**. That shaded block can now be acted upon. Once you are done with block activity, UNMARK the block (so that you don't inadvertently lose some code) by pressing CTRL + **kh**.

Use CTRL + **qf** to locate specific variable names or constants. To keep matters simple, always go to the beginning of your program before using this command, and PRESS ⟨ENTER⟩ when asked for the options. We recommend that you ignore the options until you have several months' experience with PowerBASIC.

Use CTRL + **qa** to locate specific variable names or constants and replace them with some other variable name or constant. To keep matters simple, always go to the beginning of your program before using this command and press **g** ⟨ENTER⟩, when asked for the options. The **g** option means that the entire program is searched to find (and change, if you key **y** to the request for change) each occurrence of the string. We recommend that you ignore the other options until you have several months experience with PowerBASIC.

8.3 FIND

The *Find* keys are CTRL + **qf**. You use them to locate specific variable names, expressions, and line labels or numbers. If you don't remember (or don't know) the entire name or number that you are searching for, key in the part that is known. PowerBASIC will find every occurrence of the segment that you specified.

To use the *Find* keys,

PRESS ⟨CTRL + **qf**⟩

and the *Find* command pops up. Type in the name or expression that you are searching for, and

PRESS ⟨ENTER⟩

When the *Options* prompt comes up,

PRESS ⟨ENTER⟩

If the keyed item is in the program, PowerBASIC stops at the first occurrence.

PRESS ⟨CTRL + **L**⟩

and it'll stop at the next incidence. Each time CTRL + *L* is pressed, it will find another occurrence of that expression or name.

Normally, you will want to search the entire module for the item, and upper/lower case is not an issue. So we recommend that you ignore these options of the *Find* at the start.

In some cases, the *Whole Word* (**w**) option is a handy tool. When this is specified, it means that the keyed expression (all by itself) is exactly what PowerBASIC is searching for. If that word or expression is part of another word or expression, PowerBASIC will pass it by. The *Whole Word* option is particularly useful when searching for a particular number or a variable name that is also contained in another variable name.

8.4 FIND AND REPLACE (CHANGE)

The *Change* command works in a similar fashion to the *Find* command, with a couple of additions.

1. You must specify what you want to change the expression to.
2. You choose whether you want to verify each change or just automatically change all of them.

To use the *Change* command,

PRESS ⟨CTRL + **qa**⟩

This brings up the *Find* prompt. Key in the expression that you're looking for and

PRESS ⟨ENTER⟩

The *Replace with* prompt pops up. Key in the expression that you want to change it into and

PRESS ⟨ENTER⟩

The *Options* prompt appears.

TYPE **g** (Global, to search the entire program)
PRESS ⟨ENTER⟩

PowerBASIC assumes that you want to verify each change. We recommend that in almost every case you verify every change, rather than use the **n** option that changes everything without stopping. This avoids the problem of changing something by mistake that was unanticipated.

8.5 CUT AND PASTE

Key in these five lines:

```
a = 1
b = 2
c = 3
d = c * b + a
print "the values of a, b, c and d are "; a; b; c; d
```

Use the CTRL + **kb** and CTRL + **kk** keys to select the text that you want to move, copy, delete, or print. First you select it. Then you operate on it (move, copy, delete, or print it).
You select the text by

PRESS ⟨CTRL + **kb**⟩ at the beginning of the text
PRESS ⟨CTRL + **kk**⟩ at the end of the text

The selected text becomes highlighted.
You deselect the text by

PRESS ⟨CTRL + **kh**⟩

and the highlighting disappears.
Rather than explain the nuances of the selection process, try selecting text and deselecting text until you get the feel of the selection process.

When you are finished,

PRESS ⟨CTRL + **kh**⟩

to ensure that no blocks are marked.

8.5.1 Move Selected Text

Highlight the text to be copied using the above procedure. Then, move the cursor to the position where you want the text located and

PRESS ⟨CTRL + **kv**⟩

The highlighted text is moved.

PRESS ⟨CTRL + **kh**⟩

to clear the block.

8.5.2 Copy Selected Text

Highlight the text to be copied. Move the cursor to the first position where you want the text located and

PRESS ⟨CTRL + **kc**⟩

The highlighted text is again inserted (copied to a new location). Each time the CTRL + **kc** are used thereafter, the marked piece of code will be copied into a new location.

8.5.3 Delete Selected Text

To delete a section of program code, mark the text to be copied using the CTRL + **kb** and CTRL + **kk** keys,

PRESS ⟨CTRL + **ky**⟩

and the highlighted text will disappear.

8.6 PRINTING PROGRAM BLOCKS

To print any section of your program, just mark the text to be printed using the CTRL + **kb** and CTRL + **kk** keys. Then

PRESS ⟨CTRL + **kp**⟩

and the highlighted text is printed.

PRESS ⟨CTRL + **kh**⟩

to clear the block.
     When you want to print your entire program,

PRESS ⟨CTRL + **kh**⟩

to clear any block that might be marked. Then

PRESS ⟨CTRL + **kp**⟩

to print the entire program.

8.7 READING AND WRITING PROGRAM BLOCKS

Reading and writing text to and from the Editor and the disk is not a problem in PowerBASIC. To write a block of text onto disk, just highlight the text as explained above and

PRESS ⟨CTRL + **kw**⟩

You are then prompted for a name to give this block. Just key in the name,

PRESS ⟨ENTER⟩

and the block is saved onto disk with that name.

To read a block of text from the disk,

PRESS ⟨CTRL + **kr**⟩

You are then prompted for the name of the block on disk. Key in the name,

PRESS ⟨ENTER⟩

and that program block is brought into the Editor at the cursor location.

8.8 SYNTAX CHECKING

Syntax checking (testing program statements for correctness in form) is accomplished by:

PRESS ⟨ALT + **c**⟩

This invokes the compiler, which will catch your errors. You should catch errors as you are keying them in, not hours later when you have finished typing. To test your program for errors as you go, we recommend that you compile frequently. Doing it at the completion of every routine is a good idea.

When the *Compiler* finds an error, it will pop a message onto the screen. Determine what the error is,

PRESS ⟨ESC⟩

to clear the message, and correct the error. After you've fixed the mistake,

PRESS ⟨ALT + **c**⟩

to recompile the program. Continue until the program compiles without error.

8.9 EXAMPLE OF USING THE EDITOR

To familiarize you with the Editor, we're going to put together a program sloppily and then fix it using the features in this chapter. We would NEVER write a program in this fashion, but it is the quickest and easiest way to get you to use most of the features in one sitting.

First, type in this program:

```
input "Enter a value for the rate of interest"; i$
input "Enter the dollar amount invested in one part"; d$
input "Enter the number of months in the period"; m$
input "Enter the average number of parts on hand"; a$
dols = VAL(i$) * VAL(d$) * VAL(m$) * VAL(a$)
print dols; VAL(i$); VAL(d$), VAL(m$), VAL(a$)
end
```

Run the program to ensure that it works properly:

PRESS ⟨ALT + **r**⟩ ⟨ENTER⟩

If not, check it against this one, correct it, and run again.

8.9.1 Find and Replace

It seems silly to enter the numbers as a string, then use the **VAL** command (which you'll learn in a later chapter) to convert each string to a number for the calculation, and then use the **VAL** command again to print the results. Therefore, we'll change the string variable names to numeric variable names. We'll take out the **$** using *Find* and *Replace with* and make **i, d, m,** and **a** numbers from the very start.

PRESS ⟨CTRL + **qa**⟩

The *Find* prompt pops up.

TYPE **$** ⟨ENTER⟩

The *Replace with* prompt is displayed.

   PRESS ⟨ENTER⟩

The *Options* prompt then shows.

   TYPE **g** ⟨ENTER⟩

PowerBASIC will find each dollar sign and ask if you want to change it. Each time it asks, just

   TYPE **y**

   The program should now look like this:

```
input "Enter a value for the rate of interest"; i
input "Enter the dollar amount invested in one part"; d
input "Enter the number of months in the period"; m
input "Enter the average number of parts on hand"; a
dols = VAL(i) * VAL(d) * VAL(m) * VAL(a)
print dols; VAL(i); VAL(d), VAL(m), VAL(a)
end
```

   Next we will get rid of the VAL(.

   PRESS ⟨CTRL + **qa**⟩

The *Find* prompt pops up.

   TYPE **val(** ⟨ENTER⟩

The *Replace with* prompt is displayed.

   PRESS ⟨ENTER⟩

The *Options* prompt then shows.

   TYPE **g** ⟨ENTER⟩

PowerBASIC will find each occurrence and ask whether you want to change it. In every case,

TYPE **y**

The program should now look like this:

```
input "Enter a value for the rate of interest"; i
input "Enter the dollar amount invested in one part"; d
input "Enter the number of months in the period"; m
input "Enter the average number of parts on hand"; a
dols = i) * d) * m) * a)
print dols; i); d), m), a)
end
```

The **)** will go last.

PRESS ⟨CTRL + **qa**⟩

The *Find* prompt pops up.

TYPE **)** ⟨ENTER⟩

The *Replace with* prompt is displayed.

PRESS ⟨ENTER⟩

The *Options* prompt then shows.

TYPE **g** ⟨ENTER⟩

PowerBASIC will find the **)** and ask if you want to change it. For each request,

TYPE **y**

The program now has this appearance:

```
input "Enter a value for the rate of interest"; i
input "Enter the dollar amount invested in one part"; d
input "Enter the number of months in the period"; m
input "Enter the average number of parts on hand"; a
dols = i * d * m * a
print dols; i; d, m, a
end
```

Run the program again to make sure that it still works. If it doesn't, compare your program with the one above and make your corrections. We have several more changes to go.

8.9.2 Create a Procedure

We have decided to make the calculation and print into a procedure that is called with four arguments. First we'll type the **CALL** routine just before the **END** statement, like this:

```
input "Enter a value for the rate of interest"; i
input "Enter the dollar amount invested in one part"; d
input "Enter the number of months in the period"; m
input "Enter the average number of parts on hand"; a
dols = i * d * m * a
print dols; i; d, m, a
call printdols (i, d, m, a)
end
```

Next comes the **SUB** statement itself. We will place it right after the **END**.

```
input "enter a value for the rate of interest"; i
input "enter the dollar amount invested in one part"; d
input "enter the number of months in the period"; m
input "enter the average number of parts on hand"; a
dols = i * d * m * a
print dols; i; d, m, a
call prindols (i, d, m, a)
end
sub prindols (c1, c2, c3, c4)
```

8.9.3 Move Text

Now we will move the calculation and print from the main routine into the procedure. Move the cursor to position one on the calculation line (the one beginning with **dols**).

PRESS ⟨CTRL + **kb**⟩

Now move the cursor to position one two lines down (beginning with **call**).

PRESS ⟨CTRL + **kk**⟩

Then move the cursor to the bottom of the program and

PRESS ⟨CTRL + **kv**⟩
PRESS ⟨CTRL + **kh**⟩

The screen should look like this:

```
input "enter a value for the rate of interest"; i
input "enter the dollar amount invested in one part"; d
input "enter the number of months in the period"; m
input "enter the average number of parts on hand"; a
call prindols (i, d, m, a)
end
sub prindols (c1, c2, c3, c4)
dols = i * d * m * a
print dols; i; d; m; a
```

Move to the bottom of the program, and

TYPE **end sub** ⟨ENTER⟩

Rerun the program and make sure that it works:

PRESS ⟨ALT + **r**⟩

Notice that the values displayed on the *Run* screen are now zeroes.

8.9.4 Changing Variables

Because **i, d, m,** and **a** are now within a procedure, they have no values. Their values are now contained in the arguments **c1, c2, c3,** and **c4.** So change **i, d, m,** and **a** to **c1, c2, c3,** and **c4,** respectively. Your screen should now appear as:

```
input "enter a value for the rate of interest"; i
input "enter the dollar amount invested in one part"; d
input "enter the number of months in the period"; m
input "enter the average number of parts on hand"; a
call prindols (i, d, m, a)
end
sub prindols (c1, c2, c3, c4)
dols = cl * c2 * c3 * c4
print dols; c1; c2; c3; c4
end sub
```

With all these changes, we should test the program to make sure it still works.

PRESS ⟨ALT + **r**⟩ ⟨ENTER⟩

to run the program. If it doesn't work, check the changes, make your corrections, and run again.

8.9.5 Adding Statements

The printout of the numbers is not very clear. The numbers should be clearly labeled and spaced out nicely. To accomplish this, we'll add a title line and change the print line so that the procedure looks like this:

```
sub prindol (c1, c2, c3, c4)
dols = c1 * c2 * c3 * c4
print "cost"; TAB(10); "interest"; TAB(20); "part cost"; TAB(30);___
"months"; TAB(40); "num parts"
print dols; TAB(10); c1; TAB(20); c2; TAB(30); c3; tab(40); c4
end sub
```

Now run the program again and notice the difference in apppear-ance. If you have a problem, check it against this listing, correct it, and rerun.

8.9.6 Back to the Main Module

Last, we will set up a loop, so that the input, calculation, and print process is done until the interest rate is input as 0 (zero) by the operator:

Place a label, **getint**, on a separate line just above the first input line.

```
getint:
input "Enter a value for the rate of interest"; i
input "Enter the dollar amount invested in one part"; d
input "Enter the number of months in the period"; m
input "Enter the average number of parts on hand"; a
call prindols (i, d, m, a)
end
```

Add a **GOTO** statement just before the **END** statement:

```
getint:
input "Enter a value for the rate of interest"; i
input "Enter the dollar amount invested in one part"; d
input "Enter the number of months in the period"; m
input "Enter the average number of parts on hand"; a
call prindols (i, d, m, a)
goto getint
end
```

Put a label, **ender**, on a separate line just above the **END** statement,

```
getint:
input "Enter a value for the rate of interest"; i
input "Enter the dollar amount invested in one part"; d
input "Enter the number of months in the period"; m
input "Enter the average number of parts on hand"; a
call prindols (i, d, m, a)
goto getint
ender:
end
```

Make the input prompt (for ending the program) clearer and add an **IF** statement to check for $i = 0$ (which will be the signal that we choose to end the program).

The complete program, with the subroutine **PRINDOL**, now should look like this:

```
getint:
input "Enter a value for the rate of interest (0 to ___ quit)"; i
IF i = O THEN goto ender
```

```
input "Enter the dollar amount invested in one part"; d
input "Enter the number of months in the period"; m
input "Enter the average number of parts on hand"; a
call prindol (i, d, m, a)
goto getint
ender:
end
sub prindol (c1, c2, c3, c4)
dols = c1 * c2 * c3 * c4
print "cost"; TAB(10); "interest"; TAB(20); "part cost";—__
    TAB(30); "months"; TAB(40); "num parts"
print dols; TAB(10); c1; TAB(20); c2; TAB(30); c3; TAB(40); c4
end sub
```

Your program is complete, and you now have some real experience with the Editor. Run the program again in a final test.

CHAPTER SUMMARY

1. Use CTRL + **qf** (*Find*) to locate each occurrence of a piece of program text.

2. Use CTRL + **qa** (*Find* and *Replace with*) to replace part or all of a specific program text.

3. Move or copy portions of a program by

   - highlighting it (marking it with CTRL + **kb** and CTRL + **kk**),
   - locating where you want it to be.
   - Then,

   PRESS ⟨CTRL + **kv**⟩

   - (to move it) or

   PRESS ⟨CTRL + **kc**⟩

   - (for each copy of that text that you want).

THE BOTTOM LINE

1. BASIC is a personable language, which tells your computer to follow your instructions one at a time until it has produced a desired "report."

2. When you look at a BASIC program, break it up into sections, using the block-line method. Then look at each block, one at a time, to figure out what was done.

3. PowerBASIC gives you a complete working environment, which encourages writing programs in building-block fashion.

4. Blueprint your program before you write one line of code.

5. Data names should be meaningful, short (but not cryptic), consistent, and clear.

6. Program organization is not fluff. Organize your thoughts, assign the tasks to routines, and then program each routine.

7. Break your program up into subroutines and procedures; then use **GOSUB** and **CALL**. Use **GOTO** only to go somewhere else within the same routine.

8. **The Editor is very powerful. Use the keys as much as possible, and you'll be productive in writing and changing a program.**

EXERCISES

1. Type in the program that you wrote in chapter 7, Exercise 3.

2. Save it with several different names—at least three. Put a **REM** statement with each program name as the first statement of each program.

3. Highlight and print several small parts of the main program. Print each procedure separately. Then print the entire program.

4. Run the program. Test it well to make sure that it works perfectly.

Chapter 9

IF Statements (IF You Skip this Chapter, THEN You'll Never Write Good Programs)

9.1 The Purpose of IF Statements _____ **164**

9.2 IFs and Program Flow _____ **165**

9.3 The Three Types of IF Statements _____ **169**

9.4 The ELSE Statement _____ **170**

9.5 Block ELSE Statements _____ **175**

9.6 Complex IF Statements _____ **176**

9.7 Two BASIC Decision-Making Rules _____ **178**

9.8 Minimal Testing, Minimal Clutter _____ **179**

9.9 Indenting Rule of IFs _____ **182**

It's Wednesday evening, and you're planning Saturday's activities.

The problem is, you're going out Friday night. That's sure to increase your propensity to sleep late on Saturday. You have to take that into account in figuring out what to do Saturday.

You're also unsure of the weather, since the meteorologists are talking about a possible monsoon. But then, in your area they're only right about 30% of the time, so Saturday could just as well turn out to be bright and sunny.

As a result, there are two conditions affecting your plans for Saturday:

1. The weather

    - If it's nice, you'll go biking at sunrise; otherwise you'll picnic if you get up late.
    - If it's lousy, you'll either work indoors or watch the ball game, depending on when you wake up.

2. What time you get up

    - If it's early, you'll go biking or you'll work in the basement, depending on the weather.
    - If it's late, you'll either picnic in the sun or else watch the ball game while a storm rages outside.

These conditions and possible outcomes shape your decision. Actually, there are four combinations affecting the decision, as these statements show:

1. IF you get up early on Saturday, AND
    IF the weather is nice, THEN
        you'll bicycle up one of the High Peaks.
2. IF you get up early on Saturday, AND
    IF a monsoon hits, THEN
        you'll finish off the basement.
3. IF you sleep late, AND
    IF the weather is nice, THEN
        you'll picnic at the lake.
4. IF you sleep late, AND
    IF the monsoon hits, THEN
        you'll watch the ball game.

In real life, decision-making is filled with "if" statements, spoken or unspoken. They're just as essential to the making of decisions in BASIC programming. In BASIC, the **IF** statement is a precise way of expressing a decision—more precise than in common English. It has to be precise so that a computer can understand exactly and act correctly upon the statement.

As in real life, you can build **IFs** upon **IFs**. While a simple **IF** statement is just an "either-or," you can combine two or more **IFs** to form a complex decision-making process. Of course, you can also overdo it. If you combine too many **IF** conditions into one BASIC statement, the logic of the decision may become incomprehensible.

9.1 THE PURPOSE OF IF STATEMENTS

The purpose of an **IF** statement is to do one or more things only when a certain condition is true.

An **IF** statement in BASIC has this syntax:

IF {some condition is true} THEN {do something—that is, execute the rest of this statement line}

The **IF** statement can also be written in block form, where the statement actually continues on one or more lines following the **IF** line:

IF {some condition is true} THEN
   {do something}
END IF

We prefer to use the block form, whether or not the "do something" part of the statement (everything that follows the **THEN**) is short or not. The block form is easier to find when scanning a program printout, is easier to read, and offers more flexibility than the single-line **IF...THEN** statement.

Let's look at how an **IF** (or we can call it an **IF...THEN**) statement works.

Reading the **IF**, the program knows that what follows is a condition that must be tested. The test will prove the condition to be either true or false. For example, assume that today is January 1, 1990 and that it's 12:02:

1. IF date$ = "010190" THEN {do something}
2. IF time$ <> "12:00" THEN {do something} (<> means "is unequal to")
3. IF duedate < {30 days prior to date$} THEN {do something} (< means "is less than")
4. IF custzip% > 99999 THEN ⟨do something⟩ (> means "is greater than")

Note:

>= means "greater than or equal to", and <= means "less than or equal to."

The condition in statement 1 above would test *true*. So would the condition in statement 2 (the current time is not equal to "12:00"). In the third statement, the condition will test *true* or *false*, depending on the value of the data name **duedate** relative to **date$** (today). And statement 4, although its condition appears false, could test true. (For example, maybe the statement line is checking user input for too large a zip-code number, and the value keyed in is 120065.)

What happens if the condition tests not true? If *any* part of the condition is false, then the program proceeds to the next line. It ignores the **THEN** and everything following it.

In the following example, assume **y** = 4; will the program print "Okay"?

```
IF (2 + 2) = y THEN
   IF custzip% < 99999 THEN
      PRINT "Okay"
```

It depends on the value of **custzip%**.

The purpose of an **IF** statement is to decide whether or not to do something. Based on a test of a condition, the **IF** statement either permits or does not permit the program to proceed to—

- read some data
- write some data
- perform a calculation
- **GOTO** some other statement in the routine and do something
- **GOSUB** to a subroutine elsewhere in the program
- **CALL** a procedure elsewhere in the program
- and so on.

9.2 IFS AND PROGRAM FLOW

If the condition is true, then the computer goes on to read and act on the rest of the statement line (the part of the line following the **THEN**). Data will be read or written, calculated, or in some way massaged. Or control will go to another place in the program, should the rest of the statement be a **GOTO**, **GOSUB**, or **CALL**.

Suppose we want to write a routine that will look through the customer file and print out the name and address of every customer who has bought our top-of-the-line model (the K2), along with the date of purchase. The routine might contain the following **IF** statement:

```
IF custmodel$ = "K2" THEN
   PRINT custname$, custaddress$, custpuryr%
END IF
```

If the value assigned to variable **custmodel$** for a particular customer is anything other than "K2", then the program will print nothing. In actuality, the program stops reading the **IF** statement as soon as it sees that the current value of **custmodel$** that it encounters in the customer file is not "K2". Unless **custmodel$** *is* "K2", the program will never look at what's after the word **THEN** in the statement. It will only get to read the second part of the statement (the **THEN** part) when the first part (the **IF** part) is satisfied.

If anything in the condition part of the statement is false, program control flows *down* to the next statement line in the program. (Recall the stream-flow example of chapter 4: water *always* flows downstream.) BASIC programs *always* flow to the next statement in sequence.

An **IF** statement is like a canal lock, a gate to an irrigation ditch, or some kind of channel leading off a stream (Figure 9.1). If the alternative path is closed off, then the water continues on its way down the stream. But if the way is open, then the water can be routed off to the side of the main flow. It will pass through the lock or gate and proceed along the

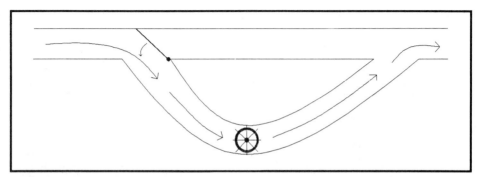

Figure 9.1

new pathway, doing whatever work it's called upon to do there. At the end, the water rejoins the stream and the downward flow.

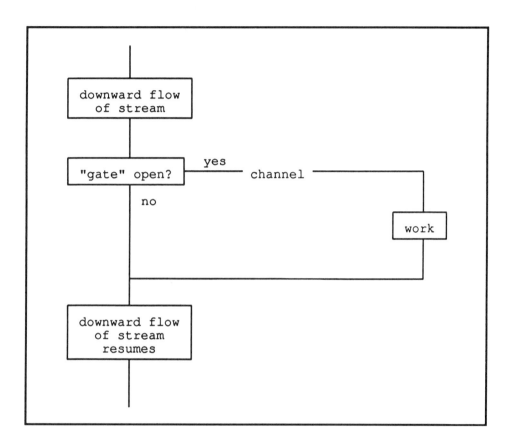

In programming terms, the "gate" in an **IF** statement is the condition that must be tested.

1. Is the condition met? Then the "gate" opens, permitting the program to continue reading the same statement line. It finds the word **THEN** and whatever else the statement says after that. (In so doing, the program may execute any of the types of instructions we mentioned above.) At the end of the **IF...THEN** statement line, the program goes down to the next statement line and resumes its downward logic.

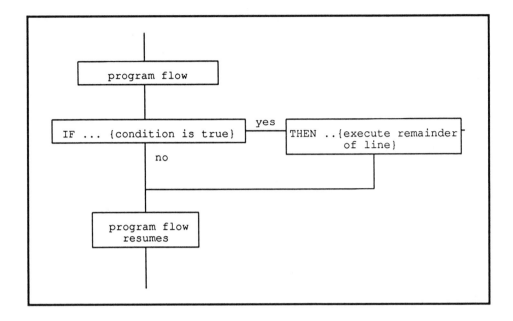

2. Is the condition not met? Then control has no choice and must turn away from the closed "gate"—to continue down the program.

This structure makes it easy for you, the programmer, to choose between alternative actions based upon some condition. Suppose, for example, that we want to print out a list of buyers of the K2 and the next-best model, the K1. A pair of **IF** statements could give you that list:

```
IF custmodel$ = "K2" THEN
   PRINT custname$, " bought K2 in ", custpuryr%
END IF
IF custmodel$ = "K1" THEN
   PRINT custname$, " bought K1 in ", custpuryr%
END IF
```

If the model the customer bought is not a K2, the program stops reading the first **IF** statement at the **custmodel$** = "K2" condition and drops down to the next program line. There, it tests again for a condition, but now the condition is **custmodel$** = "K1". If that is satisfied, we'll print something like

Freddie Burke bought K1 in 89

9.3 THE THREE TYPES OF IF STATEMENTS

There are quite a few ways to construct **IF** statements, but we'll reduce them to three types:

1. Do something with data.

```
IF {condition is true} THEN
    {do a read, write, display, or calculation/manipulation}
END IF
```

■ **EXAMPLE**

```
IF custmodel$ = "K2" THEN
        read custname$
    END IF

    IF response$ = "yes" THEN
      PRINT custname$, " answered ", response$
    END IF

    IF state$ = "NY" THEN
      total = purprice * 1.07: REM--7 percent sales tax in NY
    END IF
```

2. Alter program flow.

```
IF {condition is true} THEN
    {GOTO, CALL, or GOSUB}
```

■

■ **EXAMPLE**

```
IF custmodel$ = "K2" THEN
        GOTO 1200
    END IF

    IF custmodel$ = "K2" THEN
      CALL topline (custname$)
    END IF
```

```
IF custpuryr% > 86 THEN
    GOSUB post86purchase
END IF
```

3. Test another condition.

```
IF {condition is true} THEN
IF {another condition is true} THEN
     {do something}
  END IF
END IF                                                      ■
```

■ **EXAMPLE**

```
IF state$ = "NY" THEN
         IF city$ = "Buffalo" THEN
            PRINT city$
         END IF
  END IF                                                    ■
```

9.4 THE ELSE STATEMENT

There's a powerful add-on available to modify the **IF** statement: an **ELSE** statement. Just look at a sample **IF...THEN...ELSE**:

```
IF custpuryr% < 88 THEN
   PRINT "before 1/1/88"
ELSE PRINT "after 12/31/87"
END IF
```

You get the idea. The syntax for the **ELSE** statement is

```
IF {condition is true} THEN
   {do something}
ELSE {do something different}
END IF
```

If the condition is false, we do something different from what we'd do if it were true. Notice that this is not like the simple **IF...THEN...**

situation, where a false condition may result in doing *nothing*. With the **ELSE** statement, you have flexibility: you choose between two (or more) *definite actions*, depending on the test of the condition. Let's show this with an example.

Think back to our opening discussion of what to do on a sunny Saturday. If you want to bicycle up one of the High Peaks, you'll have to get up early. This is a case of "get up early or do nothing"—the simple **IF** situation:

```
IF {you get up early} THEN
   {bicycle}
END IF
{program continues}
```

But maybe you want to set up a definite alternative plan. If you don't get up early, you'll still have time for a picnic in the park nearby. The situation is now, "get up early and do one thing, else do another thing" (instead of "get up early or do nothing"). Using the **ELSE** statement, we can "program" the decision like this:

```
IF {you get up early} THEN
   {bicycle}
ELSE {picnic}
END IF
```

The **ELSE** statement has two broad uses:

- It can select one process or another (as opposed to selecting one process or nothing).
- It can divert program flow depending on the test of a condition.

First, let's see how selection of alternative processes is accomplished.

9.4.1 ELSE Statements and Alternative Process Selection

Here's a question for you. To make Saturday's bad-weather decision (a choice between two definite actions) of whether to finish off the basement or else watch the ball game, could you use a simple **IF** statement (one **IF...THEN**, no **ELSE**)?

```
{program begins}
IF {you get up early} THEN
  {finish off basement}
END IF
{watch ball game}
{program continues}
```

The indenting is required for legibility. Now, follow the logic for the two possible cases of getting up early or not:

1. If condition tests **FALSE** (you don't get up early)

    Program does *not* execute **THEN**, so you don't finish off basement; goes on to next line, and you watch ball game.

    Result: you watch ball game.

2. If condition tests **TRUE** (you get up early):

    Program *does* execute **THEN**; you finish off basement; program goes on to **END IF**; goes on to next line; and you *also* watch ball game.

    Result: you do *both*! Of course, that's not possible.

The logic only works for the false-condition case. In the true-condition case, you'll end up doing two actions, and that's not the desired outcome.

What about using two simple **IF** statements?

```
IF {you get up early} THEN
  {finish off basement}
END IF
IF {you don't get up early} THEN
  {watch ball game}
END IF
```

The pair of simple **IF**s works fine. One or the other action will be performed, but never both (so long as the two test conditions are mutually contradictory—you cannot get up *both* early and not early).

However, consider a case where the condition is defined a little differently—not just "early" or "not early," but with *specific values.* Let's set up a data name **wakehour**, an integer whose value ranges between 1 and 12.

```
IF wakehour < 8 THEN
  {finish off basement}
END IF
IF wakehour > 8 THEN
  {watch ball game}
END IF
```

Follow the logic for **wakehour** = 8:

1. First condition tests **FALSE** (wakehour *equals* 8, not <8):	Program does not execute first **THEN**; reads **END IF**; goes to second **IF...THEN**
2. Second condition tests **FALSE** (wakehour *equals* 8, not >8):	Program does not execute second **THEN**; reads **END IF**; goes to remaining program

Result: neither action is selected.

You can see that the only solution is a precise definition of at least one of the tests, so as to cover all three possible values of **wakehour** (that is, <8, =8, and >8). Let's make the second test more precise:

```
IF wakehour < 8 THEN
  {finish off basement}
END IF
IF wakehour >= 8 THEN (>= means "greater than or equal to")
  {watch ball game}
END IF
```

This logic works fine, although we've had to be precise about defining the tests of the condition. The **ELSE** statement can give us the same results as two simple **IF**s—and it can do so with less bother, fewer statements, and clearer lines:

```
IF wakehour < 8 THEN
  {finish off basement}
ELSE {watch ball game}
END IF
```

For a wakeup time of exactly 8:00 A.M. or any time thereafter, you'll watch the ball game.

9.4.2 ELSE Statements and Flow Diversion

The second use of the **ELSE** statement is as a flow-diverter. Using the **GOTO**, **GOSUB**, and **CALL** statements, the **ELSE** statement can be used to direct program flow to some other part of the program. But while the GO-family statements will redirect flow every time they're encountered, combining them with the **ELSE** allows you to make flow decisions with flexibility. With **ELSE**, you may choose to redirect the program flow to one of two places, or you may choose no redirection, depending on a test of a condition.

```
IF {condition is met}THEN
   {do something}
ELSE GO {somewhere}
END IF
{main program continues}
```

Note also that the "do something" and "go somewhere" can be reversed when using an **ELSE** statement:

```
IF {condition is met} THEN
   {GO somewhere}
ELSE {do something}
END IF
{main program continues}
```

Or we can go to one place, or go to another.

```
IF {condition is met} THEN
   {GO somewhere}
ELSE {go elsewhere}
END IF
{main program continues}
```

Here's a sample program application. Suppose the customer file contains buyers of only two models, the K2 and the K1. Most of our buyers have the less expensive K1. We want to give buyers of our top-of-the-line K2 something special as a measure of thanks. Here's a way to do that using an **ELSE** to divert flow:

```
REM -- program "thankyou.bas" -- created {date}
.
IF custmodel$ = "K1" THEN
   PRINT "This customer bought a K1."
ELSE GOSUB k2thanks
END IF
{program continues}
.

.
END
REM -- subroutine k2thanks follows
k2thanks:
   PRINT "This customer bought a K2. Send thank-you gift."
RETURN
```

For each customer, we test for the condition (**custmodel$** = "K1"). If it's true, we'll **PRINT** "bought a K1" and continue the program. But for a K2 owner, we redirect the program around the "This customer bought a K1" statement line and everything following it to a subroutine, **K2THANKS**.

9.5 BLOCK ELSE STATEMENTS

We mentioned that we prefer the block form of an **IF...THEN** statement. The block form is more convenient to scan and read because of its indenting. But it also simplifies writing of **IF**s when a number of lines are needed following the **THEN** or the **ELSE**. Look at the following block-form **IF**.

```
IF custpurchyr% < currentyr% THEN
   PRINT custname$, " (no purchase this year)"
   PUT #4, custname$, custpurchyr%
   REM -- FILEOUT statement to file #4 of this program,--"oldcust"
ELSE PRINT custname$, "* * * (CURRENT PURCHASE) * * *"
   PUT #5, custname$, custpurchyr%
   REM -- FILEOUT statement to file #5 of this program, "newcust"
END IF
```

The general layout of this block-form **IF** statement looks like this:

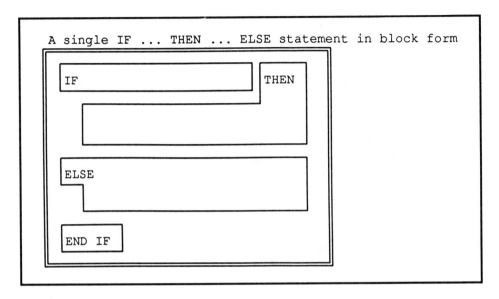

```
A single IF ... THEN ... ELSE statement in block form

IF                                      THEN

ELSE

END IF
```

As you can see from this illustration, *these lines are all one statement.*

> An **IF** statement, no matter how long, how involved, or whether or not it has an **ELSE**, is one statement.

Get into the habit of thinking of an **IF** as a block statement. One block does one thing (it makes a decision). Let's now look at how decision-making can get more sophisticated.

9.6 COMPLEX IF STATEMENTS

A complex **IF** statement is a BASIC statement containing two or more **IF** conditions. It can test a series of conditions and, assuming that all the conditions are true, do something. Conversely, if *any one* of the several conditions is false, then the program will *not* take any action. This gives a multilevel decision-making capability to your programs.

The syntax for complex **IF** statements is:

```
IF {first condition is true} THEN
IF {second condition is true} THEN
IF {third, etc., condition is true} THEN
{do something}
END IF
```

■ **EXAMPLE**

We want to send a card to our older customers (over 55) in New York.

```
IF custage% >= 55 THEN
  IF state$ = "NY" THEN
    GOSUB printgreetings
END IF
```

We want to send a card to the over-55 customers in New York who bought K2s.

```
IF custage% >= 55 THEN
  IF state$ = "NY" THEN
    IF custmodel$ = "K2" THEN
      GOSUB printgreetings
END IF                                                           ■
```

The program will only **GOSUB printgreetings** if *all* the conditions in the entire **IF** construct test true. Notice the word "entire"; in general,

---

A complex **IF** statement is all one statement.

When all the **IF** conditions are true, the program executes the rest of the statement beyond the last **THEN**. When any one of the conditions is false, the program stops at that failed condition test, ignores the rest of the complex **IF** statement, and flows down to the next program statement outside the complex **IF** construct.

Follow the program logic through another test of several conditions: New York customer, over 55, bought K2, and bought it prior to 1987.

```
IF custpurchdate% < 87 THEN
   IF custmodel$ = "K2" THEN
      IF custage% >= 55
         IF state$ = "NY" THEN
            PRINT custname$
END IF
```

The program reads in data from the record of customer Alison Arlen, who lives in Dayton, Ohio, has just turned 55, and bought a K2 back in 1986. The program logic proceeds through this complex statement as follows:

1. Is the purchase date prior to 1987?   yes
2. Is the model K2?   yes
3. Is the customer over 55?   yes
4. Does the customer live in New York?   no

The output of these program lines is nothing (one condition has tested false).

Look at the program flow through the parts of the same complex **IF** statement in the case of Dan Scampini (a New Yorker, age 30, who bought a K2 in October 1987):

1. Is the purchase date prior to 1987?   no

And that's it. The program finds the first condition false and exits the complex **IF** statement. It flows down to the next program line; the output of this operation is nothing (one condition has tested false).

9.7 TWO BASIC DECISION-MAKING RULES

We can draw some conclusions from this discussion that will make your use of **IF** statements clean, consistent, and understandable.

1. Limit a complex **IF** statement to four levels.

   See the examples just above. If the logic demands that five or more tests be conducted, then write them in two or more groups, or else on separate lines.

   A related problem is use of an **ELSE** statement in complex **IF**s. You can easily get lost if you do so—please take our word for it, and don't try to beat the odds! With this in mind, we propose rule number two:

2. Use the **ELSE** statement *only* with the *simplest* **IF** statement (one **IF,** one **ELSE**).

9.8 MINIMAL TESTING, MINIMAL CLUTTER

In the examples in this chapter you've seen some fairly simple routines and processes to be executed following **THEN**s and **ELSE**s. Now let's say a couple of words about two desirable characteristics of good **IF**-writing.

Decision making should take as little effort as possible. In terms of the computer's time and work, this simply means that you'd like to test each condition as few times as you can. Ideally, you'd like to have no unnecessary retesting of conditions; no repetitious rewriting of your programming statements; and no wasted time in having the computer make the same elementary testing decision again and again.

Because of the countless variations that may exist in any decision-making routine, even fairly simple ones, we can't give you a "cook-book" solution to how to design the statements that will test conditions. We can, though, make a recommendation based on much experience:

> Wherever possible, set up program logic to test first for the condition that is likely to prove false.

The key to this technique is to figure out which of the conditions is *most likely to be false* and test for that one first. Then, of the remaining conditions, which is the next-most-likely false one? And so on. This is not always easy, or possible. But often there is at least one clear favorite among the candidates.

Let's take as an example a four-level test:

Find owners of K2s;
in New York;
age 65 or over;
female.

Suppose we know that—

• K1s outnumber the K2s about four to one.
• Owners are fairly evenly distributed among eight states.
• Only two in one hundred owners are older than 65.
• Male and female owners are roughly equal in number.

Let's summarize the decision-making odds, starting with those least likely to be true and working down to the ones most likely to be true:

1. age   very few older customers
2. model   20% are K2s
3. state   balanced among eight
4. sex   50–50

To minimize testing, set up the condition *most likely to be false* as the first.

IF age >= 65 THEN

Then add the other conditions in roughly increasing order of likely truth:

```
If age >=65 THEN                        2 in 100
    If state$ = "NY" THEN               1 in 8
        IF custmodel$ = "K2" THEN       1 in 5
            IF sex$ = "f"THEN           1 in 2
                CALL printspecialgreets ( )
```

There will be much less repetitive testing with this sequence than if every one of the several hundred records were tested first for the 50–50 sex condition. The same applies generally to the other conditions with relatively long odds. By starting with age, this sequence will quickly eliminate all but a handful of records (the over-65 customers). The next test (the second-level **IF** statement) again eliminates all but about one-eighth of the records passing the first test, and so on.

This is a modest example, and the resulting increase in processing speed may not be detectable. But if you were testing several dozen conditions for a file with thousands of records, you'd see a difference in speed as the program ran.

Not only does this approach help the computer work faster, it also encourages clear thinking on your part and clean programming generally. And that's the point.

As for keeping your **IF** statements uncluttered and simple-to-read, here's another recommendation based on experience:

> Wherever possible, use the **IF** statement and its **THEN** and **ELSE** to redirect program flow when there are two or more actions to be performed. That is, do the actions elsewhere (e.g., in routines), not within the **IF** itself.

To see why, compare the readability of two versions of the same **IF. . . THEN. . . ELSE**.

1. All actions performed within **IF** block:

```
{program begins}
    .
    .
    .
IF custpurchyr% < currentyr% THEN
    PRINT custname$, " (no purchase this year)"
    PUT #4, custname$, custpurchyr%
    REM--custname$ into file "previous"
                    ***
            {several other statements}
                    ***
ELSE PRINT custname$, "* * * (CURRENT PURCHASE) * * *"
    PUT #5, custname$, custpurchyr%
    REM -- custname$ into file "current"
                    ***
            {several other statements
                    ***
```

```
        END IF
        {program continues}
```

2. All actions performed elsewhere:

```
        {program begins}
        IF custpurchyr% < currentyr% THEN
            GOSUB previous
        ELSE GOSUB current
        END IF
        {program continues}
        .
        .
        .
        previous:
            PRINT custname$, "(no purchase this year)"
            PUT #4, custname$, custpurchyr%
            REM -- custname$ into file "previous"
                                        ***
                        {several other statements}
                                        ***
        RETURN
        current:
            PRINT custname$, "* * * (CURRENT PURCHASE) * * *"
            PUT #5, custname$, custpurchyr%
            REM -- custname$ into file "current"
                                        ***
                        {several other statements}
                                        ***
        RETURN
```

9.9 INDENTING RULE OF IFS

As you've already noticed, we also recommend careful and consistent indenting of the statement lines in a complex **IF** statement (and elsewhere). If you indent each level of an **IF** statement two to four spaces, your printed programs will be more legible, and the decision-making process will be more comprehensible.

We suggest the following rules on indenting:

1. Indent each **IF** to show each level of the decision.

2. If the action to be taken (whatever follows the **THEN**) is brief and uncomplicated, write it on the same line as the **IF**.

3. If the action requires more than one statement, put the action in a routine and have the **IF** statement enable the routine.

To illustrate:

```
IF custage% < 18 THEN PRINT custname$

IF custpurchyr% >= 89 THEN
   IF custmodel$ = "K2" THEN
      IF state$ = "NY" THEN
         PRINT "new K2 owner from New York"
         END IF
```

CHAPTER SUMMARY

1. The purpose of an **IF** statement is to express decisions in BASIC. Such decisions allow you to—

   - read data
   - write data
   - perform calculations or manipulate data
   - **GOSUB** to a subroutine elsewhere in the program
   - **CALL** a procedure elsewhere in the program
   - **GOTO** somewhere else in the program
   - and so on

2. When the **IF** condition in a statement is true, the program reads and acts upon the rest of the statement (the word **THEN** and everything that follows it in that statement line). When the

condition is false, the program goes down to the next statement following the **IF** construct.

3. The three types of **IF** statement are:

```
IF {condition is true} THEN
   {do something with data}
IF {condition is true} THEN
   {alter program flow with CALL, GOSUB, or GOTO}
IF {condition is true} THEN
   {test another IF condition}
   ("complex if")
```

4. The **ELSE** statement is an extension of the **IF** statement that adds considerable flexibility. Instead of an "if-true-or-not" structure, the **ELSE** creates an "IF-true-then-do-this-ELSE-do-that" decision structure.

5. For all but the simplest **IF**s, use block form. Finish each block with an **END IF**.

6. A complex **IF** statement is simply a series of two or more conditions that are tested. When *all* conditions are true, the statement following the last **THEN** is executed. If *any* condition tests false, the program drops down to the next program line following the end of the complex **IF** structure.

7. Limit complex **IF**s to four levels (four **IF**s). For tests of more than four levels, recombine the levels into two or more **IF** constructions.

8. Use an **ELSE** statement only with a simple (one-level) **IF** statement.

9. Test a condition as few times as possible. For multiple tests (complex **IF**s), start with the condition *least* likely to be true.

10. Write easy-to-read **IF**s; when there are several actions to be executed, put them elsewhere, such as in routines. Indent your **IF**s for ease of reading the program.

11. At all times, keep things simple.

THE BOTTOM LINE

1. BASIC is a personable language, which tells your computer to follow your instructions one at a time until it has produced a desired "report."

2. When you look at a BASIC program, break it up into sections, using the block-line method. Then look at each block, one at a time, to figure out what each does.

3. PowerBASIC gives you a complete working environment, which encourages writing programs in building-block fashion.

4. Blueprint your program before you write one line of code.

5. Data names should be meaningful, short (but not cryptic), consistent, and clear.

6. Program organization is not fluff. Organize your thoughts, assign the tasks to routines, and then program each routine.

7. Break your program up into subroutines and procedures; then use **GOSUB** and **CALL.** Use **GOTO** only to go somewhere else within the same routine.

8. The Editor is very powerful. Use the keys as much as possible, and you'll be productive in writing and changing a program.

9. **Keep your IFs simple, and easy to read.**

EXERCISES

1. Write the **IF** statements to test for the length of each data item in the new customer program. If the data item is too long (the length defined in the blueprint), print out an error message.

2. Write the **IF** statements to test for the length of each data item in the new inventory program. If the data item is too long, print out an error message.

3. Write additional **IF** statements to test for customer type to be between 1 and 3.

4. Write additional **IF** statements to test for any inventory cost greater than $1,000.00 or less than five cents. If any items are outside these bounds, print out an error message.

Chapter 10

Loops (IF it's Worth Doing Once, THEN Do It Again.)

10.1 The Loop is the Logic Base _____ **188**

10.2 The Three Types of Loops _____ **192**

10.3 The MAIN Routine Is a Critical Loop _____ **196**

10.4 The Danger of GOTO _____ **197**

You're collating the Bikes Peak quarterly newsletter as a favor to Art. The newsletter consists of five pages and is going out to Bikes Peak's 1,000 customers. On a long table, you have five piles of paper. Each pile has 1,000 copies of one of the pages. You start at one end of the table, get the top sheet off each pile, then staple each complete newsletter and stack it at the other end.

You do this 1,000 times.

You are acting just like a computer program that is processing 1,000 customers. You keep going through the same loop—picking up each sheet, stapling, stacking, then walking back to the start, and doing it all over again. A BASIC program reads one group of data at a time, processes it, does some output, and goes back to read another group. This procedure is called a loop.

In relation to the flow of water, recall the fountain from chapter 4. It works similarly to the loop in BASIC.

10.1 THE LOOP IS THE LOGIC BASE

A computer program ONLY DOES ONE THING AT A TIME!! In order to print 1,000 customer names and addresses onto labels, it must—

1. read one customer's data,
2. print one customer's name and address onto a label, and
3. go back to (1) again, repeat (2), and keep on doing this until 1,000 customer labels have been printed.

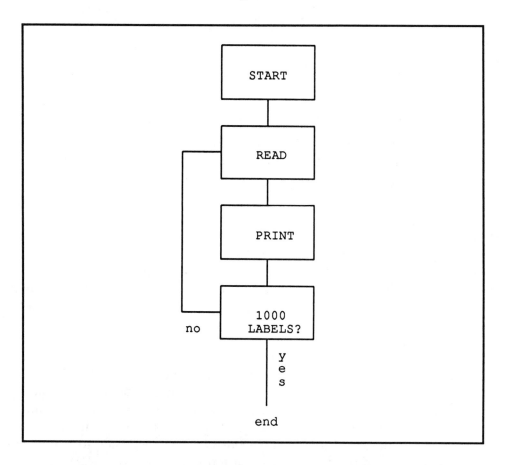

You don't need a computer to put out one, or even five labels. The real power of a computer program is its ability to process large numbers of things as easily as it processes one thing.

The same code that prints one customer label prints every customer label, because the computer program loops back to read another customer and goes through the same **PRINT** statements 1,000 times. The same loop could be changed to print 1,000,000 customer labels by simply changing one number on one statement.

The loop is the logic base of any program, because without it, only one group of data would be processed. (In this case, only one label would be printed.) Without loops, computers would have little value, because each piece of data would require its own program statements. That is, without loops, a program that processes 10,000 labels would be 1,000 times larger than a program that processes 10 labels. Using loops, the program that prints 10 labels is EXACTLY the same size as one that prints 10,000 or even 10,000,000 labels.

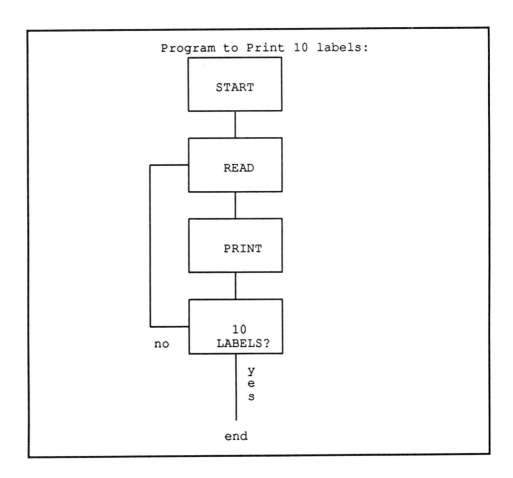

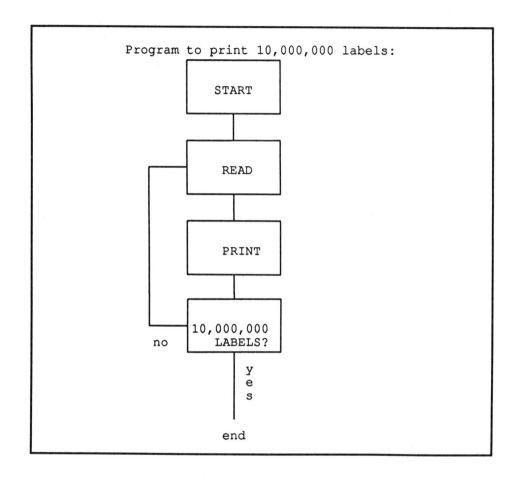

Program to print 10,000,000 labels:

Note that the only difference in the two programs is the one conditional (**IF**) statement, which tests to see how many labels have been processed.

Now here's an example of two programs that accomplish exactly the same result, one with a loop and one with no loops at all.

The program with the loop (shown on the next page) will print five labels, if there were only five records in the file. If the file contained 1,000 records, it would print 1,000 labels, and so forth.

The program without the loop (shown on the next page) will never print more than five labels, no matter how many records are in the file. In order to print 1,000 labels, the program on the left would have to have an additional 995 × 2 or (1,990) steps.

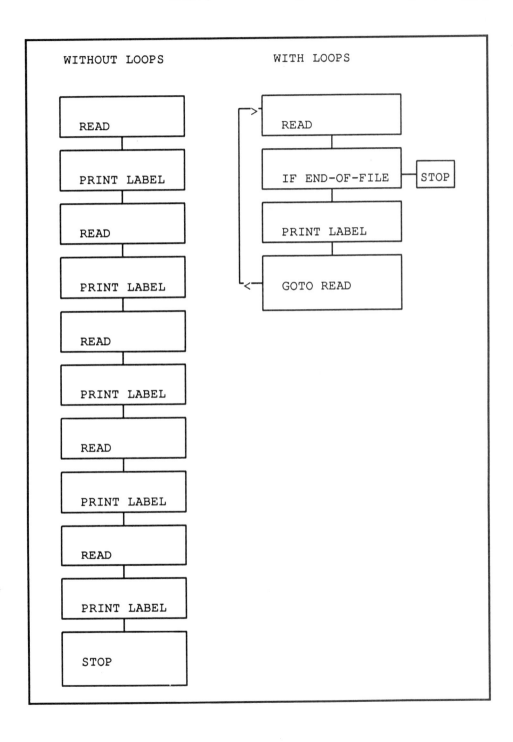

10.2 THE THREE TYPES OF LOOPS

The three types of loops are:

1. **FOR. . .TO—NEXT**
   (Fixed loop)
2. **DO UNTIL. . .—LOOP**
   (Conditional loop)
3. **IF EOF—THEN GOTO**
   (Read-until-end loop)

While loop (2) above could accomplish the work of loop (1), we prefer to use all three of these loops to identify instantly the type of loop (how it is terminated).

10.2.1 FOR. . .TO—NEXT

We use loop 1 to do something a *fixed number* of times, like 10, 100, 3,184, or any concrete number. This number could be a variable; the point is that the loop is set—it's rigid. It will be performed a specific number of times, no matter what.
Uses:

Adding up sales for a specific number of weeks or months
Totalling the sales on the lines of an invoice
Totalling the hours on a time card

The actual syntax for this first loop is:

```
FOR {variable name 1} = {variable name 2, number or expression}
                    TO {variable name 3, number or expression}

        .
        .
    {a bunch of program statements}
        .
        .

NEXT {variable name 1}
{rest of the program}
```

■ FOR. . .TO—NEXT EXAMPLES

This first section of code totals twelve months of sales into a variable named **ytdsales#**:

```
ytdsales# = 0
FOR i% = 1 to 12
   ytdsales# = ytdsales# + sales(i%)
NEXT i%
```

The next piece of program code totals fifty entries of hours into a variable named **tothours:**

```
numhours% = 50
tothours = 0
FOR i = 1 to numhours%
   tothours = tothours + hours(i%)
NEXT i%
```

10.2.2 DO UNTIL . . .

We use this second loop form to do something until a certain condition becomes true. This condition can be of any form that normally could be expressed in an **IF** statement. (Remember the conditions from chapter 9?) The test might be that a value equals 0, or that the state changes from NJ to NY, and so on. In this case, the loop has no fixed number of times to repeat. It may be performed once, 1,000 times, or 1,000,000 times—it continues looping until the specified condition is found to be true, at which point the loop is exited.

Uses:

Printing until the number of print lines exceeds what fits on a page
Printing until the value of a variable changes
Adding to a subtotal until the value of a variable changes

The syntax for this second type of loop is:

```
DO UNTIL {expression}
   .
   .
```

A group of program statements

.

.

.

LOOP

■ DO UNTIL...EXAMPLES

This first section of code totals twelve months of sales into a variable named **ytdsales#**:

```
i% = 0
ytdsales# = 0
DO UNTIL i% = 12
   i% = I% + 1
   ytdsales# = ytdsales# + sales(i%)
LOOP
```

The next piece of program code totals fifty entries of hours into a variable named **tothours**:

```
i% = 0
tothours = 0
DO UNTIL i% = 50
   i% = i% + 1
   tothours = tothours + hours(i%)
LOOP
```

This section of a program prints lines onto the printer until the number of printed lines is equal to 60:

```
n% = 0
DO UNTIL n% = 60
   LPRINT {some data}: n% = n% + 1
   LPRINT {some more data}: n% = n% + 1
LOOP
```

And this code adds to a total until the value of **custstate$** changes:

```
totcustpurch# = 0
f1 = 1
GET #1, f1
```

```
prevstate$ = custstate$
DO UNTIL custstate$ < > prevstate$
   totcustpurch# = totcustpurch# + custpurch
   prevstate$ = custstate$
   f1 = f1 + 1
   GET 1, f1
LOOP
```

Follow the logic on the example above. You will be using this kind of logic frequently in printing and totalling.

10.2.3 IF EOF THEN GOTO

We use a loop of type 3 to read a file and process a record until there is no more data to process, because we have reached the end of the file. This construct is found in major subroutines, never in procedures. It is the basis of the loop in **MAIN CONTROL**. Don't concern yourself with the detail of the **EOF** statement or the **GET** statement; you'll learn them in chapter 12. Concentrate on how the loop works; that's what's important here.

The **IF EOF** statement works just like any other **IF** statement. Actually, it is a specialized version of the **IF** statement. If the condition is true, the computer processes the statement following the **THEN**. In the case of the **IF EOF** statement, the condition that is tested is an end of file on the file specified. The statement tests as true when the end of file is found.

Uses:

To stop the processing of a file when it has reached the end.

The syntax for this type of loop is:

```
{line label 1}
   {some file read (usually a GET) statement}
   IF EOF({a file number, from 1-32}) THEN GOTO {line label 2}
   .
   {several program statements}
   .
   GOTO {line label 1 (which is the start of the IF EOF loop)}
{line label 2}
   {rest of program}
```

■ **EXAMPLE**

```
readcust:
    GET 1, f1 : REM -- read a record from the customer file
    IF EOF(1) THEN GOTO endcust
    GOSUB PRINTCUST : REM -- print a customer record
    GOTO readcust
endcust:
    {rest of program}
```
■

10.3 THE MAIN ROUTINE IS A CRITICAL LOOP

The **MAIN** routine is a loop of type 3, which controls all the processing logic of the program. It reads the major, or primary, file of the program—the one upon which all the calculations, data movement and massaging, printing, and disk writing are based.

In every program that you write in BASIC, the program processing is based on one file, even though several files are used in the program. This one file controls all of the logic in the program— processing begins when the first record of this file is read and ends when the end-of-file condition is found.

■ **EXAMPLE**

```
main:
    CLS: REM -- clear the screen
getcust:
    f1 = f1 + 1
    GET 1, f1: REM -- read the customer file
    IF EOF(1) THEN GOTO ender: REM -- if end-of-file, then get out
    GOSUB printcust: REM -- print a customer record
    GOTO getcust: REM -- go back and get another customer record
ender:
    RETURN
```
■

This **MAIN** routine reads and prints the records in the customer file until all have been read. The **EOF** statement tests file 1 (in this case, the customer file) before every read. When the **EOF** condition is found to be true (the end of file has been reached), the routine exits.

10.4 THE DANGER OF GOTO

The **GOTO**, when used in a loop, *should never alter the program flow outside of the loop.* The rule can *NEVER* be broken without having a program that will never work right!!!

The **GOTO** should only be used within a loop to skip FORWARD or BACKWARD over statements within the loop. In the read loop (type 3), using the **EOF**, it can be used only to go back to the **EOF** test. It should *never be used to jump outside of the loop.*

Uses:

Skip forward past some program statements that you don't want to execute under certain conditions (as a result of testing an **IF** statement).

Skip backward to create a loop.

■ GOTO EXAMPLES

We want to add up all of the sales for the year, except for the month of June. This first section of code totals 11 months of sales into a variable named **ytdsales#:**

```
ytdsales# = 0
FOR i% = 1 to 12
  IF i% = 6 THEN GOTO salesloop
  ytdsales# = ytdsales# + sales(i%)
salesloop:
NEXT i%
```

The next piece of program code totals 40 entries of hours into a variable named **tothours.** We'll set up the loop to skip the entries between 31 and 40 (just for purposes of example).

```
tothours = 0
FOR i% = 1 to 50
  IF i% > 30 THEN
    IF i% < 41 THEN
    GOTO skiphours
  END IF
```

```
        tothours = tothours + hours(i%)
    skiphours:
NEXT i%
```
■

Use **GOTO** statements sparingly and carefully within loops, and follow the rules. You'll never be sorry that you did.

CHAPTER SUMMARY

1. The computer only does one thing at a time. The loop is the logic base that makes programs really work.
2. The three types of loops that we will use are:
   a. **FOR. . .TO—NEXT**
      (Fixed loop—loops a specific number of times)
   b. **DO UNTIL. . .**
      (Conditional loop—loops until the condition is true)
   c. **IF EOF—THEN GOTO**
      (Read-until-end-of-file loop)
3. The **MAIN** routine is usually a read-until-end-of-file loop that controls the processing logic of the program.
4. The most dangerous place for a **GOTO** is within a loop.

   • Never use the **GOTO** to jump somewhere outside of the loop.
   • Except for jumping backward to the **EOF** test, the **GOTO** should only be used to jump forward to skip a few statements *within the loop.*

THE BOTTOM LINE

1. BASIC is a personable language, which tells your computer to follow your instructions one at a time until it has produced a desired "report."

2. When you look at a BASIC program, break it up into sections, using the block-line method. Then look at each block, one at a time, to figure out what each does.

3. PowerBASIC gives you a complete working environment, which encourages writing programs in building-block fashion.

4. Blueprint your program before you write one line of code.

5. Data names should be meaningful, short (but not cryptic), consistent, and clear.

6. Program organization is not fluff. Organize your thoughts, assign the tasks to routines, and then program each routine.

7. Break your program up into subroutines and procedures, and then use **GOSUB** and **CALL**. Use **GOTO** only to go somewhere else within the same routine.

8. The Editor is very powerful. Use the keys as much as possible, and you'll be productive in writing and changing a program.

9. Keep your **IF**s simple and easy to read.

10. **Loops are a critical structure of good programming. You can destroy that structure with the wrong use of GOTO. Use GOTO only to go somewhere else within the same loop.**

EXERCISES

1. Write the **MAIN CONTROL** loop for the New Customer program for Bikes Peak.

2. Write the **MAIN CONTROL** loop for the New Parts program for Bikes Peak.

3. Write the **MAIN CONTROL** loop that will print out the total value of the inventory of Bikes Peak.

4. Write the loop that will total the sales of each inventory item for the year. Use the examples in this chapter as an example. (We realize that we haven't yet explained tables and subscripts. They'll be covered in chapter 18.)

5. Write the procedure for (3.) above that calculates the value of the on-hand quantity of each part and then adds it to the total value.

Chapter 11

The Concept of Files (You See and Use Them Every Day)

11.1 Definition of a Data File _____ **201**

11.2 Everyday, Ordinary Files _____ **201**

11.3 Definition of a Record _____ **201**

11.4 Everyday, Ordinary Records _____ **202**

11.5 Definition of a Field _____ **202**

11.6 Everyday, Ordinary Fields _____ **203**

11.7 Types of File Structures _____ **204**

11.8 File Subject Categories _____ **208**

11.9 File Layout _____ **210**

You're trying to find that receipt for the automatic beer bottle opener that you bought Uncle Tom for Christmas. The opener doesn't work right; rather than just taking off the cap, it snaps the neck of the bottle off. You have filed all of your receipts (from forever) in the box that your television came in. And now you're looking through each receipt as you pull it out of the pile, trying to find the one for the automatic opener.

You are working with a data FILE.

11.1 DEFINITION OF A DATA FILE

A *file* is simply a collection of (generally) like things. In the case of computers, a *data file* is a collection of like data. There are other kinds of files, like program files and text files, but we won't be designing them or describing them in this book. We are working only with data files.

11.2 EVERYDAY, ORDINARY FILES

The tax forms and supporting documentation in your file cabinet
A shoebox of old, paid bills
The notes and appointments in your personal calendar
The work in your briefcase
The computer disks in the disk holder on your desk
The books in your bookcase
The records in your record case

And some not so apparent:

The phone book
A pile of cash register receipts in a drawer
A bunch of expense receipts in your wallet
The credit cards in your wallet
The coins in your coin purse
The food in your pantry
The clothing in your closet
The tools in your toolbox

11.3 DEFINITION OF A RECORD

A *record* is one of the like articles in your file.

11.4 EVERYDAY, ORDINARY RECORDS

One of the tax forms in your file cabinet
One of the paid bills in your shoebox
One set of notes on a meeting
One of the contracts in your briefcase
The disk with *Star Trek* in your disk case
The dictionary in your bookcase

And not as obvious:

One of the cash register receipts in your drawer
One of the expense receipts in your wallet
One name, address, and phone number—

Software Factory, Inc.
1675 RT 9, Clft Pk
383–1234

One can of beans in your pantry
One screwdriver from your tool box

11.5 DEFINITION OF A FIELD

A *field* is a recognizable part or piece of a record. It is the smallest unit that you normally work with. You

add,
subtract,
multiply,
divide,
display,
print,
move,
and manipulate *fields* in BASIC.

11.6 EVERYDAY, ORDINARY FIELDS

Gross income on the tax form
One item on a bill
One item on a cash register receipt
One sentence in those notes
One clause in one of the contracts
One definition in the dictionary

And the ones you don't normally think about:

The phone number 383–1234
One line on an expense receipt
One bean
The screwdriver handle

A Computer Data File (Parts file)	A Computer Data Record (Part record 1)
Record 1	Part Description
Record 2	Part Retail Price
Record 3	Part Wholesale Price
	Part Cost
Record 4	Part Quantity On Hand
Record 5	Part Quantity Sold
	Etc
Record 6	Etc
	Etc
Record 7	
Record 8	
Record 9	
Record 10	

Now that you have a feel for what files, records, and fields are all about, we'll get into...

11.7 TYPES OF FILE STRUCTURES

While there are many types of file structures, we'll limit our discussion to four of the most basic:

sequential
random
indexed
linked

A *sequential file* is one in which the records must be read in order, one by one. You first read record 1, then record 2, then record 3, then record 4, and so on until the desired record is found or until the end of file is reached. In a sequential file, no records can be skipped; all the records that precede the desired record must be read to get to the record you want. To get to record 321, the computer has to read the first 320 records in the file and then read number 321. It's a lot like a cassette tape, or VCR. The only way to get to the middle is to go through the first half of the tape.

Sequential files are normally used by beginning programmers, because they're the easiest to use. But we won't cover them, because we feel that their limitations (especially the ones mentioned in this paragraph) just don't lend themselves to good programming and systems. They're just too inefficient for most uses.

A *random file* is one that can be read both sequentially, one by one, and randomly (any one record in the file). A random file is like your compact disc player. Just as you can go to any spot on the disc, so can you go directly to any record in the file. But, if you want, you can read the entire file, one right after the other.

Note that the random file appears identical to the sequential file on the previous page. There are technical differences in using them, but it boils down to this; the only practical difference (to you, the programmer) between a sequential file and a random file is that *you can get at any single record of a random file without having to look at any other* records. Otherwise, they appear similar in nature. The next chapter

A Sequential Parts File

Record 1
Record 2
Record 3
Record 4
Record 5
Record 6
Record 7
Record 8
Record 9
Record 10

deals entirely with random files, which is what we will use for all our applications in this book.

An *indexed file* is a random file with a separate index, organized by name or number, which makes it easier to find the right record. It works on the same principle as the index in a book, which tells you on what page a certain subject is found. You see, a record in a random file can only be found by record number. That is, the 10th record in the file is record number 10, the 50th is record number 50, and so on. That's fine, if you know the record number of that customer, vendor, part, or service. But what if you only know the part name, like FENDER? If the file were indexed by part name, then the computer could

search the index,
find the part name (FENDER),

A Random Parts File

Record 1
Record 2
Record 3
Record 4
Record 5
Record 6
Record 7
Record 8
Record 9
Record 10

get the record number for FENDER,
and, finally, read the record containing the information for FENDER.

Indexed files are great to have in your system, but because of their complexity, we can't cover them here—we're just describing them for your future use beyond this book.

A *linked file* is one in which each record contains a pointer (a coupling, a connection, a reference, a location) or LINK to another record. This file type is normally used to link together all of the transactions for a particular customer, vendor, or corporation. A *transaction* is normally some form of sale or purchase, or stage of purchase or negotiation, or a meeting.

```
                        An Indexed Parts File

    ---------   Index  ---------        -------- File itself --------

       Part              Index Pointer
                         (to the record)

    +--------------+----------------+      +------------------------------+
    | brake        | (rec 9)        |      | Record 1    (gear)           |
    +--------------+----------------+      +------------------------------+
    | fender       | (rec 3)        |      | Record 2    (headlight)      |
    +--------------+----------------+      +------------------------------+
    | frame        | (rec 5)        |      | Record 3    (fender)         |
    +--------------+----------------+      +------------------------------+
    | gear         | (rec 1)        |      | Record 4    (petdl)          |
    +--------------+----------------+      +------------------------------+
    | handlebar    | (rec 7)        |      | Record 5    (frame)          |
    +--------------+----------------+      +------------------------------+
    | headlight    | (rec 2)        |      | Record 6    (seat)           |
    +--------------+----------------+      +------------------------------+
    | petdl        | (rec 4)        |      | Record 7    (handlebar)      |
    +--------------+----------------+      +------------------------------+
    | rim          | (rec 10)       |      | Record 8    (tire)           |
    +--------------+----------------+      +------------------------------+
    | seat         | (rec 6)        |      | Record 9    (brake)          |
    +--------------+----------------+      +------------------------------+
    | tire         | (rec 8)        |      | Record 10   (rim)            |
    +--------------+----------------+      +------------------------------+
```

1. The first link (in the customer/vendor/ corporation record) normally points to the last (most current) transaction (transaction record 1).
2. The link in the most current transaction record points to the previous transaction record (transaction record 2).
3. The link in the second transaction record points to the transaction prior to that, transaction record 3.
4. And so on, until there are no more transaction records.

Linked files are useful for connecting the transactions of customers/ vendors, when many transactions are involved. Because of their complexity, however, we're giving this description mainly for your understanding of files, rather than for practical application within this book.

The example below shows a linked file containing sales transactions, which have been recorded in the same order as they occurred (chronologically). But the most current sale for each customer has a pointer, or LINK, to the previous sale for that customer; that record points to the third most current sale, and so on. Try to follow the sales history, from most current to least current, for each customer by using the pointers.

Sales Transactions in a Linked File

Record Number	Name	Date of Sale	Pointer to Previous Record
112	Butkus	11/10/89	108
111	Shane	11/09/89	107
110	Scampini	11/07/89	109
109	Scampini	11/06/89	98
108	Butkus	11/04/89	105
107	Shane	11/04/89	102
106	Pratt	11/03/89	101
105	Butkus	11/03/89	104
104	Butkus	11/02/89	103
103	Butkus	11/01/89	91
102	Shane	11/01/89	83
101	Pratt	11/01/89	99

(Records 100 through 1 are not shown)

11.8 FILE SUBJECT CATEGORIES

(This section contains a brief note on tips for grouping data into files. This is not meant to be a tutorial on file design.)

When you're designing a file for your computer system, it helps to know what to put into which file. This isn't meant to be facetious;

sometimes it's hard to know what data items, or fields, to put where. This section is a start at showing you generally what kinds of files exist on computer systems, and what data items or fields go into each type of file.

Files can be classified by subject matter:

Customer/Vendor/Corporation file
Item or Service file
Transaction file

When you design a file , you should try to group data items, or fields, by the subject matter: A Customer/Vendor/Corporation file, (for example), contains

Customer/Vendor/Corporation number
Name
Address
Phone
Customer type
Notes
Credit limit
Purchases (by year, month, or week)
Bill to/pay to address
Balance
Contact names and phone numbers
Sales tax information
Total business
Discount information
Customer/Vendor since date

An Item/service file, for example, contains

Item/Service number
Description
Category
Supplier
Prices
Costs
Weight/Time
For items on hand, on order, minimum, maximum, order quantities,
    and so on.

Location
Sales by year, month, or week

A Transaction file, for example, contains

Transaction number
Transaction type
Transaction date
Transaction amount
Tax, if any
Shipping/travel, if any
Payment, if any
Pay type, if any
Description, if applicable
Discounts, if applicable

11.9 FILE LAYOUT

A file layout is just a description of the fields in each record.

Field name
Field type
Field length
Position of the field in the record

The *field name* is the variable name that you give to the field—remember chapter 5, *Types of Data and Names*? We recommend that the field name be not more than 12 characters in length and be a meaningful name so that you or any programmer will understand what the field is simply by the name.

The *field types* that we will work with are either

numeric,
alphanumeric,
or a date.

Numeric is further broken down into the integer, single-precision, double-precision, and long integer types that we saw in chapter 5. *Alphanumeric* consists of any combination of letters, numbers, and other printable characters. A *date* is simply a single-precision number that has this format: MMDDYY, where

MM is a two-digit month,
DD a two-digit day, and
YY a two-digit year.

Field length is the maximum number of letters or digits that will be stored in the field as its value. The *position* in the file is the actual space or location within the file that the field takes up. (Recall the different types of numbers from chapter 5.)

Integers take up two character positions (bytes).
Long integers take up four characters.
Single-precision numbers take up four character positions.
Double-precision numbers take up eight characters (rather than taking up a character for each digit.).

A simple file layout for a customer file might look like this:

Field name	Type	Length	Position
custnum	S	5	1–4
custname	A	30	5–34
custaddr1	A	30	35–64
custcity	A	20	65–84
custst	A	2	85–86
custzip	L	9	87–90
custtype	I	3	91–92
custbal	B	12	93–100

where the types are

A = Alpha
I = Integer
S = Small (single-precison) number
B = Big (double-precision) number
L = Long Integer

Don't worry about the detail in this last part—the next chapter will glue files and data together. Just recognize that you work with files all the time without realizing it. You'll work with them as a programmer in the same way as you always have, except that your usage is more precise.

CHAPTER SUMMARY

1. A file is a collection of (generally) like things. In the computer, a data file is a collection of like data.
2. A record is one of the like data articles in your file.
3. A field is a recognizable part or piece of a record, the smallest unit of that data item with which you normally work.
4. Four major types of file structures are

   Sequential
   Random
   Indexed
   Linked

5. Files can be classified by subject matter, such as:

   Customer/Vendor/Corporation
   Item or Service
   Transactions

6. A file layout is a description of the fields in a record:

   Field name
   Field type
   Field length
   Position within the record

THE BOTTOM LINE

1. BASIC is a personable language, which tells your computer to follow your instructions one at a time until it has produced a desired "report."
2. When you look at a BASIC program, break it up into sections, using the block-line method. Then look at each block, one at a time, to figure out what each does.

3. PowerBASIC gives you a complete working environment, which encourages writing programs in building-block fashion.
4. Blueprint your program before you write one line of code.
5. Data names should be meaningful, short (but not cryptic), consistent, and clear.
6. Program organization is not fluff. Organize your thoughts, assign the tasks to routines, and then program each routine.
7. Break your program up into subroutines and procedures, and then use **GOSUB** and **CALL.** Use **GOTO** only to go somewhere else within the same routine.
8. The Editor is very powerful. Use the keys as much as possible, and you'll be productive in writing and changing a program.
9. Keep your **IF**s simple and easy to read.
10. Loops are a critical structure of good programming. You can destroy that structure with the wrong use of **GOTO.** Use **GOTO** only to go somewhere else within the same loop.
11. **Files are no big deal. Just group like items together and describe them, and you have the start of a file.**

EXERCISES

(These exercises don't have precise answers. They're designed to start you thinking about file contents and layout.)

1. Lay out a random member file for a bowling team.

2. Lay out a random payroll file for Bikes Peak.

3. Lay out a random inventory file for the major possessions in your house.

Chapter 12

Random Files (The Only Kind You Really Need)

12.1 Definition of a Random File _____ 214

12.2 Opening a Random File _____ 215

12.3 Locating the Right Record _____ 217

12.4 Reading and Writing (GET and PUT) _____ 219

12.5 Record Layout _____ 222

12.6 Packing and Unpacking _____ 223

12.7 Creating a Random File _____ 225

12.8 Determining the End of the File _____ 226

You are trying to find a particular song on a tape. The problem is, you're not sure exactly where the song is located. You know that it's near the end of the tape, so you keep fast forwarding, playing a little bit, then fast forwarding, then playing, and so on. Damn! You just missed the start of the song. Your slow rewind doesn't work, so you rewind back a lot and then start the searching process over.

You're working with a sequential file. Whether on a tape player or on a computer, all sequential files act the same. The only way to get to a specific location on the file is to first go through every bit of information that is in front of it.

If you had the song on a compact disc, you could direct your compact disc player to go directly to the right song. You'd be working with a random file. A random file lets you go directly to any spot on the file. Again, computer sequential files act like the tape player, while computer random files function similarly to the compact disc player.

Because sequential files are both inconvenient and inflexible, (as with the tape player), we have gradually stopped using them for all business-related programming. We have found that it's just as easy to declare every file as a random file and then read it either sequentially or randomly depending on what the program calls for. Because of this, we decided not to spend a chapter on sequential files. We chose instead to devote the entire chapter to random files.

12.1 DEFINITION OF A RANDOM FILE

A *random file* is a data file in which any record can be accessed as quickly as any other record (relatively speaking—there are hardware considerations here that we're not getting into).

Assume a file of 10,000 records. If that file is a random file, the amount of time to get to the data in record 1 is roughly equal to the amount of time to get to the data in record 10,000.

12.2 OPENING A RANDOM FILE

Before any data file can be read from or written to, it must be opened. A file cabinet has to be opened before you can get at a file folder; your personal calendar has to be opened to find an appointment; and the phone book has to be opened to find a phone number. In the same way, a random file on a computer must be opened using an **OPEN** statement.

The syntax for an **OPEN** statement is:

OPEN ''R'', #{file number}, {file name}, {record length}

where—

1. ''R'' indicates that the file is opened in Random mode.

2. The *file number* is a number from 1 to 255. This number is used later in the read and write (**GET** and **PUT**) statements to tell the

computer which file to work with. Once a file name is mated to a file number in an **OPEN** statement, all reads and writes (**GET**s and **PUT**s) use that number. It's much easier than having to put the exact file name in every **GET** or **PUT**.

We recommend that you simply number your data files in every program sequentially, starting with 1 for the file that is used first. The first file (number 1) is usually the one whose reading and processing is contained in the Main Control loop. That's because the first file read is usually the primary file and controls the reading of all other files. Each file number must be unique, or the computer will be confused as to which file to read or write (**GET** or **PUT**).

3. The *file name* is the identifier (up to eight letters ptl *.DAT*), in quotes, of the random file on the computer disk. When you first create a data file (the very first time an **OPEN** statement with that file name is executed), BASIC places that file name into a directory index on the computer disk. In other words, the first time that a random file is opened, it is created on the computer disk, and the name is placed into a directory index with the name from the **OPEN** statement. Thereafter, each time the file is opened, the computer goes to the directory index to find the file location on the disk and get the data.

4. The *record length* is the number of character positions (bytes) that each record of the file contains. Remember that in the case of numeric data—

- integers take up two bytes,
- long integers take up four bytes,
- single-precision numbers take up four bytes, and
- double-precision (big) numbers take up eight bytes.

When first creating a file, leave 20 to 30 characters free for future expansion. It's a good idea to make the record size of random files some multiple of 128 characters (for technical reasons), and we allow for expansion by going to the next higher multiple of 128. (For example, if the record size of a file added up to 207, we would make the record size equal to 256, allowing 49 characters for expansion.) So our record sizes are normally 128, 256, 384, 512, 640, 768, 896, 1024, and so on.

Because disk space is so inexpensive today, we prefer to allow for the possible expansion early on. We'd rather waste a little space and *KNOW* that we can accommodate changes, rather than try to shoehorn additional data requirements into a too-small file at a later date.

■ FILE OPEN EXAMPLES:

OPEN "R", #1, "cust.dat", 128

Suppose that you had four files that you needed to use in one program:

Customers (Assume that the file name is cust.dat and the record size is 512.)
Vendors (Assume that the file name is vend.dat and the record size is 256.)
Parts (Assume that the file name is part.dat and the record size is 256.)
Service (Assume that the file name is serv.dat and the record size is 128.)

Then the **OPEN**s in the **FILEOPEN** routine would look like this:

OPEN "R", #1, "cust.dat", 512
OPEN "R", #2, "vend.dat", 256
OPEN "R", #3, "part.dat", 256
OPEN "R", #4, "serv.dat", 128

12.3 LOCATING THE RIGHT RECORD

Each record on a random file has a number. The first record is number 1, the second record is number 2, and so on. In the case of a random file, the record number is the *key* with which the computer works. You read a random file by specifying the record number as the *key* of the record you want from the computer. This record number can have a value from 1 to the number of records in the file. The record number is specified in the **GET** statement, which immediately follows this section.

The problem is, you might not want to assign numbers to your customers, vendors, parts, and services, each beginning with the number 1. If each of these began with the same number, you could have a customer number 10, a vendor number 10, a part number 10, and a service number 10. Based upon just looking at the number, you wouldn't be able to distinguish between a customer and a vendor, or between a part and a service.

So, early in the design stage you can decide to assign different numbers to each of these groups. For instance, you might want to number your customers from 1 to 5000, your vendors from 5001 to 6000, your parts from 6001 to 9000, and your services from 9001 to 10000. This gives you unique numbers for everything:

The number 10 can stand only for a customer.
The number 5010 can be only a vendor.
The number 6010 is always a part number.
The number 9010 signifies a particular service.

Then, to locate each record:

Customers: You locate a record in the random customer file by specifying the customer number (1 to 5000) as the key. This key then goes into the **GET** statement to read the customer record.

Vendors: Your vendors are numbered 5001 to 6000, which means you have 1,000 vendor numbers. The record numbers on your vendor file are numbered from 1 to 1000. Vendor number 5001 occupies record number 1, vendor 5002 has record number 2, and so on. Therefore, you locate a record in the random vendor file by calculating (vendor number − 5000) and making it the key in the **GET** statement. This gets you the vendor data that you want.

Parts: Your part numbers range between 6001 and 9000, which means that you have 3,000 parts. So the record numbers on your parts file are from 1 to 3000. Part number 6001 is in record location 1, part number 6002 is in record location 2, and so on. You locate a record in the random parts file by calculating (part number − 6000) and using it as the key in the **GET** statement.

Services: The numbers of your services are 9001−10000, so you have 1,000 services. This means that the record numbers on your service file are from 1 to 1000, with service number 9001 in record location 1, 9002 in record location 2, and so on. You can locate a record in the random service file by specifying the (service number − 9000) as the key in the **GET** statement.

Basically, you can locate a record in a random file by using any formula that works to calculate the record number (key), and then placing that number into a **GET** statement. If the formula gets you to the right record, it works. Use it.

We won't get into a series of complex formulas here for finding record keys—that's the subject matter for a different book. Just realize that you want to have the simplest formula that finds the right record.

12.4 READING AND WRITING (GET AND PUT)

You read a random file using a **GET** statement. You write a random file using a **PUT** statement.

12.4.1 GET Statement

The **GET** statement reads the specified record of the random file whose file number (the number specified in the file **OPEN**) is contained in the statement. The syntax is

GET {file number},{record number}

■ **GET EXAMPLES**

GET 1,100	Read record 100 of the file **OPEN**ed as #1.
GET 2,1000	Read record 1000 of the file **OPEN**ed as #2.
GET 3,f3	Read the record (as determined by the value of **f3**) of the file **OPEN**ed as #3. If **f3** had a value of 57, the 57th record of the file opened as #3 would be read. ■

And for the customer, vendor, part, and service files in the discussion above (12.3), to get record number 10 for each file:

- **Customer** (Assume that the Customer Number variable name is **custno,** the file number is 1, and the file key is named **f1.**)

  ```
  REM -- custno has a value of 10
  f1 = custno
  GET 1, f1
  ```

- **Vendor** (Assume that the Vendor key is called **vendno,** the file number is 2, and the file key is **f2.**)

  ```
  REM -- vendno has a value of 5010
  f2 = vendno - 5000
  GET 2, f2
  ```

- **Part** (Assume that the name of the part number is **partno,** the file number is 3, and the part key is **f3.**)

  ```
  REM -- partno has a value of 6010
  f3 = partno - 6000
  GET 3, f3
  ```

- **Service** (Assume that the service number is named **servno,** the file number is 4, and the service key is **f4.**)

  ```
  REM -- servno has a value of 9010
  f4 = servno - 9000
  GET 4, f4
  ```

12.4.2 PUT Statement

The **PUT** statement writes the specified record of the random file whose number is specified in the statement. The syntax is:

PUT {file number}, {record number}

■ PUT EXAMPLES

PUT 1,100   Write record 100 of the file **OPEN**ed as #1.
PUT 2,1000   Write record 1000 of the file **OPEN**ed as #2.
PUT 3,f3   Write the record (as determined by the value of **f3**) of the file **OPEN**ed as #3. If **f3** had a value of 57, the 57th record of the file opened as #3 would be written.   ■

And for the customer, vendor, part, and service files in the discussion above (12.3), to write record number 10 for each file:

- **Customer** (Assume that the Customer Number variable name is **custno,** the file number is 1, and the file key is named **f1.**)

```
REM -- custno has a value of 10
f1 = custno
PUT 1, f1
```

- **Vendor** (Assume that the Vendor key is called **vendno,** the file number is 2, and the file key is **f2.**)

```
REM -- vendno has a value of 5010
f2 = vendno − 5000
PUT 2, f2
```

- **Part** (Assume that the name of the part number is **partno,** the file number is 3, and the part key is **f3.**)

```
REM -- partno has a value of 6010
f3 = partno − 6000
PUT 3, f3
```

- **Service** (Assume that the service number is named **servno,** the file number is 4, and the service key is **f4.**)

```
REM -- servno has a value of 9010
f4 = servno − 9000
PUT 4, f4
```

12.5 RECORD LAYOUT

Back in chapter 11, we showed you a file layout for a customer file. This record layout for a random customer file is simply an extension of that. We've added a column to show the "packed" size of the numeric data fields:

Field name	Type	Length	Packed Length	Position
custnum	S	5	4	1–4
custname$	A	30	30	5–34
custaddr1$	A	30	30	35–64
custcity$	A	20	20	65–84
custst$	A	2	2	85–86
custzip#	L	9	4	87–90
custtype	I	3	2	91–92
custbal#	B	12	8	93–100

Where the types are

A = Alphanumeric
I = Integer
S = Small number (single-precison)
B = Big number (double-precision)
L = Long integer (up to 16 digits)

BASIC uses a **FIELD** statement to describe the layout of a random record to the computer. This **FIELD** statement specifies the name and packed length of each field in the record. Because the fields are described in the exact order in which they occur on the record, the **FIELD** statement becomes a complete definition of all the positions in a record.

The syntax for a **FIELD** statement is:

FIELD #{file number}, {packed length of 1st field} AS {name of___
1st field}$, {packed length of second field} AS {name of second___
field}$, {packed length of third field} AS {name of third___
field)$, and so on.

■ **FIELD EXAMPLE**

FIELD #1, 4 AS custnum$, 30 AS custname$, 30 AS custaddr1$, 20 AS custcity$, 2 AS__
 custst$, 4 AS custzip$, 2 AS custtype, 8 AS custbal$

So the **FILEOPEN** routine for a program that uses only this file looks like this:

FILEOPEN:
 OPEN "R", #1, "cust.dat", 128
 FIELD #1, 4 AS custnum$, 30 AS custname$, 30 AS custaddr1$, 20 AS custcity$, 2 AS__
 custst$, 4 AS custzip$, 2 AS custtype$, 8 AS custbal$
RETURN ■

12.6 PACKING AND UNPACKING

Numeric variables are *packed* before being put into a random file in order to save space. Integers are packed into the space taken up by two characters, single-precision numbers are packed into four characters, double-precision numbers are packed into eight characters, and long integers are packed into four characters. While alphanumeric variables are never packed, numeric variables must always be packed in order to put them onto a random file.

Conversely, when you read a record from a random file, you must always *unpack* the numeric variables before trying to use them in a calculation, move, or display.

The syntax for the packing commands is:

LSET {variable name}$ = MK{type of data indicator}$ ({variable name})

where **LSET** is required to do the packing, and **MKI, MKS, MKL,** and **MKD** signify the type of data being packed.

The packing commands are:

> **MKI$**—packs integer variables
> **MKS$**—packs single-precision variables
> **MKD$**—packs double-precision variables
> **MKL$**—packs long integer variables

■ PACKING EXAMPLES

(Using the sample customer file in chapter 11):

```
LSET custtype$      =      MKI$(custtype%)
LSET custnum$       =      MKS$(custnum)
LSET custbal$       =      MKD$(custbal#)
LSET custzip$       =      MKL$(custzip&)
```
■

Note that all packing statements are preceded by the word **LSET**. The **LSET** is required in BASIC in order for packing to be accomplished properly.

The syntax for unpacking is:

{variable name}$ = CV{type of data indicator} ({variable name}$)

where **CVI, CVS, CVL,** and **CVD** signify the type of data being unpacked. The unpacking commands are:

CVI—unpacks integer variables
CVS—unpacks single precision variables
CVD—unpacks double precision variables
CVL—unpacks long integer variables

■ UNPACKING EXAMPLES

(Using the customer file from chapter 11):

```
custtype%      =      CVI(custtype$)
custnum        =      CVS(custnum$)
custbal#       =      CVD(custbal$)
custzip&       =      CVL(custzip$)
```

The **FILEOPEN** and **FILEREAD** routines for the customer file from chapter 11 would look like this (For this file, we'll give the **FILEREAD** routine the name **CUSTREAD.**):

```
FILEOPEN:
  OPEN "R", #1, "cust.dat", 128
  FIELD #1, 4 AS custnum$, 30 AS custname$, 30 AS custaddr1$, 20 AS custcity$, 2 AS__
    custst$, 4 AS custzip$, 2 AS custtype$, 8 AS custbal$
  RETURN
```

```
CUSTREAD:
  GET #1, f1
  custnum = CVS(custnum$)
  custzip& = CVL(custzip$)
  custtype% = CVI(custtype$)
  custbal# = CVD(custbal$)
RETURN
```

12.7 CREATING A RANDOM FILE

As we mentioned in the OPENING A RANDOM FILE section (12.2), the first time that a random file is **OPEN**ed, the file name is recorded on the disk, and the file is created.

Most programmers simply create a random file by **OPEN**ing it, writing some records, and then **CLOS**ing the file. We recommend, however, that you write a separate program to create every random file. This program should initialize every numeric field to 0 using one of these commands:

```
LSET {fieldname}$ = MKI$(0)
LSET {fieldname}$ = MKS$(0)
LSET {fieldname}$ = MKL$(0)
LSET {fieldname}$ = MKD$(0)
```

Then set every alphanumeric field to spaces and write these "blank" records to the file. You should create this "blank" file with the maximum number of records that you expect this file to contain. This eliminates performance problems in the future and minimizes programming problems later on. It would take a chapter or two to detail the benefits, but you'll realize them after you've been programming awhile; so we won't take up our space and your time.

12.7.1 Random File Creation Program

This program creates a blank customer file for the example we have shown in this chapter and chapter 11. It creates a random access file of

1,000 records, with record numbers of 1 through 1000 and customer numbers of 1 to 1000. Note that we have over 30 characters free for future expansion.

```
REM crcust 010189
GOSUB fileopen
GOSUB main
CLOSE
END
fileopen:
   OPEN "r", 1, "cust.dat", 128
   FIELD 1, 4 AS custnum$, 30 AS custname$, 30 AS custaddr1$,__
      20 AS custcity$, 2 AS custst$, 4 AS custzip$, 2 AS custtype$
RETURN
main:
   GOSUB clearcust
   FOR f1 = 1 TO 1000: REM -- loop to write 1000 blank cust records
      LSET custnum$ = MKS$(f1)
      PUT 1, f1
      PRINT f1
   NEXT f1
RETURN
clearcust:
   REM -- set up a blank record
   LSET custname$ = " "
   LSET custaddr1$ = " "
   LSET custcity$ = " "
   LSET custst$ = " "
   LSET custzip$ = MKL$(0)
   LSET custtype$ = MKI$(0)
RETURN
```

12.8 DETERMINING THE END OF THE FILE

When you are reading a random file sequentially, you just add one to the record number time after time to get to the next record. However, if you don't stop this process, the computer can read past the end of the file and read bad data that doesn't belong to that file.

There are two ways to prevent this:

1. Use an **IF** statement to test if the record number is beyond the number of records you have allowed for that file, or
2. use an **IF EOF** statement to test for reading beyond the end-of-file.

The syntax of the **IF** statement for testing the record number to be beyond the maximum is

IF {record number} > {maximum number of records} THEN GOTO {line label}

where

{**record number**} is the current record number that is about to be read,

{**maximum number of records**} is the number of blank records in the file, and

{**line label**} is a label at which processing of that file will end. It usually is the label on the statement that ends the **READ** loop.

■ IF EXAMPLES

IF f1 > 1000 THEN GOTO quit1
IF recnum1 > 5000 THEN GOTO ender

The syntax of the **IF EOF** statement for end-of-file testing is:

IF EOF({file number}) THEN GOTO {line label}

where

{**file number**} is the number of the file when it was **OPEN**ed, and

{**line label**} is a label at which processing of that file will end. It usually is the label of the statement that exits the **READ** loop. ■

■ IF EOF EXAMPLES

IF EOF(1) THEN GOTO quit1
IF EOF(3) THEN GOTO ender

Note:

The **EOF** test must be performed *after the file is read!!*

If we had a program that printed out the customer file from chapter 11, the **MAIN** routine (major processing loop from chapter 6) could look like this:

Using **IF...**

```
main:
   f1 = f1 + 1
   IF f1 > 1000 THEN GOTO ENDMAIN
   GOSUB getcust: REM -- reads a customer record
   GOSUB princust: REM -- prints a customer record
   GOTO main
endmain:
   RETURN
```

Using **IF EOF. . .**

```
main:
   f1 = f1 + 1
   GOSUB getcust: REM -- reads a customer record
   IF EOF(1) THEN GOTO ENDMAIN
   GOSUB princust: REM -- prints a customer record
   GOTO main
endmain:
   RETURN
```

As you can see, with the exception of the end-of-file test, the routines are identical.

CHAPTER SUMMARY

1. A random file is one in which any record can be accessed as quickly as any other.
2. Before a random file can be used, it must first be opened.
3. The record number is simply the sequence number of the record in a random file. Use the record number to locate a particular piece of data. You may have to perform a calculation to find the record number.

4. You read a random file using **GET**. You write a random file using **PUT**.
5. A **FIELD** statement provides the record layout for a random file.
6. Numbers in random files must be packed before they are written. They must be unpacked after being read, before they can be used.
7. Create a "blank" random file first. Then use it for storing data.
8. Test for an end-of-file condition (no more records to be read) using

   IF {record number} > {the number of records in the file}

   or

   IF EOF({file number} **)**

THE BOTTOM LINE

1. BASIC is a personable language, which tells your computer to follow your instructions one at a time until it has produced a desired "report."
2. When you look at a BASIC program, break it up into sections, using the block-line method. Then look at each block, one at a time, to figure out what each does.
3. PowerBASIC gives you a complete working environment, which encourages writing programs in building-block fashion.
4. Blueprint your program before you write one line of code.
5. Data names should be meaningful, short (but not cryptic), consistent, and clear.
6. Program organization is not fluff. Organize your thoughts, assign the tasks to routines, and then program each routine.
7. Break your program up into subroutines and procedures, and then use **GOSUB** and **CALL**. Use **GOTO** only to go somewhere else within the same routine.
8. The Editor is very powerful. Use the keys as much as possible, and you'll be productive in writing and changing a program.
9. Keep your **IF**s simple and easy to read.

10. Loops are a critical structure of good programming. You can destroy that structure with the wrong use of **GOTO**. Use **GOTO** only to go somewhere else within the same loop.

11. Files are no big deal. Just group like items together and describe them, and you have the start of a file.

12. **Learn to use random files well; you won't need any other kind of file.**

EXERCISES

1. Write the **OPEN** statements for the Bikes Peak Customer file and the Inventory (Parts) file.

2. Write the **FIELD** statement for the Bikes Peak Customer file. Remember to convert the numeric fields to integer, single-precision, and double-precision fields. These will probably not take up the same amount of space as you originally blueprinted in chapter 4.

3. Write the **FIELD** statement for the Bikes Peak Inventory file. Remember to convert the numeric fields to integer, single-precision, and double-precision fields. These will probably not take up the same amount of space as you originally blueprinted in chapter 4.

4. Write the unpack statements for the Bikes Peak Customer file.

5. Write the unpack statements for the Bikes Peak Inventory file.

6. Now, combine these pieces and write the program to create a blank Bikes Peak Customer file for 100 customers.

7. Write the program to create the blank Bikes Peak Inventory file for 100 parts.

Chapter 13

Input from the Keyboard (The Key Is to Key in Correctly)

13.1 Editing Is Critical _____ **232**

13.2 Editing Levels _____ **233**

13.3 Error Messages _____ **239**

13.4 Screen Neatness Techniques _____ **244**

You offered to help Art with his mailing list. He bought a list of 10,000 names from _Free Wheelin_, the bike magazine. Art needs to get the names into the computer as quickly as possible, so that the announcements for the new bike, "Everest," can get out. So you get the world's fastest keypuncher, Punchin' Pam, to do the job. Pam accomplishes the task in just two days. You and Art are ecstatic!

One week later the announcements start coming back—"Return to Sender, No Such Address." Over 3,000 of them. You wasted over $1,200 in printing and mailing costs. After a brief analysis, you find that the addresses have been keyed in wrong. You should have hired Meticulous Mary, who would have taken about a week and done the job right.

Garbage in, garbage out. The most critical element (and most overlooked detail) in computer processing is validation (editing) of data. Processing of bad data is not just a waste of time, it's the most common means of projecting a wrong number, failing to balance, and causing an accounting disaster. This chapter will help you avoid these problems.

13.1 EDITING IS CRITICAL

In management, you're taught to nip the problem in the bud. This means that you catch a problem before it grows into a catastrophe requiring drastic emergency measures.

In programming, you nip the problem in the bud by thoroughly testing every piece of data BEFORE it is accepted into a program, BEFORE it is written onto a file. You accomplish this by editing each entry for length, type, ranges, and maybe even specific values.

If you don't do this with EVERY PIECE OF DATA being accepted into the program from the keyboard and EVERY FILE that you are working with for the first time, you stand a chance of the program's "blowing up" (stopping completely, with no chance of restarting it). This can really create problems, especially when you've processed and written one-third of the records and left two-thirds unprocessed.

Programs "blow up" when—

- The program tries to divide by zero (remember your algebra?),
- tries to read a record number of zero,
- tries to read a negative record number,
- and for other reasons too numerous to list, but you get the idea.

13.2 EDITING LEVELS

There are five levels of editing that we'll cover:

Length—Test the data for the maximum and minimum number of characters allowed for that field (variable name). If the length is more than allowed, reject the data item. If the length is less than allowed, reject the item.

Type (numeric)—Test each character in the data item to be a number between 0 and 9. If not, reject the item.

Type (date)—Test the date to ensure that each month has a value between 1 and 12 and that the number of days for that month is between 1 and the maximum number of days in that month. If not, reject the item.

Ranges—Test the data item for a maximum and minimum value, if applicable. If your customer numbers range between 1 and 2000, for example, test for that range before accepting a customer number. If the only acceptable customer types range between 1 and 6, test the customer type for that range. Test everything that you can for proper ranges before acceptance.

Specific Values—Test for one of a series of specific values for a field or variable name before accepting that item. If the only acceptable categories of bike parts are K1 and K2, then reject anything else.

13.2.1 BASIC Examples for Length, Type, Range, and Specific Value Testing

We're going to demonstrate editing before explaining the details of each statement that we use. Rather than bog you down with details, we're going to show you the logic first and the detail later. In all cases, we'll assume that input is coming from the keyboard. To keep things simple, we'll use this input statement for all input:

LINE INPUT "{some prompt}"; i$

where

LINE INPUT are BASIC reserved words that get data into a program by keyboard entry.

{some prompt} is any appropriate prompt that tells the person keying in the input what data the program expects to be entered.

i$ is the variable name that is given the data keyed in at the keyboard.

When the computer encounters a **LINE INPUT** statement, it

prints the prompt {**some prompt**},

waits for data to be keyed in, and,

when the ENTER key is pressed, continues with the next program statement.

Note:

Take each of the following examples one at a time. Read the example and try to guess at every line's purpose. Then, get into PowerBASIC on your computer, type in the first routine example, run the routine, and test it by keying in both valid and invalid data. Remember to work on (read, type, run, and test) each routine separately.

After keying in the routine, to run it, just

PRESS ⟨ALT⟩ + ⟨**r**⟩⟨ENTER⟩, and it'll run.

When you're through with one routine and ready to key in the next program statements, make sure that you save the previous routine by

PRESS ⟨ALT⟩ + ⟨**f**⟩⟨ENTER⟩ then
PRESS ⟨**w**⟩⟨ENTER⟩

When you are prompted for a name by PowerBASIC, enter **EX** followed by the example number (no spaces, please). Then

PRESS ⟨ENTER⟩

The program is now saved with that name. You can save the first seven examples as **EX1, EX2, EX3,** and so on. Later in this chapter, you'll retrieve them and make changes to them.

Ready? Here's the first routine.

■ LENGTH TEST EXAMPLES:

(**LEN** is a BASIC function that finds the length of an alphanumeric variable [string]. It'll be explained in detail later.) ■

■ EXAMPLE 1: LENGTH

(Save when done as **EX1**.)

```
getin:
    LINE INPUT "enter customer name"; i$
    IF LEN(i$)>30 THEN GOTO getin
    IF LEN(i$)<1 THEN GOTO getin
    PRINT "OK"
```
■

■ EXAMPLE 2: LENGTH

(Save when done as **EX2.**)

```
getin:
    LINE INPUT "enter customer state (2 characters)"; i$
    IF LEN(i$)>2 THEN GOTO getin
    IF LEN(i$)<1 THEN GOTO getin
    PRINT "OK"
```
■

■ EXAMPLE 3: LENGTH

(Save when done as **EX3.**)

```
getin:
    LINE INPUT "enter customer phone number"; i$
    IF LEN(i$)>10 THEN GOTO getin
    IF LEN(i$)<1 THEN GOTO getin
    PRINT "OK"
```
■

In the first example, we tested for the length of **i$** (the customer name, in this case) to be less than 1 or greater than 30. If either condition is true, the program will go back and ask for the data again.

In the second example, we tested for the length of **i$** (the state) to be less than 1 or greater than 2. If either condition is true, the program asks for the data again.

In the third example, we tested for a length less than 1 or greater than 10. If either condition is found, the program asks for the data again.

Note that in each case we used the **LEN** function to determine the length of the input variable, **i$.** The **LEN** function calculates the *length* of the variable inside the parentheses and returns the number for use in a BASIC statement.

■ EXAMPLE 4: TYPE TEST EXAMPLE (NUMERIC TEST)

(Save when done as **EX4.**)

```
getin:
    LINE INPUT "enter customer phone number"; i$
    i1% = LEN(i$):REM -- get the length of i$
    IF i1%>10 THEN GOTO getin
```

```
    IF i1%<1 THEN GOTO getin
numtest%=0:REM -- set a test flag to 0
FOR i%=1 TO i1%:REM -- set up a loop to check for numeric
    IF ASC(MID$(i$,i%,1))<48 THEN numtest%=1:REM -- test for <0
    IF ASC(MID$(i$,i%,1))>57 THEN numtest%=1:REM -- test for >9
NEXT i%
IF numtest%>0 THEN GOTO getin:REM -- if any of the characters were less than 0 or greater
than 9, then go back to getin__
    PRINT "OK"
REM -- rest of program
```

In this *numeric test* example, we first checked for proper length. That's because, if the length is wrong, there's no sense in checking further; it's wrong and has to be re-entered.

We then went through a loop that selects each character of the item and confirms it to be a number between 0 and 9. If the character is not a number, we gave **numtest%** a value of 1.

After the loop is completed, we test **numtest%** for a value >0. If it were greater than 0, it would mean that at least one non-numeric character had been found; therefore, the program goes back to **getin** to ask for valid numeric input.

Note that we used the **ASC** and **MID$** functions to test for numeric. **ASC** converts a character to its ASCII value. (*0* has an ASCII value of 48, 1 has a value of 49, and so on.) **MID$** selects a particular character within a string. (In this case we looked at each character, beginning with the first on the left.) We'll explain their exact use in the next chapter. Please just go over this example for general understanding, rather than exact detail. ∎

∎ EXAMPLE 5: TYPE TEST EXAMPLE (DATE TEST)

(Save when done as **EX5.**)

```
getin:
    LINE INPUT "enter customer since date"; i$
    i1%=LEN(i$):REM -- get the length of i$
    IF i1%>6 THEN GOTO getin
    IF i1%<1 THEN GOTO getin
    numtest%=0:REM -- set a test flag to 0
```

```
FOR i% = 1 TO i1%:REM -- set up a loop to check for numeric
   IF ASC(MID$(i$,i%,1))<48 THEN numtest% = 1:REM -- test for <0
   IF ASC(MID$(i$,i%,1))>57 THEN numtest% = 1:REM -- test for >9
NEXT i%
IF numtest%>0 THEN GOTO getin:REM -- if any of the characters were less than 0 or __
greater than 9, then go back to getin
IF i1%<5 THEN GOTO getin:REM -- if the length is <5 then goto getin
IF i1% = 5 THEN i$ = "0" + i$:REM -- make it a six character field
w1% = VAL(LEFT$(i$,2)):REM -- get the value of the month
IF w1%<1 THEN GOTO getin:REM -- if month <1, goto getin
IF w1%>12 THEN GOTO getin:REM -- if month >12, goto getin
w2% = VAL(MID$(i$,3,2)):REM -- get the value of the day
IF w2%<1 THEN GOTO getin:REM -- if day <1, goto getin
IF w2%>31 THEN GOTO getin:REM -- if day >31, goto getin
w3% = VAL(RIGHT$(i$,2)):REM -- get the value of the year
IF w3%>93 THEN GOTO getin:REM -- if year >93, goto getin
PRINT"OK"
```

The *date test* example is testing for a five- or six- character date without any slashes or dashes between month, day, and year. The format that this routine expects is *MMDDYY*, where

MM is a one- or two-character number (1–12) signifying month,
DD is the two-character number (01–31) of the day, and
YY is the two-character number of the year.

The example first checks for a valid length. If the length is wrong, the data input is invalid and has to be re-entered. The next test is for numeric validity. If the entry isn't numeric, it couldn't possibly pass a date test; and besides, it's wrong and has to be keyed again. Then the actual date test goes into action. The month is isolated and tested for a value between 1 and 12. If this test is failed, the test goes no further; the entry is wrong and must be re-keyed. If the month test is passed, the day is separated, then tested for a value between 1 and 31. If this test is failed, the program goes back to ask for valid input. If the input passes the day test, the routine finds the year and tests for a value greater than 93. If greater, the routine rejects the data and goes back to ask for a valid date. If the year is 93 or less, the date is considered valid, and the program continues. ∎

■ EXAMPLE 6: RANGE TEST

(Save when done as **EX6.**)

```
getin:
    LINE INPUT "enter customer type"; i$
    IF LEN(i$)>1 THEN GOTO getin:REM -- if length >1, goto getin
    IF LEN(i$)<1 THEN GOTO getin:REM -- if length <1, goto getin
    IF i$< "A" THEN GOTO getin:REM -- if type < "A", goto getin
    IF i$>"C" THEN GOTO getin:REM -- if type > "C", goto getin
    PRINT "OK"
```

The *range test* example checks for length before anything else, because if the length is wrong, further testing is a waste. If the length is all right, it then checks for a value betweeen "A" and "C" (which means that "A", "B", or "C" would be acceptable). If the entry is less than "A" (which means it's not a letter) or more than "C" (any letter beyond "C" in the alphabet), it is rejected. ■

■ EXAMPLE 7: SPECIFIC VALUE TEST EXAMPLE

(Save when done as **EX7.**)

```
getin:
    LINE INPUT "enter customer type"; i$
    IF LEN(i$)>1 THEN GOTO getin:REM -- if length >1, goto getin
    IF LEN(i$)<1 THEN GOTO getin:REM -- if length <1, goto getin
    IF i$ = "A" THEN GOTO goodtype:REM -- if type = "A", leave test
    IF i$ = "C" THEN GOTO goodtype:REM -- if type = "C", leave test
    GOTO getin:REM -- go back and get a a valid customer type
goodtype:
    PRINT "OK"
    REM -- continue with program
```

The *test for specific values* example begins with the usual length test. If that test is passed, the data is then tested for a specific value, "A". If that value is found, the entry is considered valid, and the routine leaves the test. If not, the routine next tests for the value of "C". If found, it leaves the test. If not, the program goes back to **getin** for valid input. It'll accept "A" or "C", but not "B". ■

13.3 ERROR MESSAGES

In the examples above, when we detected an error in an input data item, we simply went back and asked for the input data again. When you program for real-world applications, it's a good idea to tell the operator that an error has been detected, and what that error is. Since the operator may not be looking at the computer screen while typing in, we suggest that you "ring the bell." Key this into your computer and run it:

```
PRINT CHR$(7)
```

Then try this:

```
FOR i% = 1 TO 10
   PRINT CHR$(7)
NEXT i%
```

The "bell" rings much longer, because in effect you rang it ten times. While we don't recommend ten rings for an error, one or two are sure to make anyone notice that an error has occurred.

Now that you've notified the operator that there is an error, you should tell him or her what that error is. Based on our tests, we have six possible error messages. An example of each is:

"Too long"
"Too short"
"Not numeric"
"Bad date"
"Out of range"
"Not one of the acceptable values"

We now add these features to the same tests, and we'll have some nice error routines with clear messages. Try each of them separately in PowerBASIC on your machine. Key in both valid and invalid data to test the error testing and messages.

■ **EXAMPLE 8: LENGTH EXAMPLES WITH ERROR MESSAGES**

First retrieve **EX1**:

```
PRESS ⟨ALT⟩ + ⟨f⟩⟨ENTER⟩
PRESS ⟨L⟩⟨ENTER⟩
TYPE EX1 ⟨ENTER⟩
```

Then change the statements to look like this:

```
getin:
  LINE INPUT "enter customer name"; i$
  IF LEN(i$)>30 THEN
    PRINT CHR$(7);"Too long"
    GOTO getin
  END IF
  IF LEN(i$)<1 THEN
    PRINT CHR$(7);"Too short"
    GOTO getin
  END IF
  PRINT "OK"
```

(Save it as **EX8**.)

■ **EXAMPLE 9: LENGTH EXAMPLE**

First retrieve **EX2**. Then make the changes to look like:

```
getin:
LINE INPUT "enter customer state (2 characters)"; i$
  IF LEN(i$)>2 THEN
    PRINT CHR$(7);"Too long"
    GOTO getin
  END IF
  IF LEN(i$)<1 THEN
    PRINT CHR$(7);"Too short"
    GOTO getin
  END IF
  PRINT "OK"
```

(Save it as **EX9**).

■ EXAMPLE 10: LENGTH EXAMPLE

First retrieve **EX3.** Then change it to look like:

```
getin:
    LINE INPUT "enter customer phone number"; i$
    IF LEN(i$)>10 THEN
        PRINT CHR$(7);"Too long"
        GOTO getin
    END IF
    IF LEN (i$)<1 THEN
        PRINT CHR$(7);"Too short"
        GOTO getin
    END IF
    PRINT "OK"
```

(Save it as **EX10.**)

Notice the special setup of the block **IF** statement. The **IF** condition is on one line with the corresponding **THEN,** followed by indented statements (each on a separate line) and ending with **END IF.** If the condition is true, all statements up to the **END IF** are run.   ■

■ EXAMPLE 11: TYPE EXAMPLE: NUMERIC TEST WITH ERROR MESSAGES

Open **EX4** and make these changes:

```
getin:
    LINE INPUT "enter customer phone number"; i$
    i1% = LEN(i$):REM -- get the length of i$
    IF i1%>10 THEN
        PRINT CHR$(7);"Too long"
        GOTO getin
    END IF
    IF i1%<1 THEN
        PRINT CHR$(7);"Too short"
        GOTO getin
    END IF
    numtest% = 0:REM -- set a test flag to 0
    FOR i% = 1 TO i1%:REM -- set up a loop to check for numeric
        IF ASC(MID$(i$,i%,1))<48 THEN numtest% = 1:REM -- test for <0
        IF ASC(MID$(i$,i%,1))>57 THEN numtest% = 1:REM -- test for >9
```

```
    NEXT i%
    IF numtest%>0 THEN
        PRINT CHR$(7); PRINT"Not numeric"
        GOTO getin
    END IF
    PRINT "OK"
```

(Save it as **EX11.**)

■ EXAMPLE 12: TYPE EXAMPLE: DATE TEST WITH ERROR MESSAGES

Bring in **EX5** and make the changes to look like:

```
getin:
    LINE INPUT "enter customer since date"; i$
    i1% = LEN(i$):REM -- get the length of i$
    IF i1%>10 THEN
        PRINT CHR$(7);"Too long"
        GOTO getin
    END IF
    IF i1%<1 THEN
        PRINT CHR$(7);"Too short"
        GOTO getin
    END IF
    numtest% = 0:REM -- set a test flag to 0
    FOR i% = 1 TO i1%:REM -- set up a loop to check for numeric
        IF ASC(MID$(i$,i%,1))<48 THEN numtest% = 1:REM -- test for <0
        IF ASC(MID$(i$,i%,1))>57 THEN numtest% = 1:REM -- test for >9
    NEXT i%
    IF numtest%>0 THEN
        PRINT CHR$(7);"Not numeric"
        GOTO getin
    END IF
    IF i1%<5 THEN GOTO getin:REM -- if the length <5 then goto getin.
    IF i1% = 5 THEN i$ = "0" + i$:REM -- make it a six character field
    w1% = VAL(LEFT$(i$,2)):REM -- get the month
    IF w1%<1 THEN
        PRINT CHR$(7);"Bad date"
        GOTO getin
    END IF
    IF w1%>12 THEN
```

```
    PRINT CHR$(7);"Bad date"
    GOTO getin
END IF
w2% = VAL(MID$(i$,3,2)):REM -- get the day
IF w2%<1 THEN
    PRINT CHR$(7);"Bad date"
    GOTO getin
END IF
IF w2%>31 THEN
    PRINT CHR$(7);"Bad date"
    GOTO getin
END IF
w3% = VAL(RIGHT$(i$,2)):REM -- get the year
IF w3%>93 THEN
    PRINT CHR$(7);"Bad date"
    GOTO getin
END IF
PRINT "OK"
```

(Save it as **EX12.**)   ∎

∎ EXAMPLE 13: RANGE TEST EXAMPLE

Read in **EX6** and change it.

```
getin:
    LINE INPUT "enter customer type"; i$
    IF LEN(i$)>1 THEN
        PRINT CHR$(7);"Too long"
        GOTO getin
    END IF
    IF LEN(i$)<1 THEN
        PRINT CHR$(7);"Too short"
        GOTO getin
    END IF
    IF i$<"A" THEN
        PRINT CHR$(7);"Out of range"
        GOTO getin
    END IF
    IF i$>"C" THEN
```

```
        PRINT CHR$(7);"Out of range"
        GOTO getin
   END IF
   PRINT "OK"
```

(Save it as **EX13.**)   ■

■ EXAMPLE 14: SPECIFIC VALUES TEST EXAMPLE WITH ERROR MESSAGES

Open **EX7** and change it.

```
getin:
    LINE INPUT "enter customer type"; i$
    IF LEN(i$)>1 THEN
       PRINT CHR$(7);"Too long"
       GOTO getin
    END IF
    IF LEN(i$)<1 THEN
       PRINT CHR$(7);"Too short"
       GOTO getin
    END IF
    IF i$="A" THEN GOTO goodtype:REM -- if type = "A", leave test
    IF i$="C" THEN GOTO goodtype:REM -- if type = "C", leave test
    PRINT CHR$(7);"Not one of the acceptable entries"
    GOTO getin
goodtype:
    PRINT "OK"
    REM -- continue with program
```

(Save it as **EX14.**)

You should now have a good idea of what goes into good editing.

13.4 SCREEN NEATNESS TECHNIQUES

The routines above work nicely, but each time an entry is incorrect, two more lines are printed on the screen. If someone were entering six data items, just a few mistakes would cause the screen to fill, and then start scrolling upward with each new line printed. (Once the screen is filled, every time data is printed on the bottom line of the screen, the screen moves everything up one line, and the top line is lost.) We aren't going to cover screen layout in this chapter, but we will show you how to go back to a specific location on the screen. This can avoid a screen cluttered with old error messages and bad data that now have no meaning. When an error is found, you can go back to the location of original data entry on the screen without having to scroll several lines upwards. Your screen will show only valid data, rather than a mixture of bad data, good data, and error messages.

In this section, we'll refer to the "cursor," which is just the blinking underline (or blinking block, or solid block, or solid underline) that shows you where you are (the current location) on the screen.

In the examples below, we're introducing three new BASIC commands. In brief, this is what they do:

POS—gets the column position of the cursor
CSRLIN—gets the line position of the cursor
LOCATE—places the cursor in a specific spot on the screen

We use **POS** and **CSRLIN** to identify the spot to return to in case of an error; then, if an error occurs, **LOCATE** the cursor back on that spot. The new data can then be keyed in over the old, erroneous data.

We'll explain the details of **LOC**, **CSRLIN** and **POS** in chapter 16. (Don't look ahead, it'll confuse, not help.) Just follow the logic and the **REM** statements, and you'll have an understanding of how it works.

■ LENGTH EXAMPLE WITH ERROR MESSAGES AND NO SCROLLING

Retrieve a previous example (**EX8**) and type in the changes. Then save this as **EX15.** Run it and test it to see how it works.

```
x% = POS(0):REM -- get and save current column position
y% = CSRLIN:REM -- get and save current line
getin:
  LINE INPUT "enter customer name"; i$
  IF LEN(i$)>30 THEN
    PRINT CHR$(7);"Too long";TAB(79);""
    LOCATE y%,x%:REM -- go to original line & col
    GOTO getin
  END IF
```

```
IF LEN(i$)<1 THEN
   PRINT CHR$(7);"Too short";TAB(79);""
   LOCATE y%,x%:REM -- go to original line & col
   GOTO getin
END IF
PRINT TAB(79);"":REM -- clear any previous error message by printing a blank line
PRINT "OK"
```

■

■ TYPE EXAMPLE: NUMERIC TEST WITH ERROR MESSAGES AND NO SCROLLING

Retrieve **EX11,** make the changes, save it as **EX16,** and test it.

```
x% = POS(0):REM -- get and save current column position
y% = CSRLIN:REM -- get and save current line
getin:
   LINE INPUT "enter customer phone number"; i$
   i1% = LEN(i$):REM -- get the length of i$
   IF i1%>10 THEN
      PRINT CHR$(7);"Too long";TAB(79);""
      LOCATE y%,x%:REM -- goto original line & col
      GOTO getin
   END IF
   IF i1%<1 THEN
      PRINT CHR$(7);"Too short";TAB(79);""
      LOCATE y%,x%:REM -- goto original line & col
      GOTO getin
   END IF
   numtest% = 0:REM -- set a test flag to 0
   FOR i% = 1 TO i1%:REM -- set up a loop to check for numeric
      IF ASC(MID$(i$,i%,1))<48 THEN numtest% = 1:REM -- test <0
      IF ASC(MID$(i$,i%,1))>57 THEN numtest% = 1:REM -- test >9
   NEXT i%
   IF numtest%>0 THEN
      PRINT CHR$(7); PRINT"Not numeric";TAB(79);""
      locate y%,x%:REM -- goto original line & col
      GOTO getin
   END IF
   PRINT TAB(79);"":REM -- clear any previous error messages by printing a blank line
   PRINT "OK"
```

CHAPTER SUMMARY

1. Editing is critical to good results in programming.
2. Typical editing includes length verification, numeric validation, date validation, range testing, and specific value confirmation.
3. Short, clear error messages are important.
4. Keep the screen clear and uncluttered with unnecessary data and messages.

THE BOTTOM LINE

1. BASIC is a personable language, which tells your computer to follow your instructions one at a time until it has produced a desired "report."
2. When you look at a BASIC program, break it up into sections, using the block-line method. Then look at each block, one at a time, to figure out what each does.
3. PowerBASIC gives you a complete working environment, which encourages writing programs in building-block fashion.
4. Blueprint your program before you write one line of code.
5. Data names should be meaningful, short (but not cryptic), consistent, and clear.
6. Program organization is not fluff. Organize your thoughts, assign the tasks to routines, and then program each routine.
7. Break your program up into subroutines and procedures, and then use **GOSUB** and **CALL**. Use **GOTO** only to go somewhere else within the same routine.
8. The Editor is very powerful. Use the keys as much as possible, and you'll be productive in writing and changing a program.
9. Keep your **IF**s simple and easy to read.
10. Loops are a critical structure of good programming. You can destroy that structure with the wrong use of **GOTO**. Use **GOTO** only to go somewhere else within the same loop.

11. Files are no big deal. Just group like items together and describe them, and you have the start of a file.
12. Learn to use random files well; you won't need any other kind of file.
13. **Edit "live" (new) data thoroughly, or your program dies.**

EXERCISES

1. Design the new customer program that you blueprinted in Exercise 1 of chapter 4. Type it in and test it. Don't worry about editing for now; we'll do that in the next chapter.

2. Design the new inventory program that you blueprinted in Exercise 2 of chapter 5. Type it in and test it. Don't worry about editing for now; we'll do that in the next chapter.

Chapter 14

Writing Reusable Edit Procedures (Recycle Your Work)

14.1 Writing Reusable Edit Procedures _____ **249**

14.2 LINE INPUT Statement _____ **262**

14.3 LEN Function _____ **263**

14.4 String Processing Functions _____ **264**

Picture a truly custom homebuilder. The members of this company consider themselves "artists," building everything from scratch. They even build all the doors and windows themselves. Their name: Lightning Home Builders. True to their name, they never do anything the same way twice.

Sound ridiculous? Sure, but that's what you see a lot of programmers doing. They write each program from scratch, rather than building "doors" and "windows" to reuse over and over. In this chapter, we're going to write procedures that you can reuse with a lot of your programs.

14.1 WRITING REUSABLE EDIT PROCEDURES

Notice that the editing is getting to be a pain, and an awful lot of work. It really is, but thorough editing is one of the most important functions of programming, so get used to it.

We do have some ways to cut down on the tedium of writing the code, though. You've probably noticed that there seems to be a lot of repetition in the coding of these edits. You're right, and what we do in a case like this is to use a procedure that we can call repeatedly, rather than typing the same code over and over.

We'll set up three procedures:

1. An error routine to ring the bell, print the error message, and locate the cursor at the original entry
2. A numeric testing routine that checks each character to be between 0 and 9
3. A date testing routine that checks for a valid month, day, and year.

Note:

These are simple routines that are usable. Appendix E in the back of this book has more complex and more thorough editing routines for your use in future programming work. (Don't look ahead until you're done with all the exercises in this chapter.)

14.1.1 The Error Routine (It's a Procedure)

```
SUB printerr (e$,r%,c%):REM -- e$ is the error message
                    REM -- r% is the line number, and
                    REM -- c% is the column number
                    REM -- at which to locate.
    PRINT CHR$(7);e$;TAB(79);"":REM -- ring the bell &
                            REM -- print error message
    LOCATE r%,c%:REM -- set the cursor at the original location
END SUB
```

The *error procedure* has three arguments passed to it from the main program:

e$ is the error message that will be printed on the screen,
r% is the line (row) on the screen where the cursor will be placed to ask for input, and
c% is the column position on the screen where the cursor will be placed to ask for input.

The *error procedure* gets the three arguments, rings the bell, prints the error message, places the cursor at the specified location, and then returns.

14.1.2 The Numeric Testing Routine (It's Also a Procedure)

```
SUB numtest (n$,lgth%,e%):REM -- n$ is the data, lgth% is the
                          REM -- length of the data item, and
                          REM -- e% is an error flag (0=no error,
                          REM -- 1=error)
  e%=0:REM -- set the error flag to 0 (no error)
  FOR i%=1 TO lgth%:REM -- set up a loop to check for numeric
  IF ASC(MID$(n$,i%,1))<48 THEN e%=1:REM -- test for <0
  IF ASC(MID$(n$,i%,1))>57 THEN e%=1:REM -- test for >9
  NEXT i%
END SUB
```

The *numeric test* procedure accepts three arguments:

n$ is the data item exactly as it was input in the main program.
lgth% is the length of the data item, from the main program.
e% is the error flag that is returned to the main program. If a numeric error is found, **e%** will have a value of 1. If the numeric test is passed, **e%** will have a value of 0.

The *numeric test* routine gets the arguments and then performs the numeric test, using a loop to check each character in the data item. If the character is less than 0 or greater than 9, then the error flag, **e%**, is set to 1. Once the loop is complete, the procedure exits.

14.1.3 The Date Testing Routine (Also a Procedure)

```
SUB datest (dat$,lgth%,e%):REM -- dat$ is the date, lgth% is the
                          REM -- length of the date, and
                          REM -- e% is an error flag
                          REM -- (0=no error, 1=error)
  e%=1:REM -- set error flag to 1 (we're assuming that, until the
          REM -- date passes all the tests, an error has been
          REM -- found).
```

```
            IF lgth%<5 THEN GOTO quitdate:REM -- if the length <5 then
                                    REM -- leave the procedure with
                                    REM -- the error flag e% set
                                    REM -- to an error
        IF lgth%=5 THEN dat$="0"+dat$:REM -- make it a six-character
                                    REM -- field
            w1%=VAL(LEFT$(dat$,2)):REM -- get the month
            IF w1%<1 THEN GOTO quitdate
            IF w1%>12 THEN GOTO quitdate
            w2%=VAL(MID$(dat$,3,2)):REM -- get the day
            IF w2%<1 THEN GOTO quitdate
            IF w2%>31 THEN GOTO quitdate
            w3%=VAL(RIGHT$(dat$,2)):REM -- get the year
            IF w3%>93 THEN GOTO quitdate
            e%=0:REM -- reset error flag to 0 (no errors found)
    quitdate:REM -- just a label to go to
    END SUB
```

The *date test* procedure accepts three arguments:

dat$ is the date, exactly as it was passed from the main program.
lgth% is length of the date, as determined in the main program.
e% is the error flag that is returned to the main program. If **e%** is 0,
then no errors have been found. If an error is detected, then **e%** is
made equal to 1.

Once the **DATEST** procedure gets the arguments, it first sets the error
flag, **e%**, to 1. This action is based on the assumption that if any errors
are found, the procedure will immediately be exited. (Later on, if all
tests are passed, the flag is reset to 0.) Next, **DATEST** checks the length
for fewer than five characters. If true, the procedure is exited. If not, the
month is verified to be between 1 and 12; the day is examined for values
between 1 and 31; and the year is tested for a value of 93 or less. If the
data item fails any of these tests, the procedure simply exits with the
error flag **e%** set to 1, indicating an error. If the item passes every test, the
procedure resets the error flag to 0 and then returns flow to the main
program.

Get into PowerBASIC. Type in each of the three routines above and
save them under their routine names.

In the examples below, call up (retrieve) the saved routines and type
in the additional code to complete the example. Then run and test them

in PowerBASIC, in the same manner as you did in the previous chapter. You'll find that with our new set of routines, we can minimize our coding and do the editing in an efficient manner.

14.1.4 Length Test with Editing Routines

```
    y% = CSRLIN
    x% = POS(0)
getin:
    LINE INPUT"enter customer name";i$
    IF LEN(i$)>30 THEN
       CALL printerr("Too long",y%,x%)
       GOTO GETIN
    END IF
    IF LEN(i$)<1 THEN
       CALL printerr("Too short",y%,x%)
       GOTO GETIN
    END IF
    PRINT TAB (79);""
END : REM -- end the program
SUB printerr (e$,r%,c%):  REM -- e$ is the error message
                          REM -- r% is the line number, and
                          REM -- c% is the column number
                          REM -- at which to locate.
    PRINT CHR$(7);e$;TAB(79);"":REM -- ring the bell &
                          REM -- print error message
    LOCATE r%,c%:REM -- set the cursor at the original location
END SUB
```

14.1.5 Numeric Test with Editing Routines

```
    y% = CSRLIN
    x% = POS(0)
getin:
    LINE INPUT"enter customer phone number";i$
    i1% = LEN(i$)
    IF i1%>10 THEN
       CALL printerr("Too long",y%,x%)
       GOTO getin
```

```
      END IF
      IF i1%<1 THEN
        CALL printerr("Too short",y%,x%)
        GOTO getin
      END IF
      CALL numtest(i$,i1%,er%)
      IF er%>0 THEN
        CALL printerr("Not numeric",y%,x%)
        GOTO getin
      END IF
      PRINT TAB (79);""
    END : REM end the program
    SUB numtest (n$,lgth%,e%):REM -- n$ is the data, lgth% is the
                            REM -- length of the data item, and
                            REM -- e% is an error flag (0=no error,
                            REM -- 1=error)
      e%=0:REM -- set the error flag to 0 (no error)
      FOR i%=1 TO lgth%:REM -- set up a loop to check for numeric
      IF ASC(MID$(n$,i%,1))<48 THEN e%=1:REM -- test for <0
      IF ASC(MID$(n$,i%,1))>57 THEN e%=1:REM -- test for >9
      NEXT i%
    END SUB
    SUB printerr (e$,r%,c%):  REM -- e$ is the error message
                            REM -- r% is the line number, and
                            REM -- c% is the column number
                            REM -- at which to locate.
      PRINT CHR$(7);e$;TAB(79);"":REM -- ring the bell &
                                REM -- print error message
      LOCATE r%,c%:REM -- set the cursor at the original location
    END SUB
```

14.1.6 Date Test with Editing Routines

```
    y%=CSRLIN
    x%=POS(0)
getin:
    LINE INPUT"enter customer since date";i$
    i1%=LEN(i$)
    IF i1%>6 THEN
      CALL printerr("Too long",y%,x%)
      GOTO getin
```

```
      END IF
      IF i1%<1 THEN
         CALL printerr("Too short",y%,x%)
         GOTO getin
      END IF
      CALL numtest(i$,i1%,er%)
      IF er%>0 THEN
         CALL printerr("Not numeric",y%,x%)
         GOTO getin
      END IF
      CALL datest(i$,i1%,er%)
      IF er%> O THEN
         CALL printerr("Bad date",y%,x%)
         GOTO getin
      END IF
      PRINT TAB (79);""
END : REM end the program
SUB numtest (n$,lgth%,e%):REM -- n$ is the data, lgth% is the
                          REM -- length of the data item, and
                          REM -- e% is an error flag (0=no error,
                          REM -- 1=error)
   e%=0:REM -- set the error flag to 0 (no error)
   FOR i%=1 TO lgth%:REM -- set up a loop to check for numeric
   IF ASC(MID$(n$,i%,1))<48 THEN e%=1:REM -- test for <0
   IF ASC(MID$(n$,i%,1))>57 THEN e%=1:REM -- test for >9
   NEXT i%
END SUB
SUB datest (dat$,lgth%,e%):REM -- dat$ is the date, lgth% is the
                          REM -- length of the date, and
                          REM -- e% is an error flag
                          REM -- (0=no error, 1=error)
   e%=1:REM -- set error flag to 1 (we're assuming that, until the
          REM -- date passes all the tests, an error has been
          REM -- found).
   IF lgth%<5 THEN GOTO quitdate:REM -- if the length<5 then
                                REM -- leave the procedure with
                                REM -- the error flag e% set
                                REM -- to an error
   IF lgth%=5 THEN dat$="0"+dat$:REM -- make it a six-character
                                REM -- field
   w1%=VAL(LEFT$(dat$,2)):REM -- get the month
   IF w1%<1 THEN GOTO quitdate
```

```
        IF w1%>12 THEN GOTO quitdate
        w2% = VAL(MID$(dat$,3,2)):REM -- get the day
        IF w2%<1 THEN GOTO quitdate
        IF w2%>31 THEN GOTO quitdate
        w3% = VAL(RIGHT$(dat$,2)):REM -- get the year
        IF w3%>93 THEN GOTO quitdate
        e% = 0:REM -- reset error flag to 0 (no errors found)
quitdate:
REM -- just a label to go to
END SUB
SUB Printerr (e$,r%.c%):  REM -- e$ is the error message
                          REM -- r% is the line number, and
                          REM -- c% is the column number
                          REM -- at which to locate.
    PRINT CHR$(7);e$;TAB(79);"":REM -- ring the bell &
                                  REM -- print error message
    LOCATE r%,c%:REM -- set the cursor at the original location
END SUB
```

Now we can combine all these routines and fit all of the data for one customer, even if a few mistakes are made, onto one input screen. So we're going to write the routine that gets all the data for a new customer and writes it to the customer record.

After reading and analyzing the subroutine below, call up your procedures, type the rest into your computer using PowerBASIC, and then run and test it. Be sure to clear your previous routines first by

    PRESS ⟨ALT⟩ + ⟨f⟩⟨ENTER⟩
    PRESS ⟨N⟩⟨ENTER⟩

before starting this routine.

14.1.7 New Customer Routine

```
        GOSUB getnewcust
END
getnewcust:
    y% = CSRLIN
    x% = POS(0)
getin1:
```

```
      LINE INPUT"enter customer last name";i$
      IF LEN(i$)>15 THEN
         CALL printerr("Too long",y%,x%)
         GOTO getin1
      END IF
      IF LEN(i$)<1 THEN
         CALL printerr("Too short",y%,x%)
         GOTO getin1
      END IF
      PRINT TAB (79);""
      LSET custlname$=i$
      y%=CSRLIN
      x%=POS(0)
getin2:
      LINE INPUT"enter customer first name";i$
      IF LEN(i$)>12 THEN
         CALL printerr("Too long",y%,x%)
         GOTO getin2
         END IF
      IF LEN(i$)<1 THEN
         CALL printerr("Too short",y%,x%)
         GOTO getin2
      END IF
      PRINT TAB (79);""
      LSET custfname$=i$
      y%=CSRLIN
      x%=POS(0)
getin3:
      LINE INPUT"enter 1st customer address line";i$
      IF LEN(i$)>30 THEN
         CALL printerr("Too long",y%,x%)
         GOTO getin3
      END IF
      IF LEN(i$)<1 THEN
         CALL printerr("Too short",y%,x%)
         GOTO getin3
      END IF
      PRINT TAB (79);""
      LSET custaddr1$=i$
      y%=CSRLIN
      x%=POS(0)
```

```
getin4:
  LINE INPUT"enter 2nd customer address line";i$
  IF LEN(i$)>30 THEN
    CALL printerr("Too long",y%,x%)
    GOTO getin4
  END IF
  IF LEN(i$)<1 THEN
    CALL printerr("Too short",y%,x%)
    GOTO getin4
  END IF
  PRINT TAB(79);""
  LSET custaddr2$=i$
    y%=CSRLIN
    x%=POS(0)
getin5:
  LINE INPUT"enter customer city";i$
  IF LEN(i$)>20 THEN
    CALL printerr("Too long",y%,x%)
    GOTO getin5
  END IF
  IF LEN(i$)<1 THEN
    CALL printerr("Too short",y%,x%)
    GOTO getin5
  END IF
  PRINT TAB (79);""
  LSET custcity$=i$
  y%=CSRLIN
  x%=POS(0)
getin6:
  LINE INPUT"enter customer state";i$
  IF LEN(i$)>2
    THEN CALL printerr("Too long",y%,x%)
    GOTO getin6
  END IF
  IF LEN(i$)<1 THEN
    CALL printerr("Too short",y%,x%)
    GOTO getin6
  END IF
  PRINT TAB(79);""
  LSET custstat$=i$
  y%=CSRLIN
```

```
       x% = POS(0)
getin7:
   LINE INPUT"enter customer zip code";i$
   i1% = LEN(i$)
   IF i1%>9 THEN
      CALL printerr("Too long",y%,x%)
      GOTO getin7
   END IF
   IF LEN(i$)<1 THEN
      CALL printerr("Too short",y%,x%)
      GOTO getin7
   END IF
   CALL numtest(i$,i1%,er%)
   IF er%>0 THEN
      CALL printerr("Not numeric",y%,x%)
      GOTO getin7
   END IF
   PRINT TAB(79);""
   LSET custzip$ = MKL$(VAL(i$))
   y% = CSRLIN
   x% = POS(0)
getin8:
   LINE INPUT"enter customer phone number";i$
   i1% = LEN(i$)
   IF i1%>10 THEN
      CALL printerr("Too long",y%,x%)
      GOTO getin8
   END IF
   IF LEN(i$)<1 THEN
      CALL printerr("Too short",y%,x%)
      GOTO getin8
   END IF
   CALL numtest(i$,i1%,er%)
   IF er%>0 THEN
      CALL printerr("Not numeric",y%,x%)
      GOTO getin8
   END IF
   PRINT TAB(79);""
   LSET custphone$ = MKD$(VAL(i$))
   y% = CSRLIN
   x% = POS(0)
```

```
getin9:
  LINE INPUT "enter customer type";i$
  IF LEN(i$)>1 THEN
    CALL printerr("Too long",y%,x%)
    GOTO getin9
  END IF
  IF LEN(i$)<1 THEN
    CALL printerr("Too short",y%,x%)
    GOTO getin9
  END IF
  IF i$ = "A" THEN GOTO goodtype:REM -- if type = "A", get out
  IF i$ = "C" THEN GOTO goodtype:REM -- if type = "C", get out
  CALL printerr("Not 1 of the acceptable entries",y%,x%)
  GOTO getin9
goodtype:
  PRINT TAB (79);""
  LSET custtype$ = i$
  y% = CSRLIN
  x% = POS(0)
getin10:
  LINE INPUT"enter customer notes";i$
  IF LEN(i$)>60 THEN
    CALL printerr("Too long",y%,x%)
    GOTO getin10
  END IF
  PRINT TAB(79);""
  LSET custnotes$ = i$
  y% = CSRLIN
  x% = POS(0)
getin11:
  LINE INPUT"enter customer since date";i$
  i1% = LEN(i$)
  IF i1%>6 THEN
    CALL printerr("Too long",y%,x%)
    GOTO getin11
  END IF
  IF LEN(i$)<1 THEN
    CALL printerr("Too short",y%,x%)
    GOTO getin11
  END IF
  CALL numtest(i$,i1%,er%)
```

```
        IF er%>0 THEN
           CALL printerr("Not numeric",y%,x%)
           GOTO getin11
        END IF
        CALL datest(i$,i1%,er%)
        IF er%>0 THEN
           CALL printerr("Bad date",y%,x%)
           GOTO getin11
        END IF
        PRINT TAB(79);""
        LSET custdate$ = MKS$(VAL(i$))
        REM -- PUT 1,f1:REM -- write the customer record
RETURN
SUB numtest (n$,lgth%,e%):REM -- n$ is the data, lgth% is the
                             REM -- length of the data item, and
                             REM -- e% is an error flag (0=no error,
                             REM -- 1=error)
     e%=0:REM -- set the error flag to 0 (no error)
     FOR i%=1 TO lgth%:REM -- set up a loop to check for numeric
     IF ASC(MID$(n$,i%,1))<48 THEN e%=1:REM -- test for <0
     IF ASC(MID$(n$,i%,1))>57 THEN e%=1:REM -- test for >9
     NEXT i%
END SUB
SUB datest (dat$,lgth%,e%):REM -- dat$ is the date, lgth% is the
                             REM -- length of the date, and
                             REM -- e% is an error flag
                             REM -- (0=no error, 1=error)
     e%=1:REM -- set error flag to 1 (we're assuming that, until the
              REM -- date passes all the tests, an error has been
              REM -- found).
     IF lgth%<5 THEN GOTO quitdate:REM -- if the length <5 then
                                     REM -- leave the procedure with
                                     REM -- the error flag e% set
                                     REM -- to an error
     IF lgth%=5 THEN dat$="0"+dat$:REM -- make it a six-character
                                     REM -- field
     w1%=VAL(LEFT$(dat$,2)):REM -- get the month
     IF w1%<1 THEN GOTO quitdate
     IF w1%>12 THEN GOTO quitdate
     w2%=VAL(MID$(dat$,3,2)):REM -- get the day
     IF w2%<1 THEN GOTO quitdate
```

```
    IF w2%>31 THEN GOTO quitdate
    w3% = VAL(RIGHT$(dat$,2)):REM -- get the year
    IF w3%>90 THEN GOTO quitdate
    e% = 0:REM -- reset error flag to 0 (no errors found)
quitdate:
REM -- just a label to go to
END SUB
SUB printerr (e$,r%,c%): REM -- e$ is the error message
                         REM -- r% is the line number, and
                         REM -- c% is the column number
                         REM -- at which to locate.
    PRINT CHR$(7);e$;TAB(79);"":REM -- ring the bell &
                                      REM -- print error message
    LOCATE r%,c%:REM -- set the cursor at the original location
END SUB
```

Now run this on your computer and see how it works. Enter all combinations of data, good and bad. Your subroutine should be able to handle it without blowing up (just stopping dead).

We'll now get into the detail of some new statement types that have been introduced in this chapter.

14.2 LINE INPUT STATEMENT

The **LINE INPUT** statement is the only input statement that we use to get input from the keyboard. It is the most versatile, allowing commas, quotes, semicolons, and almost anything as input without blowing up. Once the input is entered, the editing is up to you.

The **LINE INPUT** statement has this syntax:

LINE INPUT "{some prompt}";{some string variable}

where

> {**some prompt**} is any combination of letters, numbers, and special characters (except quotation marks, because the prompt must have quotes at the beginning and the end) that the programmer uses to tell the operator of the program which data item to enter.

{**some string variable**} is the string variable name into which the input will be placed. (A string is a group of letters and/or numbers and/or other characters. A string variable is a variable that contains a string.)

■ LINE INPUT EXAMPLE

LINE INPUT "Please enter customer name"; i$

The prompt could be a string variable, rather than a character string in quotes. This next example, using a string variable, produces the same results as the previous one:

p$ = "Please enter customer name"
LINE INPUT p$;i$ ■

In both cases the value keyed in will be given to the string variable **i$**. We have a convention that we use regarding input from the keyboard:

i$ = any input
i1% = length of the input data
w1%, w2%, and **w3%** are work variables, used for testing data.

Use any convention that seems clear to you, but set up standard names for your keyboard input variables NOW. Write them down and always use them.

14.3 LEN FUNCTION

The **LEN** function is used to determine the length of a string variable. The format for the **LEN** function is:

{variable name 1} = LEN({variable name 2})

where {**variable name 1**} is a numeric variable that is given the value of the length of the string {**variable name 2**} within the parentheses.

■ **LEN FUNCTION EXAMPLE**

    i1% = LEN(i$)

The length of the string variable, **i$**, is found and given to the integer variable **i1%**. ■

14.4 STRING PROCESSING FUNCTIONS

The *string processing functions* are used to—

1. convert any one string character into the ASCII representation (the number, in computer language) of that character.
2. convert a string into a number.
3. isolate any one or more specific characters within a string so that these characters can be tested or manipulated.
4. combine any two or more strings, or parts of strings, together.

Using the *string processing functions*, any part of any string can be separated, combined, and/or converted for use.

14.4.1 ASC Function

The **ASC** function gets the ASCII value of the first character in a string. The ASCII value of a character is a number between 0 and 255. The character 0 has an ASCII value of 48, the character 1 has a value of 49, the character 2 has an ASCII value of 50, the character 9 has a value of 57, the character A has a value of 65, and so on. (Refer to appendix B in your PowerBASIC, User's Manual for ASCII character codes). Once the numeric (ASCII) value has been obtained, it is normally used for editing or validation purposes. In the **NUMTEST** procedure example above, we used the **ASC** function to test for numeric characters between 0 and 9 (between ASCII values 48 and 57). We went through the string **i$** and checked each character to confirm that it was a valid ASCII number.

The syntax for the **ASC** function is:

{variable name 1} = ASC({string variable name 2})

where {**variable name 1**} is the numeric ASCII value of the first character of {**string variable name 2**}.

The function **ASC**({**string variable name 2**}) can also be used as a number in a calculation, an IF statement, or a PRINT statement.

■ ASC FUNCTION EXAMPLES

```
w1% = ASC(i$)
IF ASC(i$)<48 THEN PRINT"error"
PRINT ASC(i$)
```
■

14.4.2 VAL Function

The **VAL** function is used to convert a string variable, or part of a string variable, to a numeric variable. This is particularly valuable for the editing of numeric data entered as a string, probably using the **LINE INPUT** statement. Once the data is checked and found valid, it is converted into numeric format for use in calculations.

The syntax for the **VAL** function is:

{variable name 1} = VAL({string variable name 2})

where {**variable name 1**} is a numeric variable that is given the numeric value of {**string variable name 2**}.

The function **VAL** {**variable name 2**}) can also be used as a number in a calculation, **IF** statement, or **PRINT** statement.

■ VAL FUNCTION EXAMPLES

```
i$ = "46"
w1% = VAL(i$):REM -- w1% now has a value of 46
IF VAL (i$)> 99 THEN PRINT"error": REM -- because VAL(i$) is 46, the word "error" would__
not be printed
PRINT VAL(i$):REM -- would print 46
```
■

14.4.3 MID$, LEFT$, And RIGHT$ Functions

These functions are used to select a part of a string for some form of other work. Let's use the date editing in the procedure **DATEST** as an example. Assume that the date string is exactly six characters long. (Remember that we made it six characters long by adding a 0 if necessary.)

We used **MID$** to extract the day from the date.
We used **LEFT$** to get the month from the date.
We used **RIGHT$** to get the year from the date.

The syntax for these functions is:

MID$({data name 1}, {starting position}, {number of positions})
LEFT$({data name 1}, {number of positions})
RIGHT$({data name 1}}, {number of positions})

where

{**data name 1**} is a string variable,
{**starting position**} is the location in the string of the first character we're extracting, and
{**number of positions**} is the number of characters that will be pulled out.

■ MID$, LEFT$, AND RIGHT$ EXAMPLES

Our examples use **dat$** as a six-character string that represents a date:

w2$ = MIDdat,3,2)

Here **w2$** is given the value of the two-character string that begins in position 3 in the string **dat$** and continues for two characters (positions 3 and 4). **w2$** is the string representation of the day of the month, when **dat$** is a date.

w1$ = LEFT$(dat$,2)

w1$** is given the value of the two-character string that begins in position 1, the LEFTmost position in the string **dat$, and continues for two characters (positions 1 and 2). **w1$** is the string representation for the month in the date **dat$**.

w3$ = RIGHT$(i$,2)

w3$** is given the value of the two-character string that begins in position 6 (the RIGHTmost position in the string **dat$) and continues TO THE LEFT for two characters (positions 6 and 5). **w3$** is the string representation of the year in the date **dat$**. ■

14.4.4 Concatenating Strings

The concatenation, or joining, of strings is not really a separate function. It is accomplished simply by using the plus (+) sign.
The syntax for joining two strings is:

{string 1} = {string 2} + {string 3}

where {**string 1**} is the string formed by placing {**string 3**} at the very end of {**string 2**}.

■ CONCATENATION EXAMPLES

```
a$ = "ABC":REM -- give value to a$
b$ = "DEF":REM -- give value to b$
c$ = a$ + b$: REM -- c$ now has the value of "ABCDEF"
d$ = "XYZ":REM -- give value to d$
e$ = c$ + d$: REM -- e$ now has the value of "ABCDEFXYZ"
f$ = a$ + b$ + d$: REM -- f$ now has the value of "ABCDEFXYZ"
```
■

14.4.5 Combining These Functions

In the numeric routine **NUMTEST**, we used this combination of functions:

ASC(MID$(n$,i%,1))

which means that we are extracting the **i**th character from the string **n$** and then getting the ASCII value for that character. We did this in a loop from 1 to the length of the field **n$**, which meant that we converted each character (of the field **n$**) into ASCII in order to test it for a value between 0 and 9 (ASCII values 48 and 57, respectively).

In the date test routine **DATEST**, we used this combination of functions:

```
VAL(LEFT$(dat$,2))
VAL(MID$(dat$,3,2))
VAL(RIGHT$(dat$,2))
```

where we extracted

the first two characters of the date (the month) and made them a number,

the middle two characters of the date (the day) and made them a number, and

the last two characters of the date (the year) and made them a number,

so that we could test the month, day, and year respectively.

```
w1% = VAL(LEFT$(dat$,2)):REM -- get the month
IF w1%<1 THEN GOTO quitdate
IF w1%>12 THEN GOTO quitdate
w2% = VAL(MID$(dat$,3,2)):REM -- get the day
IF w2%<1 THEN GOTO quitdate
IF w2%>31 THEN GOTO quitdate
w3% = VAL(RIGHT$(dat$,2)):REM -- get the year
IF w3%>93 THEN GOTO quitdate
e% = 0:REM -- reset error flag to 0 (no errors found)
quitdate:REM -- just a label to go to
END SUB
```

As you can see, the *string processing functions* give you the ability to do anything you want with any part of any string.

CHAPTER SUMMARY

1. Develop standard editing routines and error messages. Use them ALL the time. Improve them all the time.
2. Keep the screen clear and uncluttered of unnecessary messages.

3. Use the **LINE INPUT** statement for all your input. It gives you the most control and flexibility.
4. The **LEN** function finds the length of a string.
5. The **ASC** function gets the ASCII value of the first character in a string.
6. The **VAL** function converts a string into a number.
7. The **MID$, LEFT$,** and **RIGHT$** functions isolate some part of a string.
8. The plus sign (+) tacks one string onto the end of another.

Note:

Realize that the numeric test should allow for decimal points and minus signs, and the date test should check each month for its own maximum number of days (April not more than 30, February not more than 29, and so on). The routines in Appendix E have these features. They weren't put into this chapter because we felt that their complexity would muddy up this chapter.

THE BOTTOM LINE

1. BASIC is a personable language, which tells your computer to follow your instructions one at a time until it has produced a desired "report."
2. When you look at a BASIC program, break it up into sections, using the block-line method. Then look at each block, one at a time, to figure out what each does.
3. PowerBASIC gives you a complete working environment, which encourages writing programs in building-block fashion.
4. Blueprint your program before you write one line of code.
5. Data names should be meaningful, short (but not cryptic), consistent, and clear.
6. Program organization is not fluff. Organize your thoughts, assign the tasks to routines, and then program each routine.
7. Break your program up into subroutines and procedures, and then use **GOSUB** and **CALL**. Use **GOTO** only to go somewhere else within the same routine.

8. The Editor is very powerful. Use the keys as much as possible, and you'll be productive in writing and changing a program.
9. Keep your **IF**s simple and easy to read.
10. Loops are a critical structure of good programming. You can destroy that structure with the wrong use of **GOTO**. Use **GOTO** only to go somewhere else within the same loop.
11. Files are no big deal. Just group like items together, and describe them, and you have the start of a file.
12. Learn to use random files well; you won't need any other kind of file.
13. Edit "live" (new) data thoroughly, or your program dies.
14. **Set up standard edit procedures and always use them.**

EXERCISES

1. Take the edit procedures, **PRINTERR, NUMTEST,** and **DATEST** and put them into the New Customer and New Inventory item programs for Bikes Peak. Put in **CALL** statements to those three routines to handle all the editing for each program.

2. Look at Appendix B in your PowerBASIC User's manual and design and write a procedure that will convert lower-case letters to upper-case letters.

3. Design and write a procedure that tests for the proper number of days in each month (not just 1–31).

4. Design and write a procedure that allows for a minus sign and a decimal point in its numeric test.

Chapter 15

Using the Printer (Lay It on the Line)

15.1   The Beginning Is the End _____ 272

15.2   The Value (and Lack of Value) in Printed Output _____ 272

15.3   Different Types of Page Layouts _____ 275

15.4   Rules for Laying Out a Page _____ 275

15.5   PRINT Formats _____ 276

15.6   FORMAT Statement _____ 276

15.7   LPRINT, LPRINT USING Statements _____ 277

15.8   TAB Function _____ 279

15.9   CHR$ Function _____ 279

15.10 Commas and Semicolons _____ 280

15.11 WIDTH Statement _____ 280

You're helping Chuck design a new inventory report. The old one was pretty good, but Chuck has decided that he wants to have all the information he could ever need on one report. So you and he come up with a design that has all the data on every inventory item:

```
                BIKES PEAK INVENTORY REPORT
INVENTORY NUMBER 123 INVENTORY DESCRIPTION BRAKE CABLE
RETAIL PRICE 19.99 DEALER PRICE 14.00 COST 6.22 ON HAND 35
NUMBER BOUGHT THIS YEAR 371 NUMBER SOLD THIS YEAR 336
JANUARY SALES 6 FEBRUARY SALES 11 MARCH SALES 119
APRIL SALES 157 MAY SALES 43 JUNE SALES 0 JULY SALES 0
AUGUST SALES 0 SEPTEMBER SALES 0 OCTOBER SALES 0
```

NOVEMBER SALES 0 DECEMBER SALES 0
INVENTORY NUMBER 211 INVENTORY DESCRIPTION MOUNT MARCY TIRE
RETAIL PRICE 29.95 DEALER PRICE 18.00 COST 11.76 ON HAND 106
NUMBER BOUGHT THIS YEAR 144 NUMBER SOLD THIS YEAR 38
JANUARY SALES 0 FEBRUARY SALES 3 MARCH SALES 7
APRIL SALES 14 MAY SALES 14 JUNE SALES 0 JULY SALES 0
AUGUST SALES 0 SEPTEMBER SALES 0 OCTOBER SALES 0
NOVEMBER SALES 0 DECEMBER SALES 0

Almost unreadable, isn't it? But it's all there. Every bit of the data on every item of inventory. So much, in fact, that you really have to look hard to figure out where each item is.

This report brings to mind the story of the guy who insisted that he had to have a report with every bit of information on every item his company sold. The company was a billion-dollar company, and the report was six inches thick. Each week he had his secretary put the new report into his binder, but he never used it, because he couldn't read it—so he called people to get his figures. (In designing a printed report, you never use anything that isn't essential—the simpler the better.) This chapter will help avoid this mistake.

15.1 THE BEGINNING IS THE END

The report is the reason the program is being written. So the logical place to begin, in program design, is with the design of the report. Once the report is fully defined, you can work backwards to get the data the report requires and then define the program. (Refer to chapter 4, Program Blueprints).

15.2 THE VALUE (AND LACK OF VALUE) IN PRINTED OUTPUT

Printed output does have a value (sometimes). Printed output is valuable when three conditions are met:

1. The information is up-to-date.
2. The information is easily recognizable.
3. The report is instantly available to the people who need it.

1. **UP-TO-DATE.** Many large companies have extensive MIS systems, with reports on every aspect of the company's operations. Literally hundreds of reports are produced every week. The problem with many of these reports is that the information is woefully out-of-date. By the time the data is entered by the Data Entry section, verified, processed, and the reports printed and distributed, the information is five days old. Line managers who have to make decisions based on current information wind up keeping their own manual updates to the information or asking their people what the real status is. The value of the reports is more historical than decision-making, rendering them of little value to line managers. Printed information must be current enough so that the people who use the report can depend on the information in it.

   In the case of Bikes Peak, Barb needs a new report every day as she visits dealers to sell bikes and parts. If her report weren't current, it would be worthless. But because of the amount of data on the report above, it would take an hour to print. Sometimes Barb is on the road for a week straight, and she wouldn't be able to get a daily report of this size sent to her.

   Chuck, however, needs a report only once a week to review what's moving and what isn't, for projecting Bikes Peak's needs to their suppliers.

2. **EASILY RECOGNIZABLE.** Different people usually require different reports. Look back at the Bikes Peak report at the start of this chapter. It is hard to read, and it has information on only two inventory items. How long would it take you to find a sales figure, when the full report crowds eight items onto every page?

   A report must be carefully designed to make the needed data LEAP OUT to the attention of the person who uses it. This means that both the purpose of each report and the data in it must be carefully defined.

   Donna realized that not one, but two purposes were involved with inventory reporting:

   • Barb needs to know what Bikes Peak has on hand and current pricing information.

● Chuck needs sales history and on-hand information to be able to project his needs to Bikes Peak's suppliers.

As a result, she designed two separate reports:

5/18/90   page 3
BIKES PEAK Inventory status (for Barb)

	ITEM	COST	DEALER	RETAIL	ONHND
123	BRAKE CABLE	6.22	14.00	19.95	35
211	MOUNT MARCY TIRE	11.76	18.00	29.95	106

and

5/18/90   page 10
BIKES PEAK Inventory Movement (for Chuck)

123 BRAKE CABLE   lyr   623   tyr   336   onhd 35

Jan	Feb	Mar	Apr	May	Jun	Jul	Aug	Sep	Oct	Nov	Dec
6	11	119	157	43	0	0	0	0	0	0	0

211 MOUNT MARCY TIRE   lyr   0   tyr   38   onhd 106

Jan	Feb	Mar	Apr	May	Jun	Jul	Aug	Sep	Oct	Nov	Dec
0	3	7	14	14	0	0	0	0	0	0	0

Note that Barb's report is simple and gives her only the numbers she needs. That's important, because she's under pressure in many sales situations, and she can't waste time wading through a lot of history to get the vital information. The most important number, the *on-hand quantity*, is at the right margin, where she can see it quickly. Barb knows what items Bikes Peak has too many of (probably should sell at a discount) and what items not to push to the dealers (there aren't any on hand to sell).

Chuck's report is also more readable. He can easily see his inventory movement by month and look at last year's figure to project what to order over the next six months.

Because Barb and Chuck each have a report specifically designed for ease of recognition, they can do their job quicker and better.

Note:

When each person has a different job, the minimum of information well presented is the most valuable.

3. **INSTANTLY AVAILABLE.** When you're in the field, in the warehouse, or on the production floor, a report on your desk is worthless. Barb is on the road for a week at a time, and she needs a new report each day. Because the new report is concise, Barb will have it faxed to her every day. She'll always have a current report WITH HER on the road. Because each page has a date and a page number, she'll never be working with the wrong numbers.

15.3 DIFFERENT TYPES OF PAGE LAYOUTS

We'll describe two basic types of page layouts:

Columnar
Labeled data

COLUMNAR layout is used in Barb's report. Each line represents a different item, and the data is lined up in columns for ease of reading. Each page has headers or titles to identify each item. This is the easiest report to lay out, because it is always readable. Use it whenever you can put all the data for one item on a single line.

LABELED DATA is used for Chuck's report. Because the data for each item can't fit on one line, we've used three lines to print the movement of an inventory item. Each piece of data is labeled unless it is naturally obvious.

This type of report is really difficult to lay out because data isn't in columns and each of the lines is different. Ease of readability is hard to accomplish. A lot of trial and error may be involved. But it's worth it. Once you have a good format, the data becomes instantly usable to the readers.

15.4 RULES FOR LAYING OUT A PAGE

1. Keep it simple—NEVER have information on the printed report that is not immediately useful to the person or persons the report is designed for. The report should be understood at a glance.

2. Make it a columnar report, if possible. It's better to use smaller print and fit everything for one item on a single line than to have multiple lines per item.

3. If you can't make the report purely columnar and it has to be a labeled text report, line up as many columns as possible. This will enhance readability, because the eye likes to look at data in straight lines.

4. Line up alpha on the left. (Justify.)

5. Line up numbers on the right, or by decimal point. (Justify.)

6. Keep labels short, but not cryptic. You don't want to take up more space for labels than data. And you need white space in a labeled text report to give a neat appearance.

7. Eliminate truly obvious labels like NAME, STREET, CITY, STATE, ZIP, PHONE, CUSTOMER NUMBER, ITEM NUMBER, ITEM DESCRIPTION, and so forth.

15.5 PRINT FORMATS

The lack of print formats used to be a shortcoming of BASIC. Originally, you could print numbers in a format that was acceptable only to engineers, mathematicians, and students. Today, with the use of the **FORMAT** statement, programmers can easily produce the same report in BASIC that can be done in COBOL, the most common business language used on large mainframes in major corporations. You can present numbers in a clear, readable fashion.

15.6 FORMAT STATEMENT

The **FORMAT** statement is actually a layout for the line. It works as a template for the **LPRINT** statement (which is explained in the next section). **FORMAT** provides "windows" through which data is printed onto paper. The "windows" are specified using special characters to define the type and size of the data that is printed.

Where there is blank space or text in a **FORMAT** statement, that blank space or text is printed. The text in a **FORMAT** statement is the labels or titles in the line. The blank space in a **FORMAT** statement is the blank space in the printed line.

The syntax for a **FORMAT** statement is:

{data name 1}$ = "#### \   \   ! $$###.## $$#,###.##"

where

{data name 1}	is a string variable,
#	signifies that a number will be printed;
\	means that alphanumeric characters will be printed;
!	signifies that a single alphanumeric character will be printed;
$$###	means that a dollar sign will be printed immediately before the first digit of the number;
###.##	indicates that a decimal number is printed with the decimal point and number of decimal places specified (in this case, 2); and
#,###	prints a number with a comma if the number is large enough to warrant it. If not, the number alone is printed.

■ FORMAT EXAMPLE

LIN1$; = "#### \   \ $$#,###.## $$###.## $$###.##__
#####"

The **FORMAT** statement is used in conjunction with the **LPRINT** statement to put reports out onto the printer. (Examples of the relationship between the **LPRINT** and the **FORMAT** statement will follow immediately after we describe the **LPRINT** statement.) ■

15.7 LPRINT, LPRINT USING STATEMENTS

LPRINT is the statement that actually prints the line on the paper. The format is the shape of the layout. **LPRINT** has the data to print in that format. There are a lot of variations of **LPRINT**, but we can boil them down to two forms that can do everything.

The first form has this syntax:

LPRINT {data name 1}; TAB ({position 1}); {data name 2}; TAB ({position 2}); {data name 3};__

where {**data name 1**}, {**data name 2**}, and {**data name 3**} are variable names to be printed, and {**position 1**} and {**position 2**} are columns that are "tabbed" to before printing {**data names 2** and **3**}, respectively.

The second form has this syntax:

LPRINT USING {format name}; {data name 1}; {data name 2}; {data name 3}

where {**format name**} is the name of a previously defined **FORMAT** statement, and {**data names 1, 2, and 3**} are variable names to be printed.

■ LPRINT EXAMPLES

(Form 1)

LPRINT partnum;TAB(6);partdesc$;TAB(40);partcost

(Form 2)

LPRINT USING LIN1$; partnum; partdesc$; partcost; partdlrpr; partretpr; partonhd   ■

These are the **FORMAT** and **LPRINT** statements that will produce the reports for Barb.

FORMATS

```
lin1$ = "\          \                      page ###"
lin2$ =              "BIKES PEAK Inventory Status (for Barb)"
lin3$ = "          ITEM                COST  DEALER  RETAIL  ONHND"
LIN4$ = "###     \        \     ###.##  ###.##  ###.##  ###.##"
```

LPRINTS

LPRINT USING lin1$; dat$; pagnum: REM -- prints date & page number
LPRINT lin2$: REM -- prints the report title

LPRINT lin3$: REM -- prints the column headers
LPRINT USING lin4$; partnum; partdesc$; partcost; partdlrpr; partretpr; partonhd :REM -- this___
prints one item line

15.8 TAB FUNCTION

The **TAB** function is used to position the printer to a specific column before printing a variable or title. The format for the **TAB** function is:

TAB ({position})

where {**position**} is a number between 1 and 255 that represents the print column at which to locate.

■ TAB EXAMPLE

LPRINT TAB(10);partnum

TAB never stands alone. It must be used within an **LPRINT** statement. ■

15.9 CHR$ FUNCTION

The **CHR$** function is used with **LPRINT** to—

print 1 or more blank lines,
start a new page, and
give special print commands to your prirnter.

LPRINT prints one blank line.
LPRINT CHR$(10) prints two blank lines.
LPRINT CHR$(10);CHR$(10) prints three blank lines.
LPRINT CHR$(10);CHR$(10);CHR$(10) prints four blank lines, and
so forth.

LPRINT CHR$(12) starts a new page on the printer.

LPRINT CHR$(**{number 1}**);CHR$({number 2}**);** and so on with different values for {**number 1**} and {**number 2**} (which are ASCII numbers) instruct your printer to do different things, like—

change the font (type) style

change the font (type) size

print graphics

and many other things that vary with the brand of printer that you have. Since the commands are different with each printer, we won't go into them. Consult your printer manual for details.

15.10 COMMAS AND SEMICOLONS

Most books go into a discussion on the use of commas and semicolons with **LPRINT** statements. Because we feel that the use of the comma in an **LPRINT** statement frequently results in poor printed output, we won't discuss its application. Instead, we'll simply say that, in an **LPRINT** statement (not an **LPRINT USING** statement), when you **TAB** to a position, follow it with a semicolon and follow every variable name with a semicolon (except the last thing on the print line). If you do this, you'll avoid the sloppiness that results from using commas in an **LPRINT** statement.

But, for the best quality printer output, **LPRINT USING** combined with **FORMAT** is a better choice than **LPRINT**s with **TAB**s.

15.11 WIDTH STATEMENT

The **WIDTH** statement is used to tell PowerBASIC the width of the print line in characters. If no **WIDTH** is specified, then the line is assumed to be 80 characters wide.

The syntax is:

WIDTH "{printer port}",{number of characters}

where {**printer port**} is the port on your computer that is connected by a cable to the printer (usually **LPT1:**) and {**number of characters**} is the maximum number of characters that will be put onto a print line (1–255). The number of characters you can specify depends on the size of the print type and the maximum number of characters that your printer can put with that size type.

■ WIDTH EXAMPLE

WIDTH "LPT1:", 132   ■

CHAPTER SUMMARY

---

1. Begin at the end. Begin your program design with the design of the report.
2. Printed output is valuable when—

   - the information is up-to-date,
   - the information is easily recognizable, and
   - the information is instantly available.

3. There are two basic types of page layouts:

   - Columnar
   - Labeled data

4. Rules for laying out a page:

   - Keep it simple.
   - Make it columnar, if possible.
   - If not columnar, line up as many columns as possible.
   - Line up alpha data to the left of the column, numbers to the right of the column, or by decimal point.
   - Keep labels short, but not cryptic.
   - Eliminate labels on obvious data.

5. The **FORMAT** statement is a template for the line.

6. The **LPRINT** statement provides the data for the **FORMAT** statement to produce printed output.
7. The **TAB** function positions to a specified column.
8. The **CHR$** function is used with **LPRINT** to—

   - print one or more blank lines,
   - start a new page, and
   - give special commands to your printer.

9. Don't use commas; use semicolons in your **LPRINT** statements.
10. The **WIDTH** statement sets the maximum width of a print line.

THE BOTTOM LINE

1. BASIC is a personable language, which tells your computer to follow your instructions one at a time until it has produced a desired "report."
2. When you look at a BASIC program, break it up into sections, using the block-line method. Then look at each block, one at a time, to figure out what each does.
3. PowerBASIC gives you a complete working environment, which encourages writing programs in building-block fashion.
4. Blueprint your program before you write one line of code.
5. Data names should be meaningful, short (but not cryptic), consistent, and clear.
6. Program organization is not fluff. Organize your thoughts, assign the tasks to routines, and then program each routine.
7. Break your program up into subroutines and procedures, and then use **GOSUB** and **CALL**. Use **GOTO** only to go somewhere else within the same routine.
8. The Editor is very powerful. Use the keys as much as possible, and you'll be productive in writing and changing a program.
9. Keep your **IF**s simple and easy to read.
10. Loops are a critical structure of good programming. You can destroy that structure with the wrong use of **GOTO**. Use **GOTO** only to go somewhere else within the same loop.
11. Files are no big deal. Just group like items together and describe them, and you have the start of a file.

12. Learn to use random files well; you won't need any other kind of file.
13. Edit "live" (new) data thoroughly, or your program dies.
14. Set up standard edit procedures and always use them.
15. **Design each report for a specific purpose, with the minimum amount of data to achieve that purpose.**

EXERCISES

1. Write the program that prints out Barb's Inventory report. If you haven't already put data into the inventory file using the New Inventory program, do so. Get at least 11 inventory items into the file and then run the print program.

2. Write the program that prints out Chuck's report. Run it.

Chapter 16

Displaying to the Screen (It's Your Screen Test)

16.1   Start at the End _____ 286

16.2   The Value of Screen Output _____ 286

16.3   Screen Layout Techniques _____ 287

16.4   Color, Underlining, and Blinking _____ 288

16.5   Ten Common Screen Mistakes _____ 289

16.6   Keep it Simple _____ 290

16.7   PRINT Formats _____ 290

16.8   FORMAT Statements _____ 290

16.9   PRINT and PRINT USING Statements _____ 291

16.10 TAB Function _____ 293

16.11 Commas and Semicolons _____ 293

16.12 Use of CHR$ for Spacing Lines _____ 293

16.13 CLS Statement _____ 294

16.14 Locating a Point on the Screen _____ 294

16.15 The COLOR Statement _____ 296

16.16 The ONLY Criterion _____ 297

This is the first layout of Bikes Peak's customer data screen. It's supposed to show all the information Art needs when talking with a customer on the phone.

```
****************************BIKES PEAK***********************
***************************CUSTOMER DATA BASE********
***************************SCREEN DISPLAY**************
CUSTOMER NAME CHUCKER BUCKER       NUMBER 12345
CUSTOMER ADDRESS 1675 ROUTE 9      APARTMENT 69      CLIFTON
  PARK NY 12065       PHONE 1235551212  LAST YEAR         342.61
THIS YEAR     1247.11 TYPE R 21187     22889
2    21189     0 0    1 112187
NOTES WILL BUY ANYTHING NEW AND DIFFERENT
```

Does this look a little confusing to you? It did to everyone else, including Art, who designed it in the first place. The folks at Bikes Peak found that when jumping onto the computer to look up a customer, it took several minutes to figure out what each data item was. Once they were working with the lookup for 15 minutes, it wasn't a problem. But the first few lookups were tough. So Art called in his programmer friend Donna, who took the above layout home and, using the rules in this chapter, came up with this:

```
                 CUSTOMER INFORMATION
1234      CHUCKER BUCKER      type R      phone 1235551212
          1675 ROUTE 9                    cust since    21187
          APARTMENT 69                    last mail     22889
          CLIFTON PART NY 12065

WILL BUY ANYTHING NEW AND DIFFERENT

                                         bike purchases
                                         num         date
                total purchases          k1    2    21189
          this year    1247.11           k2    0         0
          last year     342.61           k3    1    112187
```

Notice the difference in the presentation of the exact same data? The methods for good screen layout are similar to the labeled text type of printout. You'll see many similarities between the previous chapter and this one.

Note:

We won't get into screen graphics, because it could take up an entire book in itself.

16.1 START AT THE END

Just as a printed page is a report, so is the display of data on a computer screen. Since the screen display is the reason for writing the program, you begin with its design. Once the screen layout is determined, you can work backwards to get the data the display needs and then define the program (just as with printed reports in chapter 15).

16.2 THE VALUE OF SCREEN OUTPUT

Screen displays, like printed reports, are valuable when three conditions are met:

1. The information is up-to-date.
2. The information is easily recognizable.
3. The screen display is instantly available to the people who need it.

1. **UP-TO-DATE.** The likelihood of obsolete data is less with a computer screen display than with a printout, because the data is the most current available (in the computer) at the time of lookup. The problem may be, however, that the most current data is not in the computer. If data is slow getting to the computer, then perhaps a screen display should not be generated at all.

   In the case of Bikes Peak, the information on the computer is current, because Chuck sees to it. So a customer lookup screen is a valuable asset whenever they're talking to a customer.

2. **EASILY RECOGNIZABLE.** This is the hardest part of a screen layout program. In many cases, people who look up information on the screen want to see all the information they can on one

screen. In other cases, this isn't advisable, especially for different classes of employees with totally different job functions.

Where you have job segmentation, you should design the screen with the MINIMUM of information to do the job. This way, the screen is uncluttered, yet each person has what he or she needs to do his or her work. Since the screen doesn't have a lot of data on it, design is easy, and the screen is more readable.

In the case of Bikes Peak, the same information on each customer is used by everybody. Everyone wants to know all the information available on every customer. And they need to make a decision or answer a question immediately, based upon that data. So screen design is critical in presenting the data in an immediately recognizable fashion.

3. **INSTANTLY AVAILABLE.** A computer screen always makes the information instantly available, right? Wrong! Due to limited hardware (too few screens)—

   - the screen may be physically in another part of the building, or in a different building.
   - several people may be contending to use one screen.

If there are enough screens, the information is instantly available. If there are not enough screens, reports should be printed onto paper for some people, while others have access to the computer screens.

Bikes Peak has only one PC (Personal Computer) and consequently only one screen. But there is a single phone line to take orders or answers from the computer, and only one person at a time needs access to the computer during the day. So the information is instantly available.

16.3 SCREEN LAYOUT TECHNIQUES

Finding the best way to lay out a screen is still an art. It varies with each type of person who will be using the screen and the screen report purpose. There are some basic techniques, however, that should always be used.

1. Tailor the screen to the individual or class of individuals who are to use it. Don't put information on the screen unless it's needed.

Superfluous data only clutters up the screen and makes the necessary data hard to find. It also makes the screen layout much more difficult. So keep it simple.

2. Group the data into categories that the computer user would want to use or see together, all in one place. Then break up the screen into sections that will accommodate the data for each category. In the example on the first page of this chapter, Donna set up the screen into three groups:

- Name and address
- Purchases
- Phone number and dates (basically miscellaneous)

3. Line data up in columns as much as possible:

Line up alpha on the (justify) left.
Line up numbers on the right, or by decimal point.

4. Keep labels short, but not so short that they're not understandable. You want a screen display to have more data than labels. By minimizing labels, you increase the blank space, making the screen more readable and easier to focus on.

5. Not everything requires a label. Eliminate unnecessary labels or prompts like NAME, STREET, CITY, STATE, ZIP, PHONE, CUSTOMER NUMBER, VENDOR NUMBER, ITEM NUMBER, ITEM DESCRIPTION, and so on.

6. Since most data is either numbers or upper-case letters, make your labels or prompts lower-case letters.

16.4 COLOR, UNDERLINING, AND BLINKING

Novices in computer programming like to use a lot of color, as well as underlining and blinking, to make data items stand out on the screen. We find that newcomers usually put too much of this into their screen work. When color, underlining, and blinking are excessive, it numbs the vision, rather than enhancing it. The screen is so busy (and everything on it is different from everything else) that you can't focus on the data you need. When color is available, moderation is the key. We have three simple rules (based on our experience) to follow on these three items:

1. Use color sparingly—too much can dazzle the eyes, making focusing on anything difficult. (We'll cover color later on in this chapter.) If you don't have a color screen, ignore the details on color.

2. Underlining seems like a great idea to draw attention to data. Actually, it's a bad idea, unless it's restricted to a few items. Underlining tends to make a screen too ''busy,'' and it makes it harder to find data that isn't underlined. When all data is underlined, it's hard to find anything. Because of this, we won't cover underlining.

3. A blinking screen will drive anyone nuts! It's bad enough to make an error; it's worse to be reminded of it by a blinking screen that you just can't read. That's how computers get punched. DON'T USE BLINK!!!!

16.5 TEN COMMON SCREEN MISTAKES

1. Poor data grouping, or none at all
2. Failure to align data items by column whenever possible
3. Too much unnecessary data
4. Too many labels
5. Multiword and too-long labels
6. Cryptic labels (no one could ever guess what they mean)
7. Not enough white space (blank space)
8. Underlining
9. Blinking
10. Too much color. Don't get the wrong idea—color is GREAT, if you have it. Sixteen different colors are not great. Use color to draw attention to certain data items. Use color to separate different groups of data that are physically close to one another. Use bright colors to show the more important data. Use color to indicate that a problem is about to happen with a particular customer, inventory item, or order. But use it carefully and sparingly. Set up some rules for color use, keep analyzing and revising them, and stick to your own rules.

16.6 KEEP IT SIMPLE

The easiest way to avoid these mistakes? KEEP IT SIMPLE!! This means that you avoid the fluff, organize the screen, and present it so that anyone can comprehend the data quickly.

16.7 PRINT FORMATS

The print formats for a screen are EXACTLY the same as those for a printer. They give the PowerBASIC programmer the power of COBOL line layout on the screen display.

16.8 FORMAT STATEMENTS

The **FORMAT** statement works as a template for the **PRINT** statement in exactly the same way as it works for the **LPRINT** in chapter 15. It provides "windows" through which data is displayed on the screen.

The syntax for a **FORMAT** statement is:

{data name 1}$ = "#### \   \ ! $$###.## $$#,###.##"

where

{data name 1}	is a string variable,
#	will print a number.
\ \	will print alphanumeric characters.
!	says that a single alphanumeric character will be printed.
$$####	lays out a dollar sign to be printed immediately before the first digit of the number.
###.##	lays out a number with the decimal point and number of decimal places specified (here, 2).

#,###   prints a number with a comma if the number is large enough to need it. If not, the number alone is printed.

■ **FORMAT EXAMPLE**

LIN1$ = "####\   \$$#,###.## $$###.## $$###.## #####"   ■

The **FORMAT** statement is used with the **PRINT** statement to put reports out onto the screen. (Examples of **PRINT** combined with **FORMAT** statements follow immediately after the **PRINT** statement description.)

16.9 PRINT AND PRINT USING STATEMENTS

PRINT is the statement that actually prints the line on the screen. We can boil all the forms of **PRINT** down to two, which can do everything:

The first form has this syntax:

PRINT {data name 1}; TAB ({position 1}); {data name 2}; TAB({position 2}); {data name 3}; . . .

where

> {**data names 1, 2, and 3**} are variable names to be printed, and {**position 1**} and {**position 2**} are columns that are positioned before printing data names 2 and 3, respectively.

The second form has this syntax:

PRINT USING {format name};{data name 1}; {data name 2}; {data name 3}

where

> {**format name**} is the name of a previously defined format statement, and
> {**data names 1, 2, and 3**} are variable names to be printed.

■ **PRINT EXAMPLES**

(Form 1)

PRINT partnum;TAB(6);partdesc$;TAB(40);partcost

(Form 2)

PRINT USING LIN1$; partnum; partdesc$; partcost; partdlrpr; partretpr; partonhd ■

These are the **FORMAT** and **PRINT** statements that will produce the screen display that Donna designed for Art.

FORMATs

```
lin1$ = "              CUSTOMER INFORMATION"
lin2$ = "####    \          \          \ type ! phone ##########"
lin3$ = "          \                  \      cust since ######"
lin4$ = "          \                  \      last mail ######"
lin5$ = "          \        \ \ \   \"
lin6$ = "\                                              \"
lin7$ = "                                        bike purchases"
lin8$ = "                                        num       date"
lin9$ = "            total purchases    k1  ###   ######"
lin10$ = "        this year #####.##    k2  ###   ######"
lin11$ = "        last year #####.##    k3  ###   ######"
```

PRINTs

```
CLS
PRINT lin1$
PRINT
PRINT USING lin2$;custnum;custfname$;custlname$;custtype$;custphone
PRINT USING lin3$;custaddr1$;custsince
PRINT USING lin4$;custaddr2$;custlastmail
PRINT USING lin5$;custcity$;custst$;custzip$
PRINT
PRINT USING lin6$;custnotes$
PRINT lin7$
PRINT lin8$
PRINT USING lin9$;custbikes%(1);custbikedol#(1)
PRINT USING lin10$;custthisyr#;custbikes%(2);custbikedol#(2)
PRINT USING lin11$;custlastyr#;custbikes%(3);custbikedol#(3)
```

16.10 TAB FUNCTION

The **TAB** function is used to position the cursor to a specific column before printing a variable or title. The format for the **TAB** function is:

TAB ({position})

where {**position**} is a number between 1 and 80 that represents the position at which to locate.

■ TAB EXAMPLE

PRINT TAB(10);partnum

(**TAB** never stands alone. It must be used within a **PRINT** statement):
■

16.11 COMMAS AND SEMICOLONS

We said enough about this in the last chapter. DON'T use commas in a **PRINT** statement. When you **TAB** to a position, follow it with a semicolon and follow every variable name with a semicolon (except for the last item on the print line). **PRINT USING** with **FORMAT** also provides the best quality screen output.

16.12 USE OF CHR$ FOR SPACING LINES

The **CHR$** function is used with **PRINT** to print one or more blank lines.

- **PRINT** prints one blank line
- **PRINT CHR$(10)** prints two blank lines
- **PRINT CHR$(10);CHR$(10)** prints three blank lines
- **PRINT CHR$(10);CHR$(10);CHR$(10)** prints four blank lines, and so forth

16.13 CLS STATEMENT

The **CLS** statement is used to clear the entire screen. When executed, it gives you a totally blank screen. It then locates the cursor at line 1, column 1.

The syntax is:

```
CLS
```

The **CLS** statement is used like the top of a new page in printing on a screen. Whenever you want to start a new "page" on the screen, use the **CLS** statement.

16.14 LOCATING A POINT ON THE SCREEN

LOCATE is used to place the cursor in a specific spot on the computer screen. **POS** and **CSRLIN** are used to find the current location of the cursor (on the screen). Since they are usually used together, we'll describe them together.

16.14.1 LOCATE

In most cases, you can work just with **LOCATE**. When your data goes on the same lines on every page (of the screen), you just clear the screen with **CLS**, then **LOCATE** and **PRINT** every line. Sometimes, however, when data length is not known or when some lines may or may not be printed (depending on some test), **POS** and **CSRLIN** are used to find out where the cursor is. Then, depending on where the cursor is, you **LOCATE** the start of the next displayed line in the right place.

The syntax for **LOCATE** is:

```
LOCATE {line number},{column number}
```

where {**line number**} is the value (1–24) of the text line where the cursor is to be placed; and {**column number**} is the value (1–80) of the column position to place the cursor. The values can be actual numbers or variables with the value range shown in the parentheses.

■ **LOCATE EXAMPLE**

```
LOCATE 1,1:REM -- places the cursor at line 1, column 1
LOCATE 24,80:REM -- places the cursor at line 24, position 80
LOCATE y%,x%:REM -- places the cursor at line y%, position x%
            REM -- where y% is a variable with a value between
            REM -- 1 and 24, and x% is a variable with a value
            REM -- between 1 and 80                              ■
```

16.14.2 CSRLIN

The syntax for **CSRLIN** is:

{variable name} = CSRLIN

where {**variable name**} is any numeric integer variable name.

■ **CSRLIN EXAMPLE**

```
y% = CSRLIN:REM -- Get the line that the cursor is on             ■
```

16.14.3 POS

The syntax for **POS** is:

{variable name} = POS(0)

where {**variable name**} is any numeric integer variable name.

■ **POS EXAMPLE**

```
x% = POS(0):REM -- get the column position of the cursor          ■
```

16.15 THE COLOR STATEMENT

The **COLOR** statement is used to set the colors of the characters, the background the characters are displayed on, and the border around the screen. When the computer screen has only one color (it is a monochrome monitor), the **COLOR** statement can set degrees of brightness or shades of the one color.

The syntax for the **COLOR** statement (on any monitor) is:

COLOR {character color number}, {background color number}, {border color number}

where

the {**character color**} can be any number or variable with a value from 0–15,
the {**background color number**} can be any number or variable with a value from 0–7,
and the {**border color number**} can be any number or variable with a value from 0–15.

Note:

In some cases, you might be able to get more colors, but this is plenty to work with.

■ **COLOR EXAMPLE**

COLOR 15,1,4:REM -- sets bright white characters on a blue background with a red border ■

Most books would give you a list of the colors and their numbers and stop at that. But it's not easy to pick the right color combinations, because the presentation varies with each screen type, its shading capabilities, and the actual colors it produces. (A red, brown, or blue, on three different color screens will be slightly different.) So here is a program for you to try on your machine (if you have a color monitor) to determine which combinations you like (or maybe those that show up at all, if you have only one color).

*************** COLOR TESTING PROGRAM ***************

```
REM screen 010190
REM note on a piece of paper the color combinations that look best
FOR i% = 0 TO 15
  FOR j% = 0 TO 7
    FOR k% = 0 TO 15
    COLOR k%, j%, i%
    PRINT "*****************************************************"
    PRINT
    PRINT "Characters ="; k%; TAB(25); "Background ="; j%; TAB(50); "Border ="; i%
    PRINT
    PRINT "*****************************************************"
    COLOR 7, 0, i%
    LINE INPUT "Press enter to continue"; i$
    NEXT k%
  NEXT j%
NEXT i%
```

****************** END OF COLOR TESTING PROGRAM ***************

Remember, don't fall into the trap of using a lot of different colors. It may be pretty, but it won't make the screen more readable.

16.16 THE ONLY CRITERION

WILL THIS MAKE THE SCREEN MORE READABLE? If not, forget it. That's your only criterion for deciding whether or not to use something for screen design.

CHAPTER SUMMARY

1. Begin a screen lookup program with the design of the screen.
2. Screen output is valuable when—

- the information is up-to-date.
- the information is easily recognizable.
- the information is instantly available.

3. Screen layout techniques:

- Tailor the screen simply for the people who use it.
- Group the data into categories; have a separate section on the screen for each category.
- Line up data in columns when you can.
- Keep labels short but recognizable.
- Eliminate unnecessary labels.
- Make labels lower-case.

4. Use color sparingly.
5. Don't underline.
6. No blinking.
7. Keep it simple.
8. **FORMAT**S are the templates for the screen lines.
9. **PRINT USING** statements work with the **FORMAT**S to produce a screen report.
10. The **TAB** function positions the cursor to a column on a line.
11. Don't use commas. Use semicolons.
12. **CHR$** is used with **PRINT** to print one or more blank lines.
13. **LOCATE** places the cursor at a specific point on the screen.
14. **POS** returns the current column position of the cursor.
15. **CSRLIN** returns the current line of the cursor.
16. The **COLOR** statement sets the colors of the characters, background, and screen border. Use **COLOR** thoughtfully.
17. The only decision that you have to make for using something in screen design is: WILL THIS MAKE THE SCREEN MORE READABLE?

THE BOTTOM LINE

1. BASIC is a personable language, which tells your computer to follow your instructions one at a time until it has produced a desired "report."

2. When you look at a BASIC program, break it up into sections, using the block-line method. Then look at each block, one at a time, to figure out what each does.
3. PowerBASIC gives you a complete working environment, which encourages writing programs in building-block fashion.
4. Blueprint your program before you write one line of code.
5. Data names should be meaningful, short (but not cryptic), consistent, and clear.
6. Program organization is not fluff. Organize your thoughts, assign the tasks to routines, and then program each routine.
7. Break your program up into subroutines and procedures, and then use **GOSUB** and **CALL**. Use **GOTO** only to go somewhere else within the same routine.
8. The Editor is very powerful. Use the keys as much as possible, and you'll be productive in writing and changing a program.
9. Keep your **IF**s simple and easy to read.
10. Loops are a critical structure of good programming. You can destroy that structure with the wrong use of **GOTO**. Use **GOTO** only to go somewhere else within the same loop.
11. Files are no big deal. Just group like items together and describe them, and you have the start of a file.
12. Learn to use random files well; you won't need any other kind of file.
13. Edit "live" (new) data thoroughly, or your program dies.
14. Set up standard edit procedures and always use them.
15. Design each report for a specific purpose, with the minimum amount of data to achieve that purpose.
16. **Will this make the screen more readable? If not, forget it.**

EXERCISES

1. Take the **FORMAT** and **PRINT** statements from the customer screen in this chapter and place them into the Customer Lookup program that you blueprinted in Exercise 2 of chapter 4. Write the program, type it in, and test it.

2. Design the layout and write the Inventory (Part) Lookup program for Bikes Peak (blueprinted in Exercise 3 of chapter 5). Type the program in and test it.

Chapter 17

Calculations (Coming up with the Right Answers)

17.1 **Where Calculations Come From** _____ **301**

17.2 **The Different Operators** _____ **302**

17.3 **Let's Concatenate(Combining Strings)** _____ **302**

17.4 **Division by Zero** _____ **303**

17.5 **What's Calculated First (The Order of Calculation in a Complex Formula)** _____ **304**

17.6 **The Use of Parentheses** _____ **304**

17.7 **Use the Right Data Types** _____ **307**

17.8 **Rounding and Presenting the Correct Answer** ____ **307**

17.9 **CINT, INT, FIX, and CLNG Functions** _____ **309**

17.10 **Math Functions** _____ **312**

17.11 **The Use of String Functions in Calculations** ____ **312**

17.12 **Date Calculations** _____ **312**

Art, Barb, and Chuck have sold over 1,000 bikes over the past year. But they realize that they don't really know what a bike costs to build. (By the way, that's not unusual—most companies don't know the real cost of building their product.) So they got out their adding machine, a pad, and paper and are itemizing the cost of their simplest, least expensive bike.

Sounds simple, doesn't it? But this process really involves a lot of calculations (what this chapter is about), which eventually will have to go into a computer program. So we're going to describe their figuring to show what goes into this kind of program.

Let's look at the conversation, and get an idea of the calculations involved.

Art: "We have to include our rent, phone, and utilities."
Barb: "We also need to add our pay and my travel expenses."
Chuck: "And besides actual parts costs, we also need to add the cost of carrying these parts for several months."

This chapter will explore how to convert these thoughts into a computer program. But first, we need to explain a bit about calculations in PowerBASIC.

17.1 WHERE CALCULATIONS COME FROM

Calculations on computers are all based on formulas that were first done with a paper and pencil. People have found that computers can do a better job than people in doing repetitive calculations; so once the formula has been worked out by hand and has been proven correct, it is put into a computer program.

Bikes Peak needs to add up all its overhead (rent, phone, utilities, payroll, travel expenses, and interest expense) and then somehow apply these costs to each bike they sell. They could do this by—

1. simply dividing the total overhead by the number of bikes they sell.
2. dividing the overhead number by the number of square feet in the barn that they rent. This produces the overhead cost per square foot of space. They can then find the number of square feet of space that all of the parts for each bike take up and multiply it by the overhead cost per square foot.
3. using any one of a dozen other methods. In any case, they have to find the correct formulas and then apply them using the computer.

17.2 THE DIFFERENT OPERATORS

The operators are: + − * / and ^, where

+ is the addition operator
− is the subtraction operator
* is the multiplication operator
/ is the division operator
^ is the exponentiation operator (raises a number to a power)

■ **OPERATOR EXAMPLES**

a = b + c:REM -- add b to c, place the result into a
a = a + b:REM -- add b to a, place the result into a

a = b − c:REM -- subtract c from b, place the result into a
a = a − b:REM -- subtract b from a, place the result into a

a = b*c:REM -- multiply b by c, place the result into a
a = a*b:REM -- multiply a by b, place the result into a

a = b/c:REM -- divide b by c, place the result into a
a = a/b:REM -- divide a by b, place the result into a

a = b^c:REM -- raise b to the c power, place the result into a
a = a^b:REM -- raise a to the b power, place the result into a

You can add, subtract, multiply, divide, and raise to a power numbers or numeric variables. You cannot add, subtract, multiply, divide, or raise to a power strings or string variables, even if the string or string variable contains numbers. (You can't add "1" + "2", or **a$ + b$**, where **a$** = "43" and **b$** = "146", for example.) ■

17.3 LET'S CONCATENATE (COMBINING STRINGS)

The addition operator can be used to join two or more strings together, forming a single string. (We covered this in chapter 14. We're just reviewing it again as an operation of the + sign.) So, c$ = a$ + b$ is a legal BASIC expression.

To be specific:

If **a$ = "CHUCKER"**,
and **b$ = "BUCKER"**,
and **c$ = a$ + b$** were executed, then
c$ would equal "CHUCKERBUCKER".

17.4 DIVISON BY ZERO

If you think back to your algebra, you'll remember that division by zero is undefined. It won't work in PowerBASIC, either. To see what happens, get into PowerBASIC and key these statements into your computer:

```
a = 0
b = 27
c = b/a
PRINT c
```

Now let's run the program.

PRESS ⟨ALT⟩ + ⟨r⟩

Now

PRESS ⟨ENTER⟩

to try this calculation on your machine.

You'll get an error message. PRESS ENTER to clear the error message. As you can see, a PowerBASIC program will "blow up" (just stop, with no chance of continuing) when it encounters division by zero. So you should always test the variable that is the divisor (the one you are dividing by) before performing a division. If the divisor variable is 0, put out a message and skip the calculation containing the division.

17.5 WHAT'S CALCULATED FIRST (THE ORDER OF CALCULATION IN A COMPLEX FORMULA)

- Exponentiation (^) is performed first.
- Then multiplication and division (* and /). Neither has precedence over the other. The order of which gets done first depends on which one is picked up first by the computer while scanning (from left to right) the program line containing the formula.
- Then addition and subtraction (+ and −). Again, neither has priority over the other. The order of execution depends on which one the computer sees first, scanning from left to right.

■ ORDER OF PRECEDENCE EXAMPLE

The sequence of calculation in

a = b + c*d − e/f

is:

1. **c** is first multiplied by **d** (we'll call it **prod1**).
2. **e** is divided by **f**. (Let's name this result **prod2**).
3. **b** and **prod1** are added together (call this **prod3**).
4. **prod2** is subtracted from **prod3**, and the answer is put into **a**.

Obviously, this hierarchy can cause you, as a programmer, a lot of grief. Calculations are sometimes performed in an order different from what you intended. The hierarchy of operations is probably the most common problem that programmers have with formulas. So, to help with this problem we have...

17.6 THE USE OF PARENTHESES

We strongly urge you to rely on the use of parentheses rather than on the precedence of operations to calculate your expressions properly. The rule of parentheses overrides the order above in this fashion:

1. The expression is calculated as the computer scans it from left to right.

2. As each left parenthesis is found, it is saved, to be matched later (in step 3 below).

3. As a right parenthesis is found, it is matched with the previous left parenthesis.

4. The expression within the parentheses is then calculated according to the rule of precedence of operations above.

5. The result of step 4 is saved temporarily somewhere in memory, and the rest of the calculation is analyzed.

6. All of the temporary results are put together in a final calculation, and the result is stored.

■ PARENTHESES EXAMPLES

We'll take the previous calculation example for the order of precedence ($a = b + c*d - e/f$) and show how the results differ completely, depending on the parentheses.

1. $a = (b+c)*d - e/f$
2. $a = b + (c*d) - e/f$
3. $a = b + c*(d-e)/f$
4. $a = (b+c)*(d-e)/f$
5. $a = (b+c*d-e)/f$

If you understand these examples intuitively, then skip around this detailed discussion to the *Hints on Parentheses*. If you have a question on 1–5 above, then read this explanation of each of the examples.

Explanation of Example 1:

- **b** is first added to **c** (we'll call it **prod1**).
- **prod1** is multiplied by **d** (call this **prod2**).
- **e** is divided by **f**. (Let's name this result **prod3**.)
- **prod3** is subtracted from **prod2,** and the answer put into **a.**

Explanation of Example 2:

- **c** is first multiplied by **d** (we'll call it **prod1**).
- **e** is divided by **f.** (Let's name this result **prod2**.)
- **b** and **prod1** are added together (call this **prod3**).
- **prod2** is subtracted from **prod3,** and the answer put into **a**.

Explanation of Example 3:

- **e** is first subtracted from **d** (we'll call it **prod1**).
- **prod1** is multiplied by **c** (Let's name this result **prod2**.)
- **prod2** is divided by **f** (call this **prod3**).
- **b** and **prod3** are added, and the answer put into **a**.

Explanation of Example 4:

- **b** is first added to **c** (we'll call it **prod1**).
- **e** is subtracted from **d** (Let's name this result **prod2**.)
- **prod1** is multiplied by **prod2** (call this **prod3**).
- **prod3** is divided by **f**, and the answer put into **a**.

Explanation of Example 5:

- **c** is first multiplied by **d** (we'll call it **prod1**).
- **b** and **prod1** are added (Let's name this result **prod2**.)
- **e** is subtracted from **prod2** (call this **prod3**).
- **prod3** is divided by **f**, and the answer put into **a**.

We have exercises to show the results in real numbers at the end of this chapter, so if the detail of this eludes you, make sure you do the parentheses exercises.

17.6.1 Hints on Parentheses

1. It's far better to use too many parentheses than too few. Don't worry about overdoing it.
2. Parentheses are for your understanding, too, and can divide a complex calculation into several smaller ones (in your mind). Don't be afraid to use them for this. Refer to Hint 1 above.
3. Make sure that you match them up! The number of left parentheses must equal the number of right parentheses.

17.7 USE THE RIGHT DATA TYPES

You have to use the right variable types on the left side of the equation when you are performing a calculation, or the answer will be incorrect.

1. Use an integer variable on the left side when you want a whole number for an answer.
2. Use a single-precision variable when you are POSITIVE that the answer will NEVER exceed five (5) digits of significance (meaning that you only care about the first five digits of the answer).
3. Otherwise, use double-precision variables on the left side of the equation. This ensures the maximum significance for the answer.

■ EXAMPLES USING DATA TYPES ON THE LEFT SIDE OF THE EQUATION

integer variable	$a\% = (b/c) + .05$
single-precision variable	$a = (b*c) - d/e$
double-precision variable	$a\# = (b + c)\hat{\,}d$

17.8 ROUNDING AND PRESENTING THE CORRECT ANSWER

Suppose you are printing a number using this format:

##########.##

- If the number is an integer, and its value is 1234, it will print as

  1234.00

- If the number is a single-precision number with a value of 12.3432, it will print as

  12.34

- If the number is a single-precision number with a value of 12.3454, it will print as

  12.35

- If the number is a double-precision number with a value of 1234.1143212345, it will print as

  1234.11

- If the number is a double-precision number with a value of 1234.1154321037, it will print as

  1234.12

Normally, you want to make your calculations as precise as possible and then round or truncate the answer for presentation. To do this:

1. Use double-precision variables on the left side of every equation when working with decimal values.
2. Then round or truncate the answer.

Sometimes, in calculating interest and discounts, you need to round each interest or discount result before adding it to a total. If you don't, the total may print out a value that is not the sum of each of the printed items. For example:

■ EXAMPLE OF NUMBERS NOT ADDING UP TO THE TOTAL

```
a = 13.234
b = 11.333
c = a + b
```

If these were printed out using this format, **#######.##**, the values would display like this:

a	would print as	13.23
b	would print as	11.33
c	would print as	24.57

(The value of **c** would actually be 24.567, which rounds up to 24.57.)
To make the total print identical to the printed value of each of the items, we'll use the long-integer variable on the left side of every equation as we are rounding each calculation. Using the same example, things will add up:

■ EXAMPLE USING LONG INTEGERS

```
a = 13.234
a& = (a + .005) *100:REM -- convert a to a rounded long integer
              REM -- the value of a& is 1323
a = a&/100:REM -- convert back to a rounded number with 2 decimal places (the value of a is
13.23)
b = 11.333
b& = (b + .005)*100:REM -- convert b TO a rounded long integer
              REM -- the value of b& is 1133
b = b&/100:REM -- convert back to a rounded number with 2 decimal places (the value of b is
11.33)
c = a + b
```

If these were printed out using this format, **#######.##**, the values would display like this:

a would print as	13.23
b would print as	11.33
c would print as	24.56,

which is actually the value of **c**.

17.9 CINT, INT, FIX, AND CLNG FUNCTIONS

The **CINT** and **INT** functions are used to convert single- and double-precision variables (actually any numeric expression) to integers. The **FIX** function is used to convert any numeric expression into a whole number. The **CLNG** function is used to convert any numeric expression into a long integer.

INT converts numbers into integers by finding the largest integer that is less than or equal to the expression it evaluates. It "rounds down."

- **INT**(45.6) would be equal to 45
- **INT**(45.2) would be equal to 45
- **INT**(-45.2) would be equal to -46
- **INT**(-45.6) would be equal to -46

CINT converts numbers into integers by rounding (.5 or greater rounds to the next higher digit, whether positive or negative), rather than truncating.

- **CINT**(45.6) would be equal to 46
- **CINT**(45.2) would be equal to 45
- **CINT**(−45.2) would be equal to −45
- **CINT**(−45.6) would be equal to −46

FIX converts a number into a whole number by taking all the digits left of the decimal point and creating a whole number. It truncates, rather than rounds, whether the expression being evaluated is positive or negative.

- **FIX**(45.6) would be equal to 45
- **FIX**(45.2) would be equal to 45
- **FIX**(−45.2) would be equal to −45
- **FIX**(−45.6) would be equal to −45

CLNG converts numbers into a large integer by rounding the numeric expression, much the same as **CINT**.

- **CLNG**(100045.6) would be equal to 100046
- **CLNG**(100045.2) would be equal to 100045
- **CLNG**(−100045.2) would be equal to −100045
- **CLNG**(−100045.6) would be equal to −100046

The syntax for the **INT** function is:

INT ({n})

where {**n**} is any numeric expression.

■ INT EXAMPLES

```
i% = INT(45.6):REM -- i% will have a value of 45


a = 234.45:REM -- give value to a
b = 123.45:REM -- give value to b
c% = INT(a + b):REM -- c% will have value of 357
```

The syntax for the **CINT** function is:

CINT ({n})

where {**n**} is any numeric expression.   ■

■ CINT EXAMPLES

i% = CINT(45.6):REM -- i% will have a value of 46

a = 234.45:REM -- give value to a
b = 123.45:REM -- give value to b
c% = CINT(a + b):REM -- c% will have a value of 358

The syntax for the **FIX** function is:

FIX ({n})

where {**n**} is any numeric expression.   ■

■ FIX EXAMPLES

i = FIX(45.6):REM -- i will have a value of 45

a = 234.45:REM -- give value to a
b = 123.45:REM -- give value to b
c = FIX(a + b):REM -- c will have a value of 357

The syntax for the **CLNG** function is:

CLNG ({n})

where {**n**} is any numeric expression.   ■

■ CLNG EXAMPLES

i& = CLNG (45.6):REM -- i& will have a value of 46

a = 234.45:REM -- give value to a
b = 123.45:REM -- give value to b
i& = CLNG(a + b):REM -- i& will have a value of 358

■ COMPARISON EXAMPLES OF INT, CINT, FIX, AND CLNG

number {n}	INT ({n})	CINT ({n})	FIX ({n})	CLNG({n})
123.4	123	123	123	123
123.7	123	124	123	124
-123.4	-124	-123	-123	-123
-123.7	-124	-124	-123	-124

17.10 MATH FUNCTIONS

PowerBASIC supports these mathematical functions: **ABS, ATN, COS, EXP, LOG, SGN, SIN, SQR,** and **TAN.**

The syntax for all of these functions is:

{fn}({n})

where

{**fn**} is any of the math functions (**ABS, ATN, COS, EXP, LOG,SGN,** SIN, SQR, or TAN), and
{**n**} is a numeric expression.

Refer to your PowerBASIC manual for further explanation if needed.

17.11 THE USE OF STRING FUNCTIONS IN CALCULATIONS

String functions are used in calculations to pick numbers that are contained within a string. Some applications are:

- Editing values keyed in by a program operator
- Picking numbers out of strings with intermixed alpha characters:
  - dates
  - zipcodes
  - phone numbers

STR$ is used to convert a number into a string that can then be processed using—

- **LEN** to get the total number of characters
- **LEFT$** to get a specific number of characters, starting with the leftmost character position
- **RIGHT$** to get a specific number of characters, starting with the rightmost character position
- **MID$** to get a specific number of characters, starting with a specified position
- **VAL** to convert a string or part of a string to a number

Refer to the end of chapter 14 for a review of these functions, if you like. Here are some examples:

```
a = 1234.56:REM -- give value to a
a$ = str$(a):REM -- string a$ = " 1234.56"
PRINT LEN(a$):REM -- will print a value of 8, (the length of the number, + one space for the
                     decimal point, and one space for the sign in front of the number.)
PRINT LEFT$(a$,3):REM -- prints 12
PRINT RIGHT$(a$,3):REM -- prints .56
PRINT MID$(a$,3,5):REM -- prints 234.5
PRINT VAL(MID$(a$,4,3)):REM -- prints 34.
```

The syntax for the **STR$** function is:

```
STR$({n})
```

where {**n**} is any numeric expression.

17.12 DATE CALCULATIONS

The primary operations involving dates are:

- Date comparisons and
- Elapsed days between two dates.

In order to compare two dates, you must change the formats of each. The format of a numeric date is six characters, in which the first two are month, the next two represent day, and the last two represent year. We'll represent this format as MMDDYY, MM being month, DD the day, and YY the last two digits of the year. In order to be able to compare dates, we have to change the date to YYMMDD, where YY is the last two digits of the year, MM is the month, and DD is the day of the month.

We accomplish this by (assume the date is in variable name **d**):

```
d$ = STR$(d):REM -- convert d to a string
w$ = MID$(d$,2):REM -- get rid of blank sign character
d$ = w$:REM -- move it back into d$
IF LEN(w$)<6 then d$ = "0" + w$:REM -- make it six characters
w$ = RIGHT$(d$,2) + LEFT$(d$,2) + MID$(d$,3,2)
REM -- convert the string into YYMMDD format
d1 = val(w$):REM -- convert it into a number
```

d1 is now a numeric variable in YYMMDD format, which you can now compare to any other date in the same format for a less-than, greater-than, or equal-to condition. Each date to be compared must first be converted into this format.

To calculate the number of elapsed days between two dates, you

1. convert both dates into YYMMDD format
2. use this routine (assume **d1** and **d2** are the dates, already in YYMMDD format):

```
****** DATE CALCULATION ROUTINE ******

REM -- datecalc 010189
REM -- this is not an exact calculation.
REM -- It assumes a 30-day month.
   d1 = 910101: REM -- date is 10191
   d2 = 891031: REM -- date is 103189
   w$ = MID$(STR$(d1), 2): REM -- make 1st date a string
   w1$ = LEFT$(w$, 2): REM -- get the year of 1st date
   w2$ = MID$(w$, 3, 2): REM -- get the month of 1st date
   w3$ = RIGHT$(w$, 2): REM -- get the day of 1st date
   x1 = VAL(w1$)
   x2 = VAL(w2$)
```

```
x3 = VAL(w3$): REM -- change year, month, and day of 1st date into separate numbers
w$ = MID$(STR$(d2), 2): REM -- make 2nd date a string
w1$ = LEFT$(w$, 2): REM -- get the year of 2nd date
w2$ = MID$(w$, 3, 2): REM -- get the month of 2nd date
w3$ = RIGHT$(w$, 2): REM -- get the day of 2nd date
x4 = VAL(w1$)
x5 = VAL(w2$)
x6 = VAL(w3$): REM -- change 2nd date into separate numbers
w1 = x1 − x4: REM -- subtract the years
w2 = x2 − x5: REM -- subtract the months
w3 = x3 − x6: REM -- subtract the days
IF w3 < 0 THEN
   w3 = w3 + 30
   w2 = w2 − 1
END IF: REM -- if the days are less than 0, add 30 to the days, and subtract 1 from the __
month
IF w2 < 0 THEN
   w2 = w2 + 12
   w1 = w1 − 1
END IF: REM -- if the months are less than 0, add 12 to the months, and subtract 1 from __
the year
   w = w1 * 365 + w2 * 30 + w3: REM -- sum the days
   PRINT w: REM--print the answer
END
```

* * * END OF DATE CALCULATION ROUTINE * * *

CHAPTER SUMMARY

1. + is the addition operator.
    − is the subtraction operator.
    * is the multiplication operator.
    / is the division operator.
    ^ is the exponentiation operator.

2. You join two or more strings into one by using the addition
    operator.

3. Avoid dividing by zero; it'll stop the program. Test the divisor before every division.

4. The order of calculation is:

- exponentiation
- multiplication, or division, whichever is found first
- addition or subtraction, whichever is found first, as the computer scans the formula from left to right.
- BUT, expressions in parentheses are calculated first, as each right parenthesis is found to match a left parenthesis.

5. Use parentheses both to determine that the formula is calculated properly and to clarify the calculation in your own mind. Don't worry about too many parentheses.

6. Consider data types in your calculations. They can affect getting the right answer.

7. Remember that BASIC can cause you rounding problems. Do your own rounding to avoid them.

8. **INT**, **CINT**, **FIX**, and **CLNG** are similar, but not identical. Be sure that you know under what circumstances to use each.

9. PowerBASIC has math functions available.

10. **STR$** converts a number into a string.

11. Reverse a date (make it YYMMDD) before comparing it to another date or calculating the number of days between two dates.

12. Calculations in computer programs come from real-life situations, which are first done with paper and pencil, and then programmed on the computer.

Note

We have simplified the operators, precedence of operations, and available functions to explain the essence of calculations better. We choose not to use the additional complexity that is available. If you want to use it, see your PowerBASIC manual.

THE BOTTOM LINE

1. BASIC is a personable language, which tells your computer to follow your instructions one at a time until it has produced a desired "report."

2. When you look at a BASIC program, break it up into sections, using the block-line method. Then look at each block, one at a time, to figure out what each does.
3. PowerBASIC gives you a complete working environment, which encourages writing programs in building-block fashion.
4. Blueprint your program before you write one line of code.
5. Data names should be meaningful, short (but not cryptic), consistent, and clear.
6. Program organization is not fluff. Organize your thoughts, assign the tasks to routines, and then program each routine.
7. Break your program up into subroutines and procedures, and then use **GOSUB** and **CALL**. Use **GOTO** only to go somewhere else within the same routine.
8. The Editor is very powerful. Use the keys as much as possible, and you'll be productive in writing and changing a program.
9. Keep your **IF**s simple and easy to read.
10. Loops are a critical structure of good programming. You can destroy that structure with the wrong use of **GOTO**. Use **GOTO** only to go somewhere else within the same loop.
11. Files are no big deal. Just group like items together, describe them, and you have the start of a file.
12. Learn to use random files well; you won't need any other kind of file.
13. Edit "live" (new) data thoroughly, or your program dies.
14. Set up standard edit procedures and always use them.
15. Design each report for a specific purpose, with the minimum amount of data to achieve that purpose.
16. Will this make the screen more readable? If not, forget it.
17. **Understand and test *all* your calculations thoroughly.**

EXERCISES

1. Let **b** = 2, **c** = 3, **d** = 4, **e** = 5, and **f** = 6. Calculate the result of each of these expressions by writing a program in Powerbasic.

   ```
   a = (b + c)*d − e/f
   a = (b + c*d) − e/f
   a = (b + c*d − e)/f
   a = b + (c*d) − e/f
   a = b + (c*d − e)/f
   ```

```
a=b+(c*d−e/f)
a=b+c*(d−e)/f
a=b+c*(d−e/f)
a=b+c*d−(e/f)
a=(b+c)*(d−e)/f
a=b+(c*d)−(e/f)
a=(b+c)*d−(e/f)
a=(b+c)*(d−e/f)
a=(b+c*d)−(e/f)
a=((b+c)*d)−(e/f)
a=((b+c)*(d−e))/f
a=(b+(c*(d−e)))/f
```

2. Find the **INT, CINT, FIX,** and **CLNG** of these numbers, and print out the results:

.01	−.01	.08	−.08
799.1	−799.1	799.5	−799.5
66777.1	−66777.1	66777.9	−66777.9 (Note—this is greater than 32,767, the largest integer.)

3. Make the date-conversion (from MMDDYY to YYDDMM) and elapsed-days routines into procedures that you can put into any program.

Chapter 18

Tables (Arrays Subscripted into the Fourth Dimension)

18.1	Frequently Seen One-Dimensional Tables	320
18.2	Frequently Seen Two-Dimensional Tables	320
18.3	And Three-Dimensional Tables	321
18.4	Defining a Table (Array)	321
18.5	Locating the Elements in a Table	324
18.6	Subscripts, and Keeping Them Straight	324
18.7	DIMensioning a Table	325
18.8	Getting Values into Arrays	326
18.9	DATA and READ Statements	326
18.10	Printing Out a Table	327
18.11	A Table within a Random File Record	328
18.12	A Complete Example	328
18.13	Common Uses of Tables in PowerBASIC	330
18.14	PowerBASIC Limitations	330

Barb is trying to figure out which train to catch. The schedule looks like this:

Train	Leaves Hometown	Arrives Mundville	Arrives Tinkerville	Arrives Villaville	Arrives NYC
Ol'Redeye	6:00 A.M.	6:41 A.M.	7:14 A.M.	7:57 A.M.	8:26 A.M.
Earlybird	7:00 A.M.	7:41 A.M.	8:14 A.M.	8:57 A.M.	9:26 A.M.
Morning Dove	8:30 A.M.	9:11 A.M.	9:44 A.M.	10:27 A.M.	10:56 A.M.
Rushhour Special	9:00 A.M.	9:41 A.M.	10:14 A.M.	10:57 A.M.	11:26 A.M.
Leisure Liner	10:30 A.M.	11:11 A.M.	11:44 A.M.	12:27 P.M.	12:56 P.M.

She needs to catch the train that gets her to New York by 11:00 A.M. Barb looks down the last column, column 5, for the arrival times. The third row has a train that arrives in NYC at 10:56 A.M. Barb then scans the row over to column 1 to find the departure time from her Hometown. She has just used a table, which in BASIC would be programmed as a two-dimensional array (table).

18.1 FREQUENTLY SEEN ONE-DIMENSIONAL TABLES

- Grocery list
- Christmas card list
- Birthday invitation list
- Playing schedule for a basketball team
- List of characters in a play
- Things to do today
- Things to take on a trip
- List of error messages
- List of reserved words in PowerBASIC

18.2 FREQUENTLY SEEN TWO-DIMENSIONAL TABLES

- Train schedules
- Bus schedules
- Television show schedules
- Calendar (for one month)

- Bowling score sheet
- Appointment book for one week (one week per sheet)
- Checkerboard
- Tic-tac-toe grid

18.3 AND THREE-DIMENSIONAL TABLES

- Appointment book (for an entire year)
- Calendar (for an entire year)
- Three-dimensional chess board
- Three-dimensional tic-tac-toe board

18.4 DEFINING A TABLE (ARRAY)

We will use the word *table* and *array* interchangeably throughout this chapter. A *table* is defined by specifying—

- the number of dimensions (eight maximum in PowerBASIC).
- the number of locations in each dimension.

Since we can't come up with a good plain-English definition of a dimension, we'll try to describe it using examples. Picture a roomful of maps. Each map is contained in a book. Each book is on a shelf, numbered sequentially. Each shelf is part of a rack with four shelves. There are three racks to a row. The room has ten rows of these racks.

Now picture yourself looking at a map in one of the books. You are on page 143 of the book, looking at a map of the Interstate that you have to drive on. The Interstate runs in a straight line, beginning at the southern part of the state and going directly north to the northern boundary of the state. The Interstate exits are numbered, beginning with 1 at the very southern tip of the state and ending with 57 at the northern tip. You have to get off at Exit 41.

The *Interstate* is a straight line, and as such, has only *one dimension* (usually length). In this case, the dimension could be either length in miles or in exit numbers. In any case, only one identifier is needed to locate a point on the Interstate.

Bird's Eye View of Map Room

The *map* you are looking at is *two-dimensional* (length and width). In most maps, a grid of letters and numbers is used to locate any point on the map.

The *map book* that you have is *three-dimensional*. To locate a point on a map, you first have to find the page (first dimension) and then the grid letter and number (the other two dimensions).

The *sequence number* of the map book on the shelf adds a *fourth dimension*.

The *shelf number* on the rack becomes a *fifth dimension*.

The *rack* requires yet another *dimension, the sixth.*

And the *row* adds the *seventh dimension, or set of identifiers.*

To completely identify a point on a map to someone who just walked into the map room (the person has to go directly to the correct point on the map without searching), you have to specify seven identifiers, one for each dimension:

- Dimension 1 (1−10) to identify the row
- Dimension 2 (1−3) to identify the rack
- Dimension 3 (1−4) to identify the shelf

A Direct View of Row 1

rack 1	rack 2	rack 3
shelf 4	shelf 4	shelf 4
shelf 3	shelf 3	shelf 3
shelf 2	shelf 2	shelf 2
shelf 1	map1 map2 map3 map4 map5 map6 map7 map8 map9 map10	shelf 1

- Dimension 4 (1–10) to identify the book
- Dimension 5 (1–{number of pages in the book}) to identify the page number
- Dimension 6 (A–Z) to identify the grid letter
- Dimension 7 (1–20) to identify the grid number

The dimensions of an array are a collection of locations that identify each element of that table. A one-dimensional table has one set of identifiers, a two-dimensional table has two sets of identifiers, a three-dimensional table has three sets of identifiers, a four-dimensional array has four sets, and so on.

There is one identifier for each location, numbered from 1 to the number of locations in each dimension. For example:

1. A list of ten items in a grocery list is a one-dimensional table, with ten locations in the single dimension. The locations are numbered 1–10.
2. A checkerboard is a two-dimensional table, with eight locations in each dimension. The locations in the first dimension are numbered 1–8. The locations in the second dimension are also numbered 1–8.
3. The train schedule above is a two-dimensional array with five locations (rows) in the first dimension and five locations (columns) in the second dimension.

18.5 LOCATING THE ELEMENTS IN A TABLE

We can locate items on the train schedule by specifying a value in each dimension:

1. The arrival time of Earlybird in Tinkertown, 8:14 A.M., is found on row 2, column 3.
2. The time that Morning Dove leaves Hometown, 8:30 A.M., is found on row 3, column 1.
3. The arrival time of Ol' Redeye in New York City, 8:26 A.M., is found on row 1, column 5.
4. The arrival of Leisure Liner in Villaville, 12:27 P.M., is found on row 5, column 4.

18.6 SUBSCRIPTS, AND KEEPING THEM STRAIGHT

These coordinates, which specify the exact location of an item in a table, are called *subscripts*. Each dimension has its own subscript. The value of the subscripts in each dimension specifies the location of each element in the array. The use of subscripts allows the computer to find any item in the array directly, without searching.

In the example, above,

1. the first subscript is 2, and the second is 3.
2. The first subscript is 3, and the second is 1.
3. The first subscript is 1, and the second is 5.
4. The first subscript is 5, and the second is 4.

Let's give the table with the train schedules a name, **Traintab$** (for use in BASIC). Then, the location of each item above is specified as:

1. Traintab$ (2,3):REM has a value of 8:14 A.M.
2. Traintab$ (3,1):REM has a value of 8:30 A.M.
3. Traintab$ (1,5):REM has a value of 8:26 A.M.
4. Traintab$ (5,4):REM has a value of 12:27 P.M.

18.7 DIMENSIONING A TABLE

Before an array can be used in BASIC, its size must be specified. This is accomplished by using the **DIM** statement. The **DIM** statement specifies the number of dimensions and the number of elements in each dimension. The **DIM** statement can only be executed once for each array in every program, so we recommend that it be placed in the **OPENFILE** or **DIMARRAY** routines, which are enabled only once.

The syntax is:

DIM {array name 1}({# of elements}, {# of elements, etc}),{array name 2}

and so on, where {**array name 1**} is the name of the table, and {**# of elements**} is the number of items in each of the dimensions.

An array can have from one to eight dimensions in PowerBASIC.

■ EXAMPLE OF DIM

DIM traintab$(5,5)

is the dimension statement for the train table in this chapter.

More than one array can be dimensioned in a **DIM** statement:

DIM traintab$(5,5), datetab(12)

This DIM statement defines **Traintab$** as having two dimensions, with five elements in each dimension. It defines **datetab** as a one-dimensional array with 12 elements. ■

18.8 GETTING VALUES INTO ARRAYS

There are several ways to get data values into the elements of a table. We'll use our **Traintab$** to illustrate:

1. Assign each value.

   traintab$(1,1) = "6:00 A.M."
   traintab$(1,2) = "6:41 A.M."
   traintab$(1,3) = "7:14 A.M."
   and so on for each element in the table.

2. Input each value.

   LINE INPUT"enter ELEMENT (1,1)";traintab$(1,1)
   LINE INPUT"enter ELEMENT (1,2)";traintab$(1,2)
   LINE INPUT"enter ELEMENT (1,3)";traintab$(1,3)

   and so forth for each element in the table.

18.9 DATA AND READ STATEMENTS

When each of these methods seems too cumbersome, and the values aren't subject to change often, the **READ** and **DATA** statements are a good way to give values to a table.

The **DATA** statement contains the values.
The **READ** statement assigns those values to the table.

■ EXAMPLE OF READ AND DATA

```
FOR i% = 1 TO 5
  FOR j% = 1 TO 5
  READ traintab$(i%,j%)
  NEXT j%
NEXT i%
DATA "6:00 A.M.","6:41 A.M.","7:14 A.M.","7:57 A.M.","8:26 A.M."
DATA "7:00 A.M.","7:41 A.M.","8:14 A.M.","8:57 A.M.","9:26 A.M."
DATA "8:30 A.M.","9:11 A.M.","9:44 A.M.","10:27 A.M.","10:56 A.M."
DATA "9:00 A.M.","9:41 A.M.","10:14 A.M.","10:57 A.M.","11:26 A.M."
DATA "10:30 A.M.","11:11 A.M.","11:44 A.M.","12:27 P.M.","12:56 P.M."
```

This will assign all the values to the table **Traintab$**, as shown in the train schedule at the beginning of the chapter.

18.10 PRINTING OUT A TABLE

The schedule at the start of this chapter could be printed (excluding the titles) by these PowerBASIC program lines:

```
FOR i% = 1 TO 5
  FOR j% = 1 TO 5
    PRINT TAB(j%*10); traintab$(i%,j%);
  NEXT j%
  PRINT
NEXT i%
```

Or it could be printed by specifying each table item:

```
PRINT TAB(10); traintab$(1,1); TAB(20); traintab$(1,2); TAB(30); traintab$(1,3); (cont'd)
PRINT TAB(10); traintab$(2,1); TAB(20); traintab$(2,2); TAB(30); traintab$(2,3); (cont'd)
PRINT TAB(10); traintab$(3,1); TAB(20); traintab$(3,2); TAB(30); traintab$(3,3); (cont'd)
PRINT TAB(10); traintab$(4,1); TAB(20); traintab$(4,2); TAB(30); traintab$(4,3); (cont'd)
PRINT TAB(10); traintab$(5,1); TAB(20); traintab$(5,2); TAB(30); traintab$(5,3); (cont'd)
```

Usually, the individual elements aren't specified in a **PRINT** statement when the entire array (or a section of it) is printed. The best way to print the entire table is to use the double loop at the start of 18.10 (previous paragraph). The only time the individual elements are specified in a **PRINT** statement is when only one or two of the table items are to be printed.

18.11 A TABLE WITHIN A RANDOM FILE RECORD

A table doesn't have to get its values from **READ** and **DATA**. It can be read into the program from a random file. For instance, sales for each customer could be saved on the customer record on disk and read in as each customer is processed.

The table first needs to be dimensioned in the **FILEOPEN** routine. Then the record is specified with the table contained in the **FIELD** statement. Once the **GET** is executed (and any necessary unpacking is done), the table is ready for use.

In the case of our train table, the **FIELD** statement containing it might look like this:

```
FIELD 1, 8 AS traintab$(1,1), 8 AS traintab$(1,2), 8 AS traintab$(1,3), (cont'd)
FIELD 1, 40 AS fill1$, 8 AS traintab(2,1), 8 AS traintab$(2,2), 8 AS traintab$(2,3), (cont'd)
FIELD 1, 80 AS fill1$, 8 AS traintab(3,1), 8 AS traintab$(3,2), 8 AS traintab$(3,3), (cont'd)
FIELD 1, 120 AS fill1$, 8 AS traintab(4,1), 8 AS traintab$(4,2), 8 AS traintab$(4,3), (cont'd)
FIELD 1, 160 AS fill1$, 8 AS traintab(5,1), 8 AS traintab$(5,2), 8 AS traintab$(5,3), (cont'd)
```

18.12 A COMPLETE EXAMPLE

The program below incorporates almost everything mentioned in this chapter. The program, **printran,** reads the train file to get the schedule (train schedule array) and then prints the entire table out on the printer.

```
REM--printran 01/01/90
stub:
```

```
      GOSUB getdate
      GOSUB fileopen
      GOSUB main
      CLOSE
      END
getdate:
   w1$ = LEFT$(DATE$,2)
   w2$ = MID$(DATE$,4,2)
   w3$ = RIGHT$(DATE$,2)
   dat$ = w1$ + "/" + w2$ + "/" + w3$
   dat = VAL(w1$) * 10000 + val(w2$) * 100 + VAL(w3$)
   tad = VAL(w3$) * 10000 + val(w1$) * 100 + VAL(w2$)
RETURN
fileopen:
   OPEN "R", #1, "trainfil.dat", 256
   DIM traintab$(5,5)
   FIELD 1, 8 AS traintab$(1,1), 8 AS traintab$(1,2), 8 AS traintab$(1,3), (cont'd)
   FIELD 1, 40 AS fill1$, 8 AS traintab(2,1), 8 AS traintab$(2,2), 8 AS traintab$(2,3), (cont'd)
   FIELD 1, 80 AS fill1$, 8 AS traintab(3,1), 8 AS traintab$(3,2), 8 AS traintab$(3,3), (cont'd)
   FIELD 1, 120 AS fill1$, 8 AS traintab(4,1), 8 AS traintab$(4,2), 8 AS traintab$(4,3), (cont'd)
   FIELD 1, 160 AS fill1$, 8 AS traintab(5,1), 8 AS traintab$(5,2), 8 AS traintab$(5,3), (cont'd)
RETURN
read1:
   GET 1, f1
RETURN
main:
   f1 = f1 + 1
   IF f1 > 100 THEN GOTO end-main
   GOSUB read1
   GOSUB prinsched
   GOTO main
end-main:
RETURN
prinsched: REM -- This is a nested loop
   FOR i% = 1 TO 5
      FOR j% = 1 TO 5
         LPRINT TAB(j%*10); traintab$(i%,j%);
      NEXT j%
      PRINT
   NEXT i%
RETURN
```

18.13 COMMON USES OF TABLES IN POWERBASIC

1. Defining sales for each month of a year, or several years
2. Defining purchases for each month, and so on
3. Defining dollars paid for each month, and so forth
4. Defining the number of days in each of 12 months
5. Defining any table of weights, dollars, and so on
6. Defining a table of error messages
7. Defining any table so that the elements can be specified using subscripts

18.14 POWERBASIC LIMITATIONS

1. Maximum of eight dimensions in any one array.
2. Maximum of 65,535 bytes total space for any one array. Each integer takes up two bytes, each single-precision number takes up four bytes, each long integer takes up four bytes, and each double-precison number takes up eight bytes. Each character in a string takes up one byte. Therefore, PowerBASIC has these limitations for each type of array (table):

   - 32,767 integers,
   - or 16,383 long integers,
   - or 16,383 single-precision numbers,
   - or 8,191 double-precision numbers,
   - or a total of 65,535 string characters.

Note:

You can *NEVER* mix data types within an array. That is:

- An integer array contains only integers.
- A long-integer array has all long integers.
- A single-precision array holds only six-digit numbers.

- A double-precision array has double-precision numbers.
- A string array contains alphanumeric characters, but none of the numeric types above.

BASIC won't allow you to mix variable types within an array. It's easier to work with these limitations than to try to work around them.

CHAPTER SUMMARY

1. Tables are something you see and work with on a daily basis.
2. A table in PowerBASIC can have from one to eight dimensions. Each dimension has a number of locations, which are specified by *subscripts*.
3. Define an array using a **DIM** statement.
4. You can get values into an array by—

   - assigning the values directly.
   - keying them in via the **LINE INPUT** statement.
   - using the combination of the **READ** and **DATA** statements.

5. You can print a table—

   - within a loop or nested loop.
   - by specifying each individual element within a series of **PRINT** statements.
   - by any combination of these two methods that works for you.

6. Use tables whenever you are working with more than three like items, to reduce coding (and potential mistakes).
7. PowerBASIC limits you to

   - eight dimensions in any one array.
   - 65,535 bytes total space for any one array:

     - 32,767 integers,
     - or 16,383 long integers,
     - or 16,383 single-precision numbers,
     - or 8,191 double-precision numbers,
     - or a total of 65,535 string characters.

THE BOTTOM LINE

1. BASIC is a personable language, which tells your computer to follow your instructions one at a time until it has produced a desired "report."
2. When you look at a BASIC program, break it up into sections, using the block-line method. Then look at each block, one at a time, to figure out what each does.
3. PowerBASIC gives you a complete working environment, which encourages writing programs in building-block fashion.
4. Blueprint your program before you write one line of code.
5. Data names should be meaningful, short (but not cryptic), consistent, and clear.
6. Program organization is not fluff. Organize your thoughts, assign the tasks to routines, and then program each routine.
7. Break your program up into subroutines and procedures, and then use **GOSUB** and **CALL**. Use **GOTO** only to go somewhere else within the same routine.
8. The Editor is very powerful. Use the keys as much as possible, and you'll be productive in writing and changing a program.
9. Keep your **IF**s simple and easy to read.
10. Loops are a critical structure of good programming. You can destroy that structure with the wrong use of **GOTO**. Use **GOTO** only to go somewhere else within the same loop.
11. Files are no big deal. Just group like items together and describe them, and you have the start of a file.
12. Learn to use random files well; you won't need any other kind of file.
13. Edit "live" (new) data thoroughly, or your program dies.
14. Set up standard edit procedures and always use them.
15. Design each report for a specific purpose, with the minimum amount of data to achieve that purpose.
16. Will this make the screen more readable? If not, forget it.
17. Understand and test *all* your calculations thoroughly.
18. **Use tables whenever you can to simplify your logic and to avoid repeatedly coding identical lines of code that process similar items.**

EXERCISES

1. Print out every character location on your computer screen, starting with location 1,1. (Hint: you have 24 lines and 80 character positions per line.)

2. Print out every character location on your computer screen, backwards, starting with location 24,80 and ending at location 1,1.

3. Create a date table with the number of days in each month. Call the date table **motab.** Create it in a subroutine named **SETMONTH**, which is envoked at the very start of a program.

4. Create the train table using **LINE INPUT** statements in a loop.

5. Create the train table using **READ** and **DATA** statements.

6. Print out the train table using a nested loop.

Chapter 19

The PowerBASIC Debugger (Cleaning up Your Act)

19.1 Taking One Step at a Time _____ 335

19.2 Skipping Some Steps _____ 336

19.3 Cut! Stopping the Action _____ 336

19.4 Watch What You're Doing! _____ 337

19.5 Action! _____ 338

19.6 Quickchange, then Action _____ 338

19.7 A Detailed Example _____ 339

19.8 Hints on Using the Debugger _____ 343

Ever write something in English perfectly the first time? You probably get quite a few short notes right on the first try, but what about a three-page letter? Or a twenty-page chapter in a book?

Writing a program is a lot more precise than writing in English. It would be equivalent to writing a chapter in a book entitled *How to Diffuse Bombs*, written for the police bomb squads. Every detail would have to be specified exactly, or the book (and its users) would be worthless. This perfect precision isn't normally found in the initial writing of any but the smallest programs. Usually, programs have mistakes—normally in logic, but sometimes just "typos" (typing mistakes)—which prevent the program from running correctly. We call these mistakes "BUGS".

No matter how hard you try, you're likely to wind up with some "bugs" in your program. Fortunately for you, PowerBASIC has plenty of power in its Debugger to find and squash them.

19.1 TAKING ONE STEP AT A TIME

First, we'll explain each of the debugging features (including the function keys). Then we'll type in a program and try each of the features with the program as a model. Since these features are found in three separate menus (*Run*, *Debug*, and *Break/watch*), we'll use the function keys in most cases, rather than jumping from menu to menu. It eliminates a step.

   PRESS ⟨ALT + **r**⟩

The *Run* menu pops up.

   We'll discuss both the menus and special function keys. Whenever a function key performs the same function as a *Run* menu item, we recommend using the function key. The fewer things that flash before your eyes, the less confusing the debug process.

19.1.1 Single-Stepping (Trace into)

Single-stepping is accomplished by pressing the F7 key. This means that each time you press the F7 key, one program statement is executed. As each statement is invoked, it is highlighted, to show you which statement has just been run.

   When you first run a program, it's a good idea to single-step through it to see how your logic actually works. If it's not possible to single-step through every part of your program (for instance, if you loop through something in a subroutine or procedure several thousand times), then press F8 instead and let the program run through the entire routine as one step. We'll explain this further in the next section.

19.2 SKIPPING SOME STEPS (STEP OVER)

You can run a block of code (a subroutine or procedure) as a single step by using F8 instead of F7. This means that once you have thoroughly tested a routine (by single-stepping and by other methods using Power-BASIC), you don't have to single-step through it again. Instead, press F8, which will single-step through each statement, while treating the **CALL** and **GOSUB** statements (and the routines they invoke) as one step. This eliminates the drudgery of restepping through each routine when you know that it's already correct.

19.3 CUT! STOPPING THE ACTION

19.3.1 Stopping the Program Manually

The combination of keys that you use to stop the execution of a program is

PRESS ⟨CTRL + BREAK⟩

You stop a running program because you want to look at the values of some variables, look at some screen output, or change something in the program.

19.3.2 The Breakpoint Feature

PRESS ⟨ALT + **b**⟩

and the *Break/watch* menu appears.

The keys that you use to mark a breakpoint statement (*Toggle breakpoint*) in your program are CTRL + F8. When the program reaches a breakpoint statement, it stops so that you can use the debugging features to check your work. You use breakpoints to stop a program so that you can check the values of different variables and look at the screen output that has been produced so far. You may also want to change some values after the breakpoint has been reached.

19.4 WATCH WHAT YOU'RE DOING!

19.4.1 Watch Window

The *Watch* window is used to display the values of certain variables as the program is being run. The *Add watch* feature in *Break/watch* (CTRL + F7) lets you add variable names to be watched, and the *Delete watch* deletes variable names to be watched.

19.4.2 Instant Watch

PRESS ⟨ALT + **d**⟩

and the *Debug* menu pops up.

The keys that you use to display the value of a variable (*Evaluate*) after you have stopped the program are

PRESS ⟨CTRL + F4⟩

So just set the cursor onto the desired variable name and

PRESS ⟨CTRL + F4⟩

Three boxes appear, the first having the variable or expression that the cursor is on. Just

PRESS ⟨ENTER⟩

and the value is displayed in the middle box.

PRESS ⟨ESC⟩ to clear the boxes.

19.4.3 Instant Screen (User screen)

PRESS ⟨ALT + **r**⟩

to get the *Run* menu.

The keys that you use to switch between your program statements and the screen output of the program are ALT + F5. You can use these keys to look at the screen output that was produced up to the point that the program was stopped.

19.5 ACTION!

The key that you can use to start your program, run it until it reaches a breakpoint, and then continue to run it to another breakpoint is F4.

The key that you use to start or restart your program in single-step mode is F7.

The key that you use to start or restart your program in step over mode (treats each subroutine or procedure as a single step) is F8.

19.6 QUICKCHANGE, THEN ACTION

PRESS ⟨ALT + **d**⟩

for the *Debug* menu.

The *Evaluate* feature (CTRL + F4) is used to change the values of variables, so that pieces of logic can be checked out more quickly. After the program has been stopped,

PRESS ⟨CTRL + F4⟩

to get into the *Evaluate* window. Then simply assign the new value to the variable in the *New value* window,

PRESS ⟨ESC⟩⟨F10⟩

to get out of the *New value* window and continue with the program.

19.7 A DETAILED EXAMPLE

Now it's time to really test the Debugger. First, we'll key in a very simple program, one that you will easily understand. Then we'll use the Debugger to test it. This will give you a good idea of how the Debugger works.

TYPE **a = 1** ⟨ENTER⟩
      b = 2 ⟨ENTER⟩
      FOR i = 1 TO 1000 ⟨ENTER⟩
      c = i * b + a ⟨ENTER⟩
      PRINT i, a, b, c ⟨ENTER⟩
      NEXT i ⟨ENTER⟩
      PRINT "finished" ⟨ENTER⟩
      END ⟨ENTER⟩

First, we'll single-step through the program.

PRESS ⟨F7⟩

Keep pressing it and watch the program run, one step (statement) at a time. If you get an error, check your program against the one in the book, make your corrections, and

PRESS ⟨F7⟩

about fifteen times. Note that as each statement is executed, it is highlighted.
    Next we'll take a look at the screen display that the program produced.

PRESS ⟨ALT + F5⟩

The screen output of the program will be staring you in the face.

PRESS ⟨ESC⟩

You are now back to the program statements.

PRESS ⟨ALT + F5⟩ again.

You have the screen display again.

PRESS ⟨ESC⟩ once more,

and you're back to the program statements.

The *Breakpoint* key sets the program line or lines at which the program will stop and gives control back to you. We'll set a *breakpoint* at the first **PRINT** line:

PRINT i, a, b, c

Using the ARROW keys, move the cursor down to that **PRINT** line and

PRESS ⟨CTRL + F8⟩

The statement line will be highlighted. Now,

PRESS ⟨F4⟩

to run the program. It'll stop at the **PRINT** line.

PRESS ⟨ALT + F5⟩

to look at the screen. You'll note that one more iteration of the loop has printed.

PRESS ⟨ESC⟩ again.

You are back at the program statements.

PRESS ⟨F4⟩ to continue.

Repeat this process a few times to get the feel of it. This run-to-breakpoint, then look-at-the-output, then run-to-breakpoint, then look-at-the-output process is a common method of testing programs.

Now, remove the *breakpoint*:

PRESS ⟨CTRL + F8⟩

The highlight disappears; the *breakpoint* is removed, and we can go on to the next feature.

We'll try the *Instant watch* keys. Using the ARROW keys, move the cursor to the **a** in the calculation line.

PRESS ⟨CTRL + F4⟩

Three boxes pop up. The first has the variable **a** in it.

PRESS ⟨ENTER⟩

The value of **a** pops up in the middle box on the screen.

PRESS ⟨ESC⟩⟨F10⟩

to clear the screen.
Move the cursor to the **b**.

PRESS ⟨CTRL + F4⟩

Then,

PRESS ⟨ENTER⟩

The value of **b** appears.

PRESS ⟨ESC⟩⟨F10⟩

to clear the screen.

Do the same for **i** and **c**. As you can see, the CTRL + F4 keys give you the ability to instantly see the value of any variable.

If you have variables that you want to watch consistently, it becomes a pain to keep moving the cursor around and pressing CTRL + F4. So PowerBASIC has an additional *Watch* feature that saves a lot of time. You add the variables or expressions that you want to monitor using the *Add Watch* command (CTRL + F7), and whenever the program is not showing the screen display, the values of the expressions or variables are shown at the bottom of the screen.

We'll add **c** and **i** to the *Watch* window.

    PRESS ⟨CTRL + F7⟩

The *Add Watch* window appears.

    TYPE **c** ⟨ENTER⟩

Again,

    PRESS ⟨CTRL + F7⟩
    TYPE **i** ⟨ENTER⟩

The values of **c** and **i** appear at the bottom of the screen. Now, again set a *breakpoint* at the **PRINT** line. Move the cursor to the **PRINT** statement in the program and

    PRESS ⟨CTRL + F8⟩

Then

    PRESS ⟨F4⟩

The program executes one iteration of the loop and stops at the **PRINT** statement. The new values of **c** and **i** appear at the bottom of the screen. Repeat this several times and note the change in the values of **c** and **i** with each iteration.

    Clear the *breakpoint* by

    PRESS ⟨CTRL + F8⟩

and we're on to the next debug feature.

    The Debugger also allows you to change the values of variables and then continue running the program. For instance, when the program has a loop that it repeats many times (like this one)—and you want to get through the loop to see how well the rest of the logic works—you can change the value of the loop counter to skip most of the iterations. Right now, the value of **i** is some low number; we're going to change it to 990 and continue running the program until it finishes.

    PRESS ⟨CTRL + F4⟩

to get into the *Evaluate* window.

Then

TYPE **i** ⟨ENTER⟩
PRESS ⟨DOWN ARROW⟩⟨DOWN ARROW⟩

Then,

TYPE **990** ⟨ENTER⟩
PRESS ⟨ESC⟩⟨F10⟩

again to get back to the main window with the program statements.
Then

PRESS ⟨F9⟩

to continue the program.
The program skips to **i = 990** and continues processing until **i =
1000,** prints **finished,** and then stops.

PRESS ⟨ENTER⟩

to get back to the program statements, and use CTRL + F4 to check the
value of **c** against what is printed on the screen.

19.8 HINTS ON USING THE DEBUGGER

All of these debug features ensure that your program can be thoroughly
tested without ever leaving PowerBASIC. Here are a few hints to help
you test your programs with the Debugger.

1. Test your program one routine at a time. Begin with the main
   routine and set up blank "dummy" routines to test the main
   logic.
2. Single-step through each routine the first time.
3. Perform the simplest test for each routine first; then go on to more
   complex tests.

4. One test is not enough for any routine; a minimum of three tests is needed for every possible logic path.
5. Use *Breakpoints* next.
6. Keep your testing as simple as possible, but test thoroughly. If the input is numeric, use simple numbers like 10, 50, 100, etc., at first so that you can easily check the answer.
7. Quantity testing is no substitute for quality testing. Running a whole bunch of numbers through the same logic is not as good as running a few numbers through all the logic paths.
8. When you're positive that it's right, make two last tests.

CHAPTER SUMMARY

1. You have a powerful Debugger at your beck and call. Use it.
2. Heed the Hints on Using the Debugger.

THE BOTTOM LINE

1. BASIC is a personable language, which tells your computer to follow your instructions one at a time until it has produced a desired "report."
2. When you look at a BASIC program, break it up into sections, using the block-line method. Then look at each block, one at a time, to figure out what was done.
3. PowerBASIC gives you a complete working environment, which encourages writing programs in building-block fashion.
4. Blueprint your program before you write one line of code.
5. Data names should be meaningful, short (but not cryptic), consistent, and clear.
6. Program organization is not fluff. Organize your thoughts, assign the tasks to routines, and then program each routine.

7. Break your program up into subroutines and procedures: then use **GOSUB** and **CALL**. Use **GOTO** only to go somewhere else within the same routine.
8. The Editor is very powerful. Use the keys as much as possible, and you'll be productive in writing and changing a program.
9. Keep your **IF**s simple and easy to read.
10. Loops are a critical structure of good programming. You can destroy that structure with the wrong use of **GOTO**. Use **GOTO** only to go somewhere else within the same loop.
11. Files are no big deal. Just group like items together and describe them, and you have the start of a file.
12. Learn to use random files well; you won't need any other kind of file.
13. Edit "live" (new) data thoroughly, or your program dies.
14. Set up standard edit procedures and always use them.
15. Design each report for a specific purpose, with the minimum amount of data to achieve that purpose.
16. Will this make the screen more readable? If not, forget it.
17. Understand and test *all* your calculations thoroughly.
18. Use tables whenever you can to simplify your logic and to avoid repeatedly coding identical lines of code that process similar items.
19. **Use ALL EIGHT hints with the PowerBASIC Debugger, and your programs will become bug-free quickly.**

EXERCISE

1. Write a small input program for Bikes Peak that lets you add the sales quantities (how many of each part were sold) from each customer order into the monthly sales for each part. (You'll have to ask the computer operator which month to put the sales into.) The program should use your input edit procedures (from chapter 14). Load the input edit procedures: then write, type, and run the program, using the Debugger to follow the logic flow and show you the values of the variables.

Chapter 20

The PowerBASIC Compiler (The Command Performance)

20.1 The Last, Shortest, and Easiest _____ 346

20.2 Starting a Program _____ 347

20.3 Stopping a Program _____ 347

20.4 Compiling a Program When You're All Done _____ 347

20.5 A Note on PowerBASIC Features That We Skipped _____ 348

Think of your program as a stage production. You've put everything together painstakingly for each scene; it all flows flawlessly, and the first performance is next week. Before you put this show (your program) in front of your audience (Bikes Peak), you'll do a complete dress rehearsal (complete run of the program) to make sure it's completely right.

You've checked your program using the PowerBASIC Debugger, and you think the program is perfect! So now you go to run it one last time, all the way through, for a final test before you compile it and make it available to Bikes Peak for regular use.

20.1 THE LAST, SHORTEST, AND EASIEST

You have reached the last and shortest chapter in the book. Because you made it this far, you are well on your way to becoming a good programmer. This chapter has only one real piece of advice for you.

> ALWAYS test for the most ridiculous situations that you can imagine.

Just before you do the final compile, test and retest. Lack of proper testing is the second major flaw in most programmers' work. Don't make it one of your major flaws. It will cost you far more if you don't test all your work completely.

Now, let's Run the program for one last test.

20.2 STARTING A PROGRAM

To begin running your program,

PRESS ⟨ALT + **r**⟩

20.3 STOPPING A PROGRAM

To stop the program,

PRESS ⟨CTRL + BREAK⟩

Debug the program further, if necessary. And, to start again from the beginning,

PRESS ⟨CTL + F2⟩⟨ALT + **r**⟩

20.4 COMPILING A PROGRAM WHEN YOU'RE ALL DONE

Once your test (or, more likely, your tests) are complete, get into the *Compile* menu, select *Destination*, and

PRESS ⟨ENTER⟩

Now, select *EXE file* and

PRESS ⟨ENTER⟩

Now, begin the compile process:

PRESS ⟨ALT + F9⟩

The program begins compiling.

PowerBASIC will check the program for errors and, if none are found, will produce a program that can be put on any compatible computer, anywhere, and run. Incidentally, the compiled program will run up to 50 times faster than the same program on the BASIC (GWBASIC, IBM BASIC, or BASICA) that came with your computer.

20.5 A NOTE ON POWERBASIC FEATURES THAT WE SKIPPED

PowerBASIC is an extremely advanced version of the BASIC language. It offers features like:

MAX and **MIN** functions for both numbers and strings;
Array (table) manipulation statements, for sorting, inserting, deleting, and scanning;
Binary Coded Decimal data type to eliminate rounding errors in financial calculations;
Extended-precision floating-point numbers for scientific calculation accuracy;
Special string functions;
A new binary file construct;

and others, too many to mention. The use of these statements belongs in an advanced programming book, so they are not explained here.

You've made it through the book, and you now have a strong base from which to write programs in BASIC, or in *ANY LANGUAGE*.

Remember, this book won't make you a programmer. It'll just give you the knowledge to become one. Only you, working at the keyboard of your computer, and the lessons the computer gives you (by showing you your syntax and logic errors) can make yourself a programmer. There's no magic in computers!!

Review THE BOTTOM LINE, and start programming.

THE BOTTOM LINE

1. BASIC is a personable language, which tells your computer to follow your instructions one at a time until it has produced a desired "report."
2. When you look at a BASIC program, break it up into sections, using the block-line method. Then look at each block, one at a time, to figure out what was done.
3. PowerBASIC gives you a complete working environment, which encourages writing programs in building-block fashion.
4. Blueprint your program before you write one line of code.
5. Data names should be meaningful, short (but not cryptic), consistent, and clear.
6. Program organization is not fluff. Organize your thoughts, assign the tasks to routines, and then program each routine.
7. Break your program up into subroutines and procedures; then use **GOSUB** and **CALL**. Use **GOTO** only to go somewhere else within the same routine.
8. The Editor is very powerful. Use the keys as much as possible, and you'll be productive in writing and changing a program.
9. Keep your **IF**s simple and easy to read.
10. Loops are a critical structure of good programming. You can destroy that structure with the wrong use of **GOTO**. Use **GOTO** only to go somewhere else within the same loop.
11. Files are no big deal. Just group like items together and describe them, and you have the start of a file.
12. Learn to use random files well; you won't need any other kind of file.
13. Edit "live" (new) data thoroughly, or your program dies.
14. Set up standard edit procedures and always use them.

15. Design each report for a specific purpose, with the minimum amount of data to achieve that purpose.
16. Will this make the screen more readable? If not, forget it.
17. Understand and test *all* your calculations thoroughly.
18. Use tables whenever you can to simplify your logic and to avoid repeatedly coding identical lines of code that process similar items.
19. Use ALL EIGHT hints with the PowerBASIC Debugger, and your programs will become bug-free quickly.
20. * * * **ALWAYS test for the most ridiculous situations that you can imagine.** * * *

Appendix A

PowerBASIC Statement Summary (Selected Statements)

ASC Gets the ASCII value of the first character in a string.

BLOCK IF An **IF** statement with its logic spread out onto several program lines.

CHAIN Loads and runs a program from another program. The control is passed to the **CHAIN**ed program.

CHR$ Used with **LPRINT** to—
print one or more lines,
start a new page, and
give special commands to your printer.

CINT Converts an expression into an integer by rounding.

CLNG Converts an expression into a long integer by rounding.

CLOSE Closes an open file.

CLS Clears the computer screen and locates the cursor at line 1, column 1.

COLOR Determines the color of the computer screen foreground (characters) and background.

CSRLIN Gets the current line position of the cursor.

CVD Unpacks a double-precision number from a random file.

CVI Unpacks an integer from a random file.

CVL Unpacks a long integer from a random file.

CVS Unpacks a single-precision number from a random file.

DATA Used in conjunction with **READ** to get data into variable names.

DIM Specifies the size of an array.

DO UNTIL ... Begins a loop, that iterates until the specified condition is true. This loop ends with **LOOP**.

ELSE The action taken when an IF condition is false.

END Ends a program.

END IF Ends the logic of a block **IF** statement.

FIELD Defines a record layout.

FIX Converts an expression into a whole number by truncating, rather than rounding.

FOR ... TO Begins a loop that will process a fixed number of times. This loop ends with a **NEXT** statement.

FORMAT A string assignment statement that lays out the print line for use by a **PRINT** or a **PRINT USING** statement.

GET Reads a record from a random file.

IF A statement that causes some processing only when the specified condition is true.

INT Converts a number into an integer by finding the largest integer that is equal to, or less than, the expression.

LEFT$ Gets a specific number of characters from the left side of a string.

LEN Finds the length of a string.

LINE INPUT Gets an input string from the keyboard.

LOCATE Positions the cursor at a specific spot on the screen.

LOOP Ends the logic of a conditional loop that began with **DO UNTIL** ....

LPRINT Prints onto paper.

LPRINT USING Prints onto paper according to the layout established by the referenced **FORMAT** statement.

MID$ Gets a specific number of characters from anywhere in the string.

MKD$ Packs a double-precision number into random file format.

MKI$ Packs an integer into random file format.

MKL$ Packs a long integer into random file format.

MKS$ Packs a single-precision number into random file format.

NEXT Ends the logic of a fixed loop that began with a **FOR ... TO**.

OPEN The statement that opens a random file for use.

POS Gets the current column position of the cursor.

PRINT Displays onto the computer screen.

PRINT USING Displays onto the computer screen according to the layout established by the referenced **FORMAT** statement.

PUT Writes a record onto a random file.

REM A comment or explanation statement by the program to the person who is reading the program code. **REM** is ignored by the computer. It is never processed.

RETURN Exits a subroutine.

RIGHT$ Gets a specific number of characters from the right side of a string.

STR$ Converts a numeric expression into a string.

TAB Used with **PRINT** or **LPRINT** to move to a specific column.

VAL Converts a string into a number.

WIDTH Sets the maximum number of characters for a print line.

Appendix B

BASIC Reserved Words

$COM	BINARY	CVE	END
$COM1	BLOAD	CVF	ENDMEM
$COM2	BSAVE	CVI	ENVIRON
$CPU	CALL	CVL	ENVIRON$
$DYNAMIC	CASE	CVMD	EOF
$ELSE	CBCD	CVMS	EQV
$ENDIF	CDBL	CVQ	ERADR
$EVENT	CEIL	CVS	ERASE
$FLOAT	CEXT	DATA	ERDEV
$IF	CFIX	DATE$	ERDEV$
$INCLUDE	CHAIN	DECLARE	ERL
$INLINE	CHDIR	DECR	ERR
$LIB	CHR$	DEF	ERROR
$LINK	CINT	DEFBCD	EXIT
$OPTION	CIRCLE	DEFDBL	EXP
$SEGMENT	CLEAR	DEFEXT	EXP2
$SOUND	CLNG	DEFFIX	EXP10
$STACK	CLOSE	DEFFLX	EXTERNAL
$STATIC	CLS	DEFINT	EXTRACT$
ABS	COLOR	DEFLNG	FIELD
ABSOLUTE	COM1	DEFQUD	FILEATTR
AND	COM2	DEFSNG	FILES
APPEND	COMMAND$	DEFSTR	FIX
AS	COMMON	DELAY	FN
ASC	COS	DIM	FOR
AT	CQUD	DO	FRE
ATN	CSNG	DRAW	FREEFILE
BASE	CSRLIN	DYNAMIC	FUNCTION
BEEP	CVB	ELSE	GET
BIN$	CVD	ELSEIF	GET$

355

GOSUB	MEMSET	PUBLIC	STRSEG
GOTO	MID$	PUT	SUB
HEX$	MKB$	PUT$	SWAP
IF	MKD$	RANDOM	SYSTEM
IMP	MKDIR	RANDOMIZE	TAB
INCR	MKE$	READ	TAN
INKEY$	MKF$	REDIM	THEN
INLINE	MKI$	REG	TIME$
INP	MKL$	REM	TIMER
INPUT	MKMD$	RESET	TO
INPUT#	MKMS$	RESTORE	TROFF
INPUT$	MKQ$	RESUME	TRON
INSTAT	MKS$	RETURN	UBOUND
INSTR	MOD	RIGHT$	UCASE$
INT	MTIMER	RMDIR	UNTIL
INTERRUPT	NAME	RND	USING
IOCTL	NEXT	RSET	USR
IOCTL$	NOT	RTRIM$	USR0
KEY	OCT$	RUN	USR1
KILL	OFF	SAVE	USR2
LBOUND	ON	SCREEN	USR3
LCASE$	OPEN	SEEK	USR4
LEFT$	OPTION	SEG	USR5
LEN	OR	SELECT	USR6
LET	OUT	SGN	USR7
LINE	OUTPUT	SHARED	USR8
LIST	PAINT	SHELL	USR9
LOC	PALETTE	SIN	VAL
LOCAL	PALETTE USING	SOUND	VARPTR
LOCATE	PEEK	SPACE$	VARPTR$
LOF	PEN	SPC	VARSEG
LOG	PLAY	SQR	VIEW
LOG10	PMAP	STATIC	WAIT
LOG2	POINT	STEP	WEND
LOOP	POKE	STICK	WHILE
LPOS	POS	STOP	WIDTH
LPRINT	PRESET	STR$	WINDOW
LPRINT #	PRINT	STRIG	WRITE
LSET	PRINT #	STRING$	WRITE #
LTRIM$	PSET	STRPTR	XOR

Appendix C

Sample Data Dictionary and Naming Rules

Rule		Examples
1. Names should be meaningful to you, the programmer. (Remember, the data type also helps explain what kind of data occupies the field name.)	Not good: Good: Better:	**fn personsfirstname y** **fnam yr%** **firstname purchyr%**
2. Names should be short; we recommend not more than 12 characters.	Not good: Good: Better:	**stad streetaddress** **stradd** **street**
3. Names should be consistent.		
a. All data items from the same file should use the file name as the first part (prefix). Thus, we recommend using short file names (up to 4 characters).	Not good: Good: Better:	**customeraddr name prtlstprc** **custadd custnam partlstprc** **custstreet custlastname partlistpric**
b. The same data item seen in several files should have the same suffix in each name.	Not good: Good: Better:	**cno pnum** **cusno prtno** **custnum partnum**
c. All items that are dates should have the same abbreviated suffix, e.g., **dt**, **dat**, or **date**.	Not good: Good: Better:	**pdt hirdt bald** **paydt hiredt baldt** **paydate hiredate balancedate**

d. All numbers that identify things, such as "customer number," "part number," "Social Security Number," etc., should have the same abbreviated suffix, e.g., **no** or **num**.

Not good:	**cusnmb prt# socialsn**
Good:	**cusno prtno ssno**
Better:	**custnum partnum ssnum**

4. Names should not be cryptic. Use vowels when necessary for clarity.

Not good:	**cutot dtsnt**
Good:	**currunpdtot dtsent**
Better:	**totunpaid datesent**

5. Make yourself a *data dictionary* with all data names for each program. Place it at the very beginning of every program. (See the next section.)

6. Make data names unique. Include enough characters to make them clear, but no more.

THE DATA DICTIONARY

```
REM -- Data Dictionary
REM -- baseprice          base price of bike
REM -- city$
REM -- custbirthdat$       customer's birthdate
REM -- custfirstnam$       customer's first name
REM -- custlastname$       customer's last name
REM -- custstreet1$        customer's street address, line 1
REM -- custstreet2$        customer's street address, line 2
REM -- disc                discount from base price (percent)
REM -- model$              model of bike purchased
REM -- purchtot            purchase price total
REM -- purchyr%            year of purchase
REM -- salestax
REM -- st$                 state
REM -- zip%                zip code
REM -- Work Variables:
REM -- accesstot           total price of accessories
REM -- c                   loop counter
REM -- subtot              subtotal
```

The data dictionary includes all the data names (variables) encountered in the program. We recommend putting them in two major groupings:

- data names that are saved in files, followed by
- "work variables" (those used in the program but not saved)

Within each grouping, list the data names in alphabetical order.

1. The recommended limit for an explanation is 50 characters.
2. Data names should include the character suffix that defines the data type.
3. Where there can be no confusion about what data item a name represents, it's safe to omit the expanded definition in the dictionary. See **city$** and **salestax** above.
4. The "work variables" are simple data names for the "little" variables used in standard routines, as well as the results of calculations typically performed within **PROCESS, SUBCALC,** and **MASSAGE** routines.

Consistency throughout all your programs is the key to proper use of data names.

Appendix D

Blueprints and Program Structures

BLUEPRINT PROCESS

Step 1.
PURPOSE: State in a single, simple sentence (no ands, ors, ifs, or commas) what the *single* major purpose of your program is. Then, break the sentence down to list the major tasks that this program is supposed to accomplish—again, each task in a single, simple sentence. If the program is so simple that there's only one task, then one sentence is enough.

Step 2.
End Result (OUTPUT): On a piece of paper, lay out each page that will be displayed on the screen or printed by the printer. If a file of data is to be saved onto disk as a result of this program, then picture on paper what the disk file contents will look like.

Step 3.
Necessary Data (INPUT): Look at the OUTPUT data (in Step 2) that must be present in order to accomplish the end result and determine its source (where it comes from—another file, a calculation, or keyboard input). As you're doing this, give meaningful names to the OUTPUT data to be created by this program.

Step 4.
Hidden Data (HIDPUT): If a calculation (formula) is involved, then determine the source of all the data contained in the formula. The

source could be another file, another calculation, or keyboard input. Keep on doing this until every piece of data has a source within the program.

Step 5.

LOGIC: A good way to look at your logic is to put it into simple block diagrams. Each block diagram should fit onto a single 8½ by 11 sheet of paper. If it doesn't fit, then the logic is probably too complex. (Remember the secret of good programming: Make it simple.) If you can't fit all the functions or procedures onto one sheet of paper, then put the major logic onto one sheet and the other (sublogic) routines on other sheets. In any case, *force* yourself to be constrained—that's the purpose of using a single 8½ by 11 sheet for block diagramming the logic. Fitting the logic onto one sheet forces simplicity.

The rules of block diagramming are simple: Put each step within a block and connect the blocks with arrows to show program flow direction.

Sample Blueprint #1

PROGRAM NAME: **mailkey1**.

PURPOSE: To key the magazine mailing list into our computer.

OUTPUT RESULT: File on disk, containing 20,000 names and addresses. The name of the file is "mail". The description is . . .

Data Name	Description	Location in File (positions)	Maximum Length
mailname	prospect's name	1–30	30
mailaddr1	1st line of address	31–60	30
mailaddr2	2nd line of address	61–90	30
mailcity	city	91–110	20
mailstate	state	111–112	2
mailzip	zip	113–121	9

INPUT (data sources): Source for all data is keyboard input. The operator of the program keys in all the information on each person and saves it onto the disk.

Data	Source
mailname	key entry
mailaddr1	key entry
mailaddr2	key entry

mailcity	key entry
mailstate	key entry
mailzip	key entry

HIDPUT (data in formulas): None.
LOGIC (block diagram):

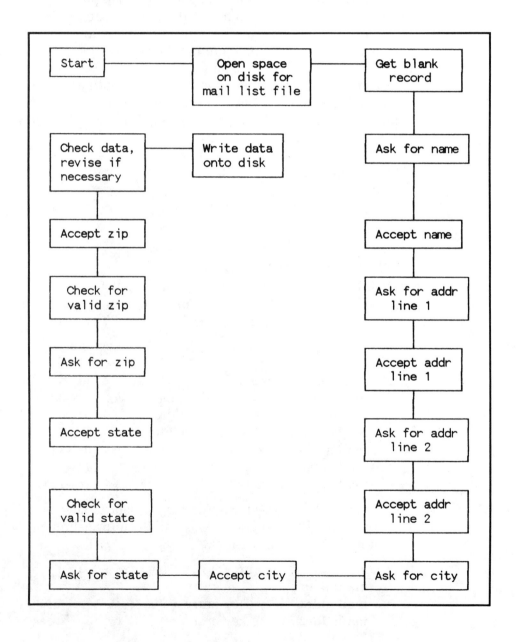

Sample Blueprint #2

PROGRAM NAME: **maillabl.**

PURPOSE: To print mailing labels for all the people in our MAIL file.

OUTPUT RESULT: One mailing label for each person.

```
CHUCK BUTKUS
1675 ROUTE 9
CLIFTON PARK   NY   12065
```

INPUT (data sources): All the data for the label is found in the file called MAIL, which is on our computer disk.

Data	Description	Source
lablname	prospect name	"mail" file
labladdr1	1st address line	"mail" file
labladdr2	2nd address line	"mail" file
lablcity	city	"mail" file
lablstate	state	"mail" file
lablzip	zip	"mail" file

HIDPUT (data in formulas): none.

LOGIC (block diagram):

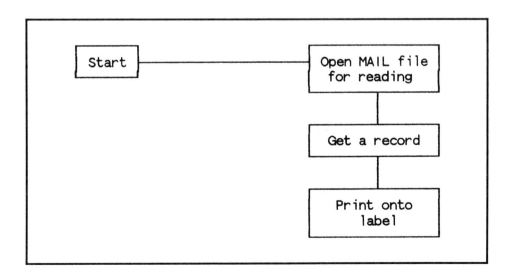

THE TEN PARTS OF THE CLASSIC PROGRAM STRUCTURE

1. **STUB**
   - Directs program flow to:
     - **DATE** routine
     - **FILEOPEN** routine
     - **MAIN** routine
   - Includes **CLOSE** statement
   - Includes **END** statement
     - (More commonly, **CHAIN**s to another program)

2. **FILEOPEN** routine
   - Opens all files
   - Establishes the layout of each file

3. **MAIN CONTROL** routine
   - Calls **FILEREAD**, **MASSAGE**, **CALC/SUBCALC**, and **OUT** routines

4. **FILEREAD** routine
   - Reads files
   - Unpacks information

5. **MASSAGE** routines
   - Any commonplace tasks that format or handle data
     - E.g., errors, input, date, etc.

6. **CALC** routine
   - Changes data
   - Produces value to be saved or displayed
   - (Optionally) calls **SUBCALC** routines

7. **SUBCALC** routines
   - Detailed calculations

8. **SCREENOUT** routine
   - Outputs information to screen

9. **PRINTOUT** routine

   - Outputs information to printer

10. **FILEOUT** routine

   - Outputs changed data back to files

RULES FOR PROGRAM STRUCTURE

1. Always use the standard **STUB**. The **STUB** is the same for every program. No new control statements go into it. ONLY THE DATA DICTIONARY DEFINITIONS OF THE VARIABLE NAMES SHOULD EVER BE ADDED. If there are no tables (an unusual program), the **GOSUB** to **DIMARRAYS** should have an **REM** in front of it. OTHER THAN THAT, THE **STUB** SHOULD NEVER CHANGE.

2. Every program should contain exactly ONE **FILEOPEN** routine, whether there are a dozen files in the program or none. ALL **OPEN**s SHOULD BE IN THIS ROUTINE. If no files are to be opened, then leave the subroutine itself with only a blank **REM**ark and a **RETURN** statement.

3. Each file that is read should have ITS OWN **FILEREAD** ROUTINE. This routine gets and unpacks one record each time it is summoned. If you have six files, then have six **FILEREAD** routines.

4. The **MAIN CONTROL** DOES NO WORK ITSELF. It just serves as the major loop, which controls getting data, processing it, and outputting it. Its function is to control all the **READ**s, **CALC**s and **WRITE**s (or **PRINT**s). Therefore, no tasks from your blueprint are assigned to **MAIN CONTROL.**

5. ALL **PRINT** tasks go to **PRINTOUT** routines. All SCREEN tasks go to **SCREENOUT** routines. Usually, one master routine for each different screen layout or printed page layout is a good idea. Each of the master routines may or may not have several other routines that it controls.

6. Each file that is written should have its own **FILEOUT** routine, with several minor routines if needed.

7. The **CALC** routine controls calculations and the movement of data. It is called from **MAIN CONTROL. SUBCALC**s, which do the actual calculations, are controlled by either the **CALC** routine or the **OUT** routines (**SCREENOUT, PRINTOUT,** or **FILEOUT**), whichever works more easily in your program. Assign calculation and data movement tasks to the **SUBCALC**s and don't worry about what controls the **SUBCALC**s until the very end. Do what works most easily in your program.
8. **MASSAGE** routines are almost always procedures that do some specific operation (massaging) on a certain type of data. They can be used many times in the same program and are usually worth saving for use in other programs.

STEPS IN CONVERTING A BLUEPRINT INTO A ROUTINE

1. Write each step of your blueprint down the left side of a piece of paper.
2. Using rules 1–8 above, assign each task to a routine.
3. You know you'll always have one **STUB,** one **FILEOPEN,** one **FILEREAD** for each file read, one **FILEOUT** for each file written, and one **MAIN CONTROL,** so...
4. Get another sheet of paper and group the tasks by each type of **SUBCALC** and **OUT** routine.
5. When you are all done, decide how many routines of each type you want, or whether you want to group several tasks into one routine.
6. Decide whether you want the **SUBCALC**s controlled by one major **CALC** or by the **OUT** routines.
7. You now have a program structure.

Appendix E

Sample Routines

1. The Error Routine (It's a Procedure)

```
SUB printerr (e$,r%,c%):  REM -- e$ is the error message
                          REM -- r% is the line number, and
                          REM -- c% is the column number
                          REM -- at which to locate.
   PRINT CHR$(7); e$; TAB(79);"":REM -- ring the bell &
                          REM -- print error message
   LOCATE r%,c%:REM -- set the cursor at the original location
END SUB
```

2. The Numeric Testing Routine (It's Also a Procedure)

```
SUB numtest (n$,lgth%,e%):REM -- n$ is the data, lgth% is the
                          REM -- length of the data item, and
                          REM -- e% is an error flag (0 = no error,
                          REM -- 1 = error)
   e% = 0:REM -- set the error flag to 0 (no error)
   FOR i% = 1 TO lgth%:REM -- set up a loop to check for numeric
   IF ASC(MID$(n$,i%,1))<48 THEN e% = 1:REM -- test for <0
   IF ASC(MID$(n$,i%,1))>57 THEN e% = 1:REM -- test for >9,
   NEXT i%
END SUB
```

3. The Date Testing Routine (Also a Procedure)

```
SUB datest (dat$,lgth%,e%):REM -- dat$ is the date, lgth% is the
                          REM -- length of the date, and
                          REM -- e% is an error flag
                          REM -- (0 = no error, 1 = error)
```

```
    e% = 1:REM -- set error flag to 1 (we're assuming that until the
            REM -- date passes all the tests, an error has been
            REM -- found).
    IF lgth%<5 THEN GOTO quitdate:REM -- if the length <5 then
                                 REM -- leave the procedure with
                                 REM -- the error flag e% set
                                 REM -- to an error
    IF lgth% = 5 THEN dat$ = "0" + dat$:REM -- make it a six-character
                                        REM -- field
    w1% = VAL(LEFT$(dat$,2)):REM -- get the month
    IF w1%<1 THEN GOTO quitdate
    IF w1%>12 THEN GOTO quitdate
    w2% = VAL(MID$(dat$,3,2)):REM -- get the day
    IF w2%<1 THEN GOTO quitdate
    IF w2%>31 THEN GOTO quitdate
    w3% = VAL(RIGHT$(dat$,2)):REM -- get the year
    IF w3%>93 THEN GOTO quitdate
    e% = 0:REM -- reset error flag to 0 (no errors found)
    quitdate:
    REM -- just a label to go to
END SUB
```

4. Procedure to Convert Lower Case to Upper Case

```
SUB upper(i$): REM i$ is the string to be converted
  l% = LEN(i$)
  FOR i% = 1 TO l%
    w1% = ASC(MID$(i$,i%,1))
    IF w1% > 96 THEN
      IF w1% <123 THEN
      MID$(i$,i%,1) = CHR$(w1%-32)
    END IF
  NEXT i%
END SUB
```

5. Procedure to Test for Number of Days in a Month

```
SUB MOTEST(d,e%): REM -- d is the date, in MMDDYY format, and
  e% is the error indicator (0 = ok, 1 = days are greater than
  allowed for that month)
  moda = INT(d/100)
  mo = INT (moda/100)
```

```
da = moda MOD 100
e% = 0
IF da >31 THEN
  e% = 1
  goto endmotest
END IF
IF mo = 2 THEN
  IF da >29 THEN
  e% = 1
  goto endmotest
END IF
IF mo = 4 THEN GOTO thirty
IF mo = 6 THEN GOTO thirty
IF mo = 9 THEN GOTO thirty
IF mo = 11 THEN GOTO thirty
thirtyone:
  IF da > 31 THEN e% = 1
  GOTO endmotest
thirty:
  IF da > 30 THEN e% = 1
endmotest:
END SUB
```

6. Procedure to Check for a Minus Sign and a Decimal Point in a Number

```
SUB numtest (n$,lgth%,e%):REM -- n$ is the data, lgth% is the
                          REM -- length of the data item, and
                          REM -- e% is an error flag (0 = no error,
                          REM -- 1 = error)
e% = 0:REM -- set the error flag to 0 (no error)
w2% = 0:REM -- set decimal point counter to 0
FOR i% = 1 TO lgth%:REM -- set up a loop to check for numeric
  w1% = ASC(MID$(n$,i%,1))
  IF i% = 1 THEN
    IF w1% = 45 THEN
    GOTO nexti
  END IF
  IF w1% = 46 THEN w2% = w2% + 1: GOTO nexti
  IF w1% < 48 THEN e% = 1:REM -- test for <0
  IF w1% > 57 THEN e% = 1:REM -- test for >9
```

```
nexti:
  NEXT i%
  IF w2% > 1 THEN e% = 1
END SUB
```

7. Date Conversion (from MMDDYY into YYMMDD) Procedure

```
SUB chgdat(d,d1)
  REM the date is in variable name d, the converted date in d1
  d$ = STR$(d):REM -- convert d to a string
  w$ = MID$(d$,2):REM -- get rid of blank sign character
  d$ = w$:REM -- move it back into d$
  IF LEN(w$)<6 then d$ = "0" + w$:REM -- make it 6 characters
  w$ = RIGHT$(d$,2) + LEFT$(d$,2) + MID$(d$,3,2)
  REM -- convert the string into YYMMDD format
  d1 = val(w$):REM -- convert it into a number
END SUB
```

8. Elapsed Days Procedure

```
SUB elapsdays (dat1,dat2,elap)
  REM -- dat1 and dat2 are the dates, elap is the elapsed days
  CALL chgdat (dat1,d1)
  CALL chgdat (dat2,d2)
  w$ = MID$(STR$(d1), 2): REM -- make 1st date a string
  w1$ = LEFT$(w$, 2): REM -- get the year of 1st date
  w2$ = MID$(w$, 3, 2): REM -- get the month of 1st date
  w3$ = RIGHT$(w$, 2): REM -- get the day of 1st date
  x1 = VAL(w1$)
  x2 = VAL(w2$)
  x3 = VAL(w3$): REM -- change year, month, and day of 1st date into separate numbers
  w$ = MID$(STR$(d2), 2): REM -- make 2nd date a string
  w1$ = LEFT$(w$, 2): REM -- get the year of 2nd date
  w2$ = MID$(w$, 3, 2): REM -- get the month of 2nd date
  w3$ = RIGHT$(w$, 2): REM -- get the day of 2nd date
  x4 = VAL(w1$)
  x5 = VAL(w2$)
  x6 = VAL(w3$): REM change 2nd date into separate numbers
  w1 = x1 - x4: REM -- subtract the years
  w2 = x2 - x5: REM -- subtract the months
  w3 = x3 - x6: REM -- subtract the days
```

```
IF w3 < 0 THEN
   w3 = w3 + 30
   w2 = w2 - 1
END IF: REM -- if days < 0, add 30 to the days, and subtract 1 from the month
IF w2 < 0 THEN
   w2 = w2 + 12
   w1 = w1 - 1
END IF: REM -- if months < 0, add 12 to the months, and subtract 1 from the year
elaps = w1 * 365 + w2 * 30 + w3: REM -- sum the days
END SUB
```

9. Create a Date Table

```
setmonths:
   DIM motab(12)
   DATA 31,29,31,30,31,30,31,31,30,31,30,31
   FOR i% = 1 TO 12
   READ motab(i%)
   NEXT i%
RETURN
```

Appendix F

Answers to Exercises

CHAPTER 2 EXERCISES

1. getnext:
```
    INPUT"Key in the first number ";num1
    INPUT"Key in the second number ";num2
    INPUT"Key in the third number ";num3
    INPUT"Key in the fourth number ";num4
    INPUT"Key in the fifth number ";num5
    INPUT"Key in the sixth number ";num6
    avg = (num1 + num2 + num3 + num4 + num5 + num6)/6
    print num1;num2;num3;num4;num5;num6" **** ";avg
    GOTO getnext
```

2.
```
    REM -- program "firsmenu.bas" -- created 010189
    GOSUB printmenu : REM -- perform the print routine

    INPUT "Number from menu"; menuselect$ : REM -- Step #2 Asks for the selection
    program$ = "bikes" + menuselect$ :REM -- form the program name
    PRINT "Selecting program "; program$
    CHAIN program$ : REM -- Step #3-runs that program
    END
printmenu:
    REM -- (Step #1- displays the menu)
    CLS : REM -- clear the screen
    PRINT "********** BIKES PEAK **********"
    PRINT "********** PROGRAMS **********"
    FOR c = 1 TO 5: PRINT: NEXT c : REM -- space 5 lines
    PRINT "1 Inventory"
```

```
PRINT "2 Customers"
PRINT "3 Mail List"
PRINT "4 Order Processing"
PRINT "5 Monthlies"
PRINT "6 Special Sales"
PRINT "7 Service Bulletins"
PRINT "8 Forecasting"
FOR c = 1 TO 4: PRINT: NEXT c : REM -- space 4 lines
RETURN
```

CHAPTER 3 EXERCISES

1. Type in and run Exercise 1 in chapter 2 above.
2. Type in and run Exercise 2 in chapter 2 above.

CHAPTER 4 EXERCISES

1. Blueprint of **new customer program** is:

> PROGRAM NAME: **newcust**
> PURPOSE: To key in all the data for a new customer.
> OUTPUT: File on disk, containing 1,000 customers. The name of the file is "cust.dat". The description is. . .

Data Name	Description	Location in File	Maximum Length
custnum	Customer number	1−4	4
custlname	Last name	5−24	20
custfname	First name	25−39	15
custaddr1	Address line 1	40−69	30
custaddr2	Address line 2	70−99	30
custcity	City	100−119	20
custstate	State	120−121	2
custzip	Zipcode	122−130	9
custphone	Phone	131−140	10
custtype	Type	141−141	1

custnotes	Notes	142–191	50
custsince	Customer since (date)	192–197	6
custlastmail	Last mailing (date)	198–203	6
custlastpurch	Last purchase	204–209	6
custthisyr	Purchases this year	210–217	8
custlastyr	Purchases last year	218–225	8
custk1bikes	Number of K1 purchases	226–227	2
custk2bikes	Number of K2 purchases	228–229	2
custk3bikes	Number of K3 purchases	230–231	2
custk1dols	Dollar value of K1 purchases	232–239	8
custk2dols	Dollar value of K2 purchases	240–247	8
custk3dols	Dollar value of K3 purchases	248–255	8

INPUT

Data Name	Source
custnum	record number
custlname	Key entry
custfname	Key entry
custaddr1	Key entry
custaddr2	Key entry
custcity	Key entry
custstate	Key entry
custzip	Key entry
custphone	Key entry
custtype	Key entry
custnotes	Key entry
custsince	Key entry
custlastmail	Mailing program puts it there
custlastpurch	Sales entry program puts it there
custthisyr	Calculation in sales entry program
custlastyr	Moved at end of year (hidput)
custk1bikes	Calculation in sales entry program

For your info only (brace covering custlastmail through custk1bikes)

custk2bikes	Calculation in sales entry program
custk3bikes	Calculation in sales entry program
custk1dols	Calculation in sales entry program
custk2dols	Calculation in sales entry program
custk3dols	Calculation in sales entry program

For your info only

HIDPUT: **custlastyr** data comes from the data name **custthisyr**. At the end of each year, a special program is run, which moves **custthisyr** to **custlastyr** and gives **custthisyr** a value of 0. This program also gives a value of 0 to the K1, K2, and K3 number and dollar fields (the last six). In this way the new year begins with these fields at 0, and last year's fields keep the historical data. Then, as sales are entered during the new year, the fields are added to.

LOGIC (block diagram):

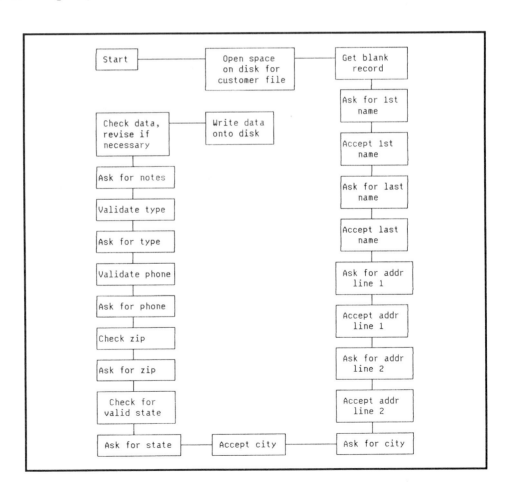

2. Blueprint of **lookup customer program** is:

PROGRAM NAME: **lookcust**
PURPOSE: To look at all the data for a customer.
OUTPUT: Screen display of the customer file.
INPUT: Customer file.
LOGIC (block diagram):

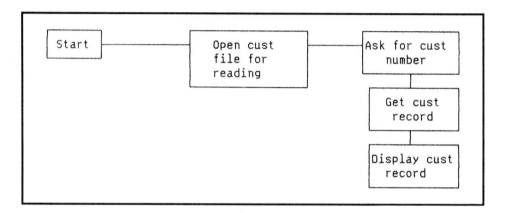

CHAPTER 5 EXERCISES

1. No right answers—just check your names against the rules.
2. Blueprint of **new inventory program** is:

PROGRAM NAME: **newinvn**
PURPOSE: To key in all the data for a new inventory item.
OUTPUT: File on disk, containing 1,000 parts. The name of the
file is "part.dat". The description is. . .

Data Name	Description	Location In File	Maximum Length
partnum	Part number	1–4	4
partdesc	Part description	5–34	30
partretail	Retail price	35–40	6
partdealer	Dealer price	41–46	6
partcost	Cost	47–52	6

partonhand	On hand	53–57	5
partminqty	Minimum quantity to be stocked	58–62	5
partlastcnt	Date of last count	63–68	6
partonorder	Number of items on order	69–73	5
partorderdat	Date of last order	74–79	6
partsales1	Number of sales Jan	80–84	5
partsales2	Number of sales Feb	85–89	5
partsales3	Number of sales Mar	90–94	5
partsales4	Number of sales Apr	95–99	5
partsales5	Number of sales May	100–104	5
partsales6	Number of sales Jun	105–109	5
partsales7	Number of sales Jul	110–114	5
partsales8	Number of sales Aug	115–119	5
partsales9	Number of sales Sep	120–124	5
partsales10	Number of sales Oct	125–129	5
partsales11	Number of sales Nov	130–134	5
partsales12	Number of sales Dec	135–139	5

INPUT:

Data Name	Source
partnum	record number
partdesc	Key entry
partretail	Key entry
partdealer	Key entry
partcost	Key entry
partonhand	Key entry
partminqty	Key entry
partlastcnt	Key entry
partonorder	Key entry
partorderdat	Key entry
partsales1	Sales entry program puts it there
partsales2	Sales entry program puts it there
partsales3	Sales entry program puts it there
partsales4	Sales entry program puts it there
partsales5	Sales entry program puts it there
partsales6	Sales entry program puts it there
partsales7	Sales entry program puts it there
partsales8	Sales entry program puts it there
partsales9	Sales entry program puts it there

partsales10	Sales entry program puts it there
partsales11	Sales entry program puts it there
partsales12	Sales entry program puts it there

LOGIC (block diagram):

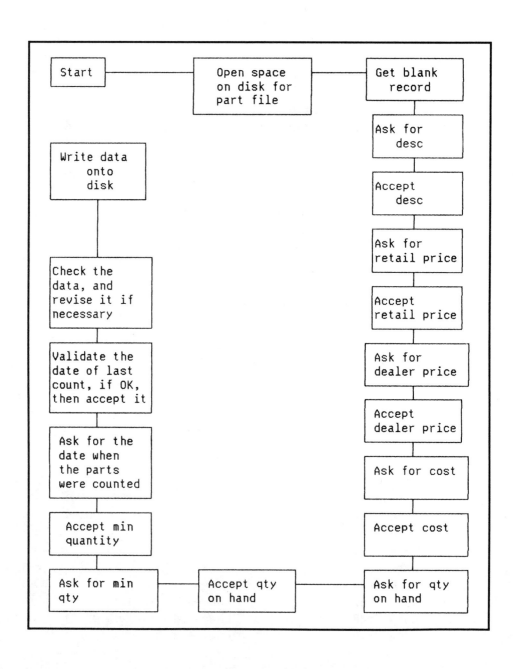

3. Blueprint of **lookup part program** is:

PROGRAM NAME: **lookpart**
PURPOSE: To look at all the data for a part.
OUTPUT: Screen display of the part file.
INPUT: Part file.
LOGIC (block diagram):

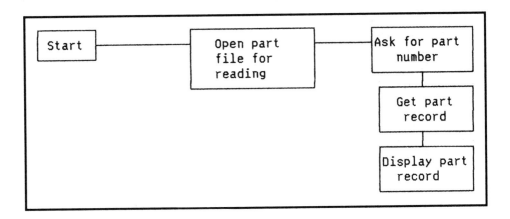

CHAPTER 6 EXERCISES

1. Form the program structure for **mailkey1**.

Steps 1 and 2

Task	Routine
Open space	**FILEOPEN**
Get blank record	**FILEREAD**
Ask for name	**SUBCALC1**
Accept name	**SUBCALC1**
Ask for address line 1	**SUBCALC1**
Accept address line 1	**SUBCALC1**
Ask for address line 2	**SUBCALC1**
Accept address line 2	**SUBCALC1**
Ask for city	**SUBCALC1**
Accept city	**SUBCALC1**
Ask for state	**SUBCALC1**

Validate state	**SUBCALC1**
Accept state	**SUBCALC1**
Ask for zip	**SUBCALC1**
Validate zip	**SUBCALC1**
Accept zip	**SUBCALC1**
Check data, revise if necessary	**CALC**
Write data onto disk	**FILEOUT**

Steps 3 and 4
Aren't needed here, because the tasks are already grouped by routine.

Step 5
We decided to have one **SUBCALC** routine, because this is a simple program.

Step 6
We will have the **SUBCALC** routine controlled by one CALC routine.

Step 7
The program structure for **mailkey1** is:

STUB
FILEOPEN
FILEREAD
MAIN
CALC
SUBCALC
FILEOUT

2(a). Form the program structure for **newcust**.

Steps 1 and 2

Task	Routine
Open space	**FILEOPEN**
Get blank record	**FILEREAD**
Ask for last name	**SUBCALC1**
Accept last name	**SUBCALC1**

Ask for first name	**SUBCALC1**
Accept first name	**SUBCALC1**
Ask for address line 1	**SUBCALC1**
Accept address line 1	**SUBCALC1**
Ask for address line 2	**SUBCALC1**
Accept address line 2	**SUBCALC1**
Ask for city	**SUBCALC1**
Accept city	**SUBCALC1**
Ask for state	**SUBCALC1**
Validate state	**SUBCALC1**
Accept state	**SUBCALC1**
Ask for zip	**SUBCALC1**
Validate zip	**SUBCALC1**
Accept zip	**SUBCALC1**
Ask for phone	**SUBCALC1**
Validate phone	**SUBCALC1**
Accept phone	**SUBCALC1**
Ask for type	**SUBCALC1**
Validate type	**SUBCALC1**
Accept type	**SUBCALC1**
Ask for notes	**SUBCALC1**
Accept notes	**SUBCALC1**
Ask for customer since date	**SUBCALC1**
Validate customer since date	**SUBCALC1**
Accept customer since date	**SUBCALC1**
Check data, revise if necessary	**CALC**
Write data onto disk	**FILEOUT**

Steps 3 and 4

Aren't needed here, because the tasks are already grouped by routine.

Step 5

We decided to have one **SUBCALC** routine, because this is a simple program and the data belongs together.

Step 6

We will have the **SUBCALC** routine controlled by one **CALC** routine.

Step 7

The program structure for **newcust** is:

STUB
FILEOPEN
FILEREAD
MAIN
CALC
SUBCALC
FILEOUT

2(b). Structure is in the block diagram.
3. Type in the **STUB** and save it.
4(a). Form the program structure for **newpart**.

Steps 1 and 2

Task	Routine
Open space	**FILEOPEN**
Get blank record	**FILEREAD**
Ask for description	**SUBCALC1**
Accept description	**SUBCALC1**
Ask for retail price	**SUBCALC1**
Accept retail price	**SUBCALC1**
Ask for dealer price	**SUBCALC1**
Accept dealer price	**SUBCALC1**
Ask for cost	**SUBCALC1**
Accept cost	**SUBCALC1**
Ask for on hand	**SUBCALC1**
Accept on hand	**SUBCALC1**
Ask for minimum quantity	**SUBCALC1**
Accept minimum quantity	**SUBCALC1**
Ask for last count date	**SUBCALC1**
Validate last count date	**SUBCALC1**
Accept last count date	**SUBCALC1**
Check data, revise if necessary	**CALC**
Write data onto disk	**FILEOUT**

Steps 3 and 4

Aren't needed here, because the tasks are already grouped by routine.

Step 5

We decided to have one **SUBCALC** routine.

Step 6

We will have the **SUBCALC** routine controlled by one **CALC** routine.

Step 7

The program structure for **newpart** is:

    STUB
    FILEOPEN
    FILEREAD
    MAIN
    CALC
    SUBCALC
    FILEOUT

4(b). Structure is in the block diagram.

CHAPTER 7 EXERCISES

1. | | |
   |---|---|
   | **STUB** | Main routine |
   | **FILEOPEN** | Subroutine |
   | **FILEREAD** | Subroutine |
   | **MAIN** | Subroutine |
   | **CALC** | Subroutine |
   | **SUBCALC** | Subroutine |
   | **FILEOUT** | Subroutine |

2. | | |
   |---|---|
   | **STUB** | Main routine |
   | **FILEOPEN** | Subroutine |
   | **FILEREAD** | Subroutine |
   | **MAIN** | Subroutine |
   | **CALC** | Subroutine |
   | **SUBCALC** | Subroutine |
   | **FILEOUT** | Subroutine |

3. Blueprint of program to **calculate and print** is:

PROGRAM NAME: **calcprin**
PURPOSE: To average any three numbers and print out the result.

OUTPUT: A printed line for each calculation, giving all three numbers and their average.
INPUT: Keyboard.
LOGIC: (block diagram)

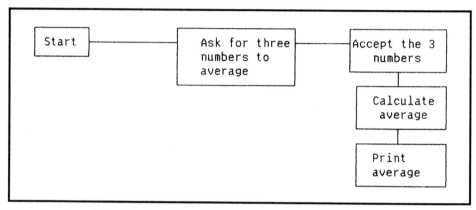

(The structure is in the logic.)

```
REM -- calcprint 10190
GOSUB main
CLOSE
END
main:
nextcalc:
    INPUT "Key in the first number";i1
    IF i1 = 999999 THEN RETURN
    INPUT "Key in the second number";i2
    IF i2 = 999999 THEN RETURN
    INPUT "Key in the third number";i3
    IF i3 = 999999 THEN RETURN
    CALL calcavg(i1,i2,i3,i4)
    CALL prinavg(i1,i2,i3,i4)
    GOTO nextcalc
RETURN
SUB calcavg (i1,i2,i3,i4)
    i4 = (i1 + i2 + i3) / 3
END SUB
SUB prinavg (p1,p2,p3,p4)
    LPRINT "Average of "; p1;", "; p2;", "; p3;" is "; p4
END SUB
```

CHAPTER 8 EXERCISES

Practice with PowerBASIC.

CHAPTER 9 EXERCISES

1. **IF** statements for **newcust** program.

   ```
   IF LEN(custnum$) > 4 THEN PRINT "Too long"
   IF LEN(custlname$) > 20 THEN PRINT "Too long"
   IF LEN(custfname$) > 15 THEN PRINT "Too long"
   IF LEN(custaddr1$) > 30 THEN PRINT "Too long"
   IF LEN(custaddr2$) > 30 THEN PRINT "Too long"
   IF LEN(custcity$) > 20 THEN PRINT "Too long"
   IF LEN(custstate$) > 2 THEN PRINT "Too long"
   IF LEN(custzip$) > 9 THEN PRINT "Too long"
   IF LEN(custphone$) > 10 THEN PRINT "Too long"
   IF LEN(custtype$) > 1 THEN PRINT "Too long"
   IF LEN(custnotes$) > 50 THEN PRINT "Too long"
   IF LEN(custsince$) > 6 THEN PRINT "Too long"
   ```

2. **IF** statements for **newpart** program.

   ```
   IF LEN(partnum$) > 4 THEN PRINT "Too long"
   IF LEN(partdesc$) > 30 THEN PRINT "Too long"
   IF LEN(partretail$) > 6 THEN PRINT "Too long"
   IF LEN(partdealer$) > 6 THEN PRINT "Too long"
   IF LEN(partcost$) > 6 THEN PRINT "Too long"
   IF LEN(partonhand$) > 5 THEN PRINT "Too long"
   IF LEN(partminqty$) > 5 THEN PRINT "Too long"
   IF LEN(partlastcnt$) > 6 THEN PRINT "Too long"
   ```

3.
   ```
   IF custtype <1 THEN PRINT" Bad customer type"
   IF custtype >3 THEN PRINT" Bad customer type"
   ```

    4. IF partcost <.05 THEN PRINT "Cost too low"
        IF partcost >1000 THEN PRINT "Cost too high"

CHAPTER 10 EXERCISES

---

1. Main control loop for **newcust**.

```
main:
nextcust:
     CLS
     GOSUB getcust: REM -- file read
     IF i$ = "end" THEN RETURN
     GOSUB dispcust: REM -- screenout
     GOSUB getdatain: REM -- calc
     GOSUB putcust: REM -- fileout
     GOTO nextcust
     RETURN
```

2. Main control loop for **newpart**.

```
main:
nextpart:
     CLS
     GOSUB getpart: REM -- file read
     IF i$ = "end" THEN RETURN
     GOSUB disppart: REM -- screenout
     GOSUB getdatain: REM -- calc
     GOSUB putpart: REM -- fileout
     GOTO nextpart
     RETURN
```

3. Main control loop for **partvalu**.

```
main:
nextpart:
     GOSUB getpart: REM -- file read
     IF i$ = "end" THEN RETURN
```

```
CALL calcvalu(partonhand, partcost, totcost#): REM -- calc
GOSUB disppart: REM -- printout
GOTO nextpart
RETURN
```

4. Loop to total the sales.

```
totsales = 0
FOR i%=1 TO 12
    totsales = totsales + partsales(i%)
NEXT i%
```

5. Procedure to calculate inventory value.

```
SUB calcvalu (qty,cost,totcost#)
    partvalu# = qty * cost
    totcost = totcost# + partvalu#
END SUB
```

CHAPTER 11 EXERCISES

1. Bowling team file layout (one of many).

Data Name	Description	Location in File	Packed Length
bowlnum	Bowler number	1–3	3
bowllname$	Last name	4–23	20
bowlfname$	First name	24–38	15
bowldayphone	Day number	39–48	10
bowlnitephone	Night phone	49–58	10
bowllastavg	Average last year	59–62	4
bowlthisavg	Average this year	63–66	4
bowllastwk	Average last week	67–70	4
bowlhigh	High game this year	71–74	4
bowllow	Low game this year	75–78	4

2. Payroll file layout (one of many).

Data Name	Description	Location in File	Packed Length
paynum	Payer number	1–3	3
paylname$	Last name	4–23	20
payfname$	First name	24–38	15
paywkphone	Work phone	39–48	10
payhomephone	Night phone	49–58	10
paywkrate	Weekly pay	59–62	4
paydeps	Number of dependents	63–66	4
paygrossweek	Gross pay last week	67–70	4
paynetweek	Net pay last week	71–74	4
payficaweek	FICA(Social Security) last week	75–78	4
payfedweek	Federal tax paid last week	79–82	4
paystweek	State tax paid last week	83–86	4
paygrossytd	Gross pay year-to-date	87–94	8
paynetytd	Net pay year-to-date	95–102	8
payficaytd	Year-to-date FICA	103–110	8
payfedytd	Year-to-date federal tax paid	111–118	8
paystytd	Year-to-date state tax paid	119–126	8

3. Major possessions file layout.

Data Name	Description	Location In File	Packed Length
possnum	Possession number	1–4	4
possdesc	Possession description	5–34	30
possprice	Purchase price	35–42	8
possdate	Date purchased	43–48	6
possvalu	Current value	49–56	8
possloc	Location	57–58	2
possinsvalu	Insured amount	59–66	8
posslastcnt	Date of last valuation	67–72	6

CHAPTER 12 EXERCISES

1. **OPEN** statement for CUST file is:

   OPEN "r", 1, "cust.dat", 256

   OPEN statement for PART file is:

   OPEN "r", 1, "part.dat", 256

2. **FIELD** statement for CUST file is:

   FIELD 1, 2 AS custnum$, 20 AS custlname$, 15 AS custfname$, 30__
   AS custaddr1$, 30 AS custaddr2$, 20 AS custcity$, 2 AS__
   custstate$, 9 AS custzip$, 8 AS custphone$, 1 AS custtype$, 50__
   AS custnotes$, 4 AS custsince$, 4 AS custlastmail$, 4 AS__
   custlastpurch$
   FIELD 1, 199 AS custfill1$, 8 AS custthisyr$, 8 AS custlastyr$,__
   2 AS custbikes$(1), 2 AS custbikes$(2), 2 AS custbikes$(3), 8__
   AS custbikedol$(1), 8 AS custbikedol$(2), 8 AS custbikedol$(3)

3. **FIELD** statement for PART file is:

   FIELD 1, 2 AS partnum$, 30 AS partdesc$, 4 AS partretail$, 4 AS__
   partdealer$, 4 AS partcost$, 4 AS partonhand$, 4 AS__
   partminqty$, 4 AS partlastcnt$, 4 AS partonorder$, 4 AS__
   partorderdat$, 4 as partsales1$, 4 AS partsales2$
   FIELD 1, 72 AS partfill1$, 4 AS partsales3$, 4 AS partsales4$,__
   4 AS partsales5$, 4 AS partsales6$, 4 AS partsales7$, 4 AS__
   partsales8$, 4 AS partsales9$, 4 AS partsales10$, 4 AS__
   partsales11$, 4 AS partsales12$

4. UNPACK statements for CUST file are:

   custnum% = CVI(custnum$)
   custphone# = CVD(custphone$)
   custsince = CVS(custsince$)
   custlastmail = CVS(custlastmail$)
   custlastpurch = CVS(custlastpurch$)

```
custthisyr# = CVD(custthisyr$)
custlastyr# = CVD(custlastyr$)
FOR i% = 1 TO 3
  custbikes(i%) = CVI(custbikes$(i%))
  custbikedol#(i%) = CVD(custbikedol$(i%))
NEXT i%
```

5. UNPACK statements for PART file are:

```
partnum% = CVI(partnum$)
partretail = CVS(partretail$)
partdealer = CVS(partdealer$)
partcost = CVS(partcost$)
partonhand = CVS(partonhand$)
partminqty = CVS(partminqty$)
partlastcnt = CVS(partlastcnt$)
partonorder = CVS(partonorder$)
partorderdat = CVS(partorderdat$)
partsales1 = CVS(partsales1$)
partsales2 = CVS(partsales2$)
partsales3 = CVS(partsales3$)
partsales4 = CVS(partsales4$)
partsales5 = CVS(partsales5$)
partsales6 = CVS(partsales6$)
partsales7 = CVS(partsales7$)
partsales8 = CVS(partsales8$)
partsales9 = CVS(partsales9$)
partsales10 = CVS(partsales10$)
partsales11 = CVS(partsales11$)
partsales12 = CVS(partsales12$)
```

6. Program to create a blank Bikes Peak customer file (CUST).

```
REM -- creacust
GOSUB fileopen
GOSUB main
CLOSE
END
fileopen:
DIM custbike$(3), custbike%(3), custbikedol$(3), custbikedol#(3)
OPEN "r", 1, "cust.dat", 256
FIELD 1, 2 AS custnum$, 20 AS custlname$, 15 AS custfname$, 30
```

```
            AS custaddr1$, 30 AS custaddr2$, 20 AS custcity$, 2 AS__
            custstate$, 9 AS custzip$, 8 AS custphone$, 1 AS custtype$, 50_
            AS custnotes$, 4 AS custsince$, 4 AS custlastmail$, 4 AS__
            custlastpurch$
            FIELD 1, 199 AS custfill1$, 8 AS custthisyr$, 8 AS custlastyr$,_
            2 AS custbikes$(1), 2 AS custbikes$(2), 2 AS custbikes$(3), 8_
            AS custbikedol$(1), 8 AS custbikedol$(2), 8 AScustbikedol$(3)
    RETURN
    main:
        GOSUB clearcus: REM -- clear the record
        FOR f1 = 1 to 100
            LSET custnum$ = MKI$(f1)
            PUT 1, f1
        NEXT f1
    RETURN
    clearcus:
        LSET custnum$ = MKI$(0)
        LSET custlname$ = " "
        LSET custfname$ = " "
        LSET custaddr1$ = " "
        LSET custaddr2$ = " "
        LSET custcity$ = " "
        LSET custstate$ = " "
        LSET custzip$ = " "
        LSET custphone$ = MKD$(0)
        LSET custtype$ = " "
        LSET custnotes$ = " "
        LSET custsince$ = MKS$(0)
        LSET custlastmail$ = MKS$(0)
        LSET custlastpurch$ = MKS$(0)
        LSET custthisyr$ = MKD$(0)
        LSET custlastyr$ = MKD$(0)
        FOR i% = 1 TO 3
            LSET custbikes$(i%) = MKI$(0)
            LSET custbikedol$(i%) = MKD(0)
        NEXT i%
    RETURN
```

7. Program to create a blank Bikes Peak part file (PART).

```
    REM -- creapart
    GOSUB fileopen
```

```
        GOSUB main
        CLOSE
        END
    fileopen:
        OPEN "r", 1, "part.dat", 256
        FIELD 1, 2 AS partnum$, 30 AS partdesc$, 4 AS partretail$, 4 AS__
        partdealer$, 4 AS partcost$, 4 AS partonhand$, 4 AS__
        partminqty$, 4 AS partlastcnt$, 4 AS partonorder$, 4 AS__
        partorderdat$, 4 as partsales1$, 4 AS partsales2$
        FIELD 1, 72 AS partfill1$, 4 AS partsales3$, 4 AS partsales4$,__
        4 AS partsales5$, 4 AS partsales6$, 4 AS partsales7$, 4 AS__
        partsales8$, 4 AS partsales9$, 4 AS partsales10$, 4 AS__
        partsales11$, 4 AS partsales12$
    RETURN
    main:
        GOSUB clearpart: REM -- clear the record
        FOR f1 = 1 to 100
            LSET partnum$ = MKI$(f1)
            PUT 1, f1
        NEXT f1
    RETURN
    clearpart:
        LSET partnum$ = MKI$(0)
        LSET partdesc$ = " "
        LSET partretail$ = MKS$(0)
        LSET partcost$ = MKS$(0)
        LSET partonhand$ = MKS$(0)
        LSET partminqty$ = MKS$(0)
        LSET partlastcnt$ = MKS$(0)
        LSET partonorder$ = MKS$(0)
        LSET partorderdat$ = MKS$(0)
        LSET partsales1$ = MKS$(0)
        LSET partsales2$ = MKS$(0)
        LSET partsales3$ = MKS$(0)
        LSET partsales4$ = MKS$(0)
        LSET partsales5$ = MKS$(0)
        LSET partsales6$ = MKS$(0)
        LSET partsales7$ = MKS$(0)
        LSET partsales8$ = MKS$(0)
        LSET partsales9$ = MKS$(0)
        LSET partsales10$ = MKS$(0)
```

```
       LSET partsales11$ = MKS$(0)
       LSET partsales12$ = MKS$(0)
     RETURN
```

CHAPTER 13 EXERCISES

1. The new customer program.

```
     REM -- newcust 010189
     GOSUB getdate
     GOSUB fileopen
     GOSUB main
     CLOSE
     END
     getdate:
     d$ = DATE$
     dat$ = LEFT$(d$, 2) + "/" + MID$(d$, 4, 2) + "/" + __
       RIGHT$(d$, 2)
     da$ = LEFT$(d$, 2) + MID$(d$, 4, 2) + RIGHT$(d$, 2)
     da = VAL(da$)
     PRINT dat$; da$, da
RETURN
fileopen:
       DIM custbike$(3), custbike%(3), custbikedol$(3), custbikedol#(3)
       OPEN "r", 1, "cust.dat", 256
       FIELD 1, 2 AS custnum$, 20 AS custlname$, 15 AS custfname$, 30 AS
       custaddr1$, 30 AS custaddr2$, 20 AS custcity$, 2 AS custst$, 9 AS__
       custzip$, 8 AS custphone$, 1 AS custtype$, 50 AS custnotes$, 4 AS__
       custsince$, 4 AS custlastmail$, 4 AS custlastpurch$
       FIELD 1, 199 AS custfill1$, 8 AS custthisyr$, 8 AS custlastyr$, 2__
       AS custbikes$(1), 2 AS custbikes$(2), 2 AS custbikes$(3), 8 AS__
       custbikedol$(1), 8 AS custbikedol$(2), 8 AS custbikedol$(3)
RETURN
errout:
       REM -- error routine
       PRINT CHR$(7); "*** error"
     RETURN
```

```
main:
  CLS
  GOSUB getcust: REM -- fileread
  IF i$ = "end" THEN RETURN
  GOSUB dispcust: REM -- screenout
  GOSUB getdatain: REM -- calc
  GOSUB putcust: REM -- fileout
  GOTO main
RETURN
getcust:
  LINE INPUT "input customer number (1-100) , or 'end' to leave__
  program "; i$
  IF i$ = "end" THEN RETURN
  f1 = VAL(i$)
  IF f1 < 1 THEN
      GOSUB errout
      GOTO getcust
  END IF
  IF f1 > 100 THEN
      GOSUB errout
      GOTO getcust
  END IF
  GET 1, f1
    custnum% = CVI(custnum$)
    custphone# = CVD(custphone$)
    custsince = CVS(custsince$)
    custlastmail = CVS(custlastmail$)
    custlastpurch = CVS(custlastpurch$)
    custthisyr# = CVD(custthisyr$)
    custlastyr# = CVD(custlastyr$)
    FOR i% = 1 TO 3
      custbikes(i%) = CVI(custbikes$(i%))
      custbikedol#(i%) = CVD(custbikedol$(i%))
    NEXT i%
  PRINT "customer name is "; custlname$; " "; custfname$
  LINE INPUT "right one, ( y or n ) "; i$
  IF i$ <> "y" THEN GOTO getcust
RETURN
dispcust:
  CLS
  PRINT custnum; TAB(8); custlname$; TAB(30); custfname$; TAB
    (50);__
```

```
            "phone"; TAB(60); custphone#
            PRINT TAB(8); custaddr2$; TAB(50); "cust since"; TAB(64);__
            custsince
            PRINT TAB(8); custaddr2$; TAB(50); "cust type"; TAB(69); custtype$
            PRINT TAB(8); custcity$; " "; custst$; " "; custzip$
            PRINT TAB(8); "** notes "; custnotes$
    RETURN
    getdatain:
        LINE INPUT "customer last name "; i$
        LSET custlname$ = i$
        LINE INPUT "customer first name "; i$
        LSET custfname$ = i$
        LINE INPUT "customer address line 1 "; i$
        LSET custaddr1$ = i$
        LINE INPUT "customer address line 2 "; i$
        LSET custaddr2$ = i$
        LINE INPUT "customer city "; i$
        LSET custcity$ = i$
        LINE INPUT "customer state "; i$
        LSET custst$ = i$
        LINE INPUT "customer zip "; i$
        LSET custzip$ = i$
        LINE INPUT "customer phone "; i$
        LSET custphone$ = MKD$(VAL(i$))
        LINE INPUT "customer type "; i$
        LSET custtype$ = i$
        LINE INPUT "notes "; i$
        LSET custnotes$ = i$
        LINE INPUT "customer since "; i$
        LSET custsince$ = MKS$(VAL(i$))
    RETURN
    putcust:
        PUT 1, f1
    RETURN
```

2. The new part program.

```
    REM -- newpart 010189
    GOSUB getdate
    GOSUB fileopen
    GOSUB main
    CLOSE
```

```
        END
        getdate:
          d$ = DATE$
          dat$ = LEFT$(d$, 2) + "/" + MID$(d$, 4, 2) + "/" + RIGHT$(d$, 2)
          da$ = LEFT$(d$, 2) + MID$(d$, 4, 2) + RIGHT$(d$, 2)
          da = VAL(da$)
          PRINT dat$; da$, da
        RETURN
        fileopen:
          OPEN "r", 1, "part.dat", 256
          FIELD 1, 2 AS partnum$, 30 AS partdesc$, 4 AS partretail$, 4 AS__
          partdealer$, 4 AS partcost$, 4 AS partonhand$, 4 AS__
          partminqty$, 4 AS partlastcnt$, 4 AS partonorder$, 4 AS__
          partorderdat$, 4 as partsales1$, 4 AS partsales2$
          FIELD 1, 72 AS partfill1$, 4 AS partsales3$, 4 AS partsales4$,__
          4 AS partsales5$, 4 AS partsales6$, 4 AS partsales7$, 4 AS__
          partsales8$, 4 AS partsales9$, 4 AS partsales10$, 4 AS__
          partsales11$, 4 AS partsales12$
        RETURN
        errout:
          REM -- error routine
          PRINT CHR$(7); "*** error"
        RETURN
        main:
          CLS
          GOSUB getpart: REM -- fileread
          IF i$ = "end" THEN RETURN
          GOSUB disppart: REM -- screenout
          GOSUB getdatain: REM -- calc
          GOSUB putpart: REM -- fileout
          GOTO main
        RETURN
        getpart:
          LINE INPUT "input part number (1-100) , or 'end' to leave program__
          "; i$
          IF i$ = "end" THEN RETURN
          f1 = VAL(i$)
          IF f1 < 1 THEN
              GOSUB errout
              GOTO getpart
          END IF
```

```
     IF f1 > 100 THEN
          GOSUB errout
          GOTO getpart
     END IF
     GET 1, f1
        partnum% = CVI(partnum$)
        partretail = CVS(partretail$)
        partdealer = CVS(partdealer$)
        partcost = CVS(partcost$)
        partonhand = CVS(partonhand$)
        partminqty = CVS(partminqty$)
        partlastcnt = CVS(partlastcnt$)
        partonorder = CVS(partonorder$)
        partorderdat = CVS(partorderdat$)
        partsales1 = CVS(partsales1$)
        partsales2 = CVS(partsales2$)
        partsales3 = CVS(partsales3$)
        partsales4 = CVS(partsales4$)
        partsales5 = CVS(partsales5$)
        partsales6 = CVS(partsales6$)
        partsales7 = CVS(partsales7$)
        partsales8 = CVS(partsales8$)
        partsales9 = CVS(partsales9$)
        partsales10 = CVS(partsales10$)
        partsales11 = CVS(partsales11$)
        partsales12 = CVS(partsales12$)
      PRINT "Part description is "; partdesc$
      LINE INPUT "right one, ( y or n ) "; i$
      IF i$ <> "y" THEN GOTO getpart
RETURN
disppart:
   CLS
   PRINT partnum; TAB(8); partdesc$; TAB(40); partretail; TAB(50);__
   partdealer; TAB(60); partcost
   PRINT TAB(8); "Onhand"; TAB(20); partonhand; TAB(40);"Minimum";__
   TAB(50);partminqty; TAB(60); "Lastcount"; TAB(70);partlastcnt
   PRINT TAB(8); "Onorder";TAB(20);partonorder; TAB(40); "Orderdate";__
   TAB(50); partorderdat
   PRINT TAB(8); "Jan"; TAB(20);partsales1
   PRINT TAB(8); "Feb"; TAB(20);partsales2
   PRINT TAB(8); "Mar"; TAB(20);partsales3
```

```
            PRINT TAB(8); "Apr"; TAB(20);partsales4
            PRINT TAB(8); "May"; TAB(20);partsales5
            PRINT TAB(8); "Jun"; TAB(20);partsales6
            PRINT TAB(8); "Jul"; TAB(20);partsales7
            PRINT TAB(8); "Aug"; TAB(20);partsales8
            PRINT TAB(8); "Sep"; TAB(20);partsales9
            PRINT TAB(8); "Oct"; TAB(20);partsales10
            PRINT TAB(8); "Nov"; TAB(20);partsales11
            PRINT TAB(8); "Dec"; TAB(20);partsales12
        RETURN
        getdatain:
            LINE INPUT "Part description"; i$
            LSET partdesc$ = i$
            LINE INPUT "Part retail price"; i$
            partretail = VAL(i$): LSET partretail$ = MKS$(partretail)
            LINE INPUT "Part dealer price"; i$
            partdealer = VAL(i$): LSET partdealer$ = MKS$(partdealer)
            LINE INPUT "Part cost"; i$
            partcost = VAL(i$): LSET partcost$ = MKS$(partcost)
            LINE INPUT "Number on hand"; i$
            partonhand = VAL(i$): LSET partonhand$ = MKS$(partonhand)
            LINE INPUT "Minimum quantity"; i$
            partminqty = VAL(i$): LSET partminqty$ = MKS$(partminqty)
            LINE INPUT "Last count"; i$
            partlastcnt = VAL(i$): LSET partlastcnt$ = MKS$(partlastcnt)
        RETURN
        putpart:
            PUT 1, f1
        RETURN
```

CHAPTER 14 EXERCISES

1(a). The **newcust** program.

```
REM -- newcust 010190
GOSUB getdate
```

```
GOSUB fileopen
GOSUB main
CLOSE
END
getdate:
  d$ = DATE$
  dat$ = LEFT$(d$, 2) + "/" + MID$(d$, 4, 2) + "/" + RIGHT$(d$, 2)
  da$ = LEFT$(d$, 2) + MID$(d$, 4, 2) + RIGHT$(d$, 2)
  da = VAL(da$)
  PRINT dat$; da$, da
RETURN
fileopen:
  DIM custbike$(3), custbike%(3), custbikedol$(3), custbikedol#(3)
  OPEN "r", 1, "cust.dat", 256
  FIELD 1, 2 AS custnum$, 20 AS custlname$, 15 AS custfname$, 30 AS__
  custaddr1$, 30 AS custaddr2$, 20 AS custcity$, 2 AS custst$, 9 AS__
  custzip$, 8 AS custphone$, 1 AS custtype$, 50 AS custnotes$, 4 AS__
  custsince$, 4 AS custlastmail$, 4 AS custlastpurch$
  FIELD 1, 199 AS custfill1$, 8 AS custthisyr$, 8 AS custlastyr$, 2__
  AS custbikes$(1), 2 AS custbikes$(2), 2 AS custbikes$(3), 8 AS__
  custbikedol$(1), 8 AS custbikedol$(2), 8 AS custbikedol$(3)
RETURN
errout:
  REM -- error routine
  PRINT CHR$(7); "*** error"
RETURN
main:
  CLS
  GOSUB getcust: REM -- fileread
  IF i$ = "end" THEN RETURN
  GOSUB dispcust: REM -- screenout
  GOSUB getdatain: REM -- calc
  GOSUB putcust: REM -- fileout
  GOTO main
RETURN
getcust:
  LINE INPUT "input customer number (1-100) , or 'end' to leave__
  program "; i$
  IF i$ = "end" THEN RETURN
  f1 = VAL(i$)
  IF f1 < 1 THEN
```

```
        GOSUB errout
        GOTO getcust
  END IF
  IF f1 > 100 THEN
        GOSUB errout
        GOTO getcust
  END IF
  GET 1, f1
    custnum% = CVI(custnum$)
    custphone# = CVD(custphone$)
    custsince = CVS(custsince$)
    custlastmail = CVS(custlastmail$)
    custlastpurch = CVS(custlastpurch$)
    custthisyr# = CVD(custthisyr$)
    custlastyr# = CVD(custlastyr$)
    FOR i% = 1 TO 3
      custbikes(i%) = CVI(custbikes$(i%))
      custbikedol#(i%) = CVD(custbikedol$(i%))
    NEXT i%
  PRINT "customer name is "; custlname$; " "; custfname$
  LINE INPUT "right one, ( y or n ) "; i$
  IF i$ <> "y" THEN GOTO getcust
RETURN
dispcust:
  CLS
  PRINT custnum; TAB(8); custlname$; TAB(30); custfname$; TAB(50);_
  "phone"; TAB(60); custphone#
  PRINT TAB(8); custaddr2$; TAB(50); "cust since"; TAB(64);_
  custsince
  PRINT TAB(8); custaddr2$; TAB(50); "cust type"; TAB(69); custtype$
  PRINT TAB(8); custcity$; " "; custst$; " "; custzip$
  PRINT TAB(8); "* * notes "; custnotes$
RETURN
getdatain:
  GOSUB getnewcust
END
getnewcust:
  y% = CSRLIN
  x% = POS(0)
getin1:
  LINE INPUT"enter customer last name"; i$
  IF LEN(i$)>15 THEN
```

```
      CALL printerr("Too long",y%,x%)
      GOTO getin1
    END IF
    PRINT TAB (79);""
    LSET custlname$ = i$
    y% = CSRLIN
    x% = POS(0)
getin2:
    LINE INPUT"enter customer first name"; i$
    IF LEN(i$)>12 THEN
      CALL printerr("Too long",y%,x%)
      GOTO getin2
    END IF
    IF LEN(i$)<1 THEN
      CALL printerr("Too short",y%,x%)
      GOTO getin1
    END IF
    PRINT TAB (79);""
    LSET custfname$=i$
    y% = CSRLIN
    x% = POS(0)
getin3:
    LINE INPUT"enter 1st customer address line"; i$
    IF LEN(i$)>30 THEN
      CALL printerr("Too long",y%,x%)
      GOTO getin3
    END IF
    IF LEN(i$)<1 THEN
      CALL printerr("Too short",y%,x%)
      GOTO getin3
    END IF
    PRINT TAB (79);""
    LSET custaddr1$ = i$
    y% = CSRLIN
    x% = POS(0)
getin4:
    LINE INPUT"enter 2nd customer address line"; i$
    IF LEN(i$)>30 THEN
      CALL printerr("Too long",y%,x%)
      GOTO getin4
    END IF
    IF LEN(i$)<1 THEN
```

```
      CALL printerr("Too short",y%,x%)
      GOTO getin4
   END IF
   PRINT TAB(79);""
   LSET custaddr2$ = i$
      y% = CSRLIN
      x% = POS(0)
getin5:
   LINE INPUT"enter customer city"; i$
   IF LEN(i$)>20 THEN
      CALL printerr("Too long",y%,x%)
      GOTO getin5
   END IF
   IF LEN(i$)<1 THEN
      CALL printerr("Too short",y%,x%)
      GOTO getin5
   END IF
   PRINT TAB (79);""
   LSET custcity$ = i$
   y% = CSRLIN
   x% = POS(0)
getin6:
   LINE INPUT"enter customer state"; i$
   IF LEN(i$)>2
      THEN CALL printerr("Too long",y%,x%)
      GOTO getin6
   END IF
   IF LEN(i$)<1 THEN
      CALL printerr("Too short",y%,x%)
      GOTO getin6
   END IF
   PRINT TAB(79);""
   LSET custstat$ = i$
   y% = CSRLIN
   x% = POS(0)
getin7:
   LINE INPUT"enter customer zip code"; i$
   i1% = LEN(i$)
   IF i1%>9 THEN
      CALL printerr("Too long",y%,x%)
      GOTO getin7
```

```
      END IF
      IF LEN(i$)<1 THEN
        CALL printerr("Too short",y%,x%)
        GOTO getin7
      END IF
      CALL numtest(i$,i1%,er%)
      IF er%>0 THEN
        CALL printerr("Not numeric",y%,x%)
        GOTO getin7
      END IF
      PRINT TAB(79);""
      LSET custzip$ = MKD$(VAL(i$))
      y% = CSRLIN
      x% = POS(0)
getin8:
      LINE INPUT"enter customer phone number"; i$
      i1% = LEN(i$)
      IF i1%>10 THEN
        CALL printerr("Too long",y%,x%)
        GOTO getin8
      END IF
      IF LEN(i$)<1 THEN
        CALL printerr( "Too short",y%,x%)
        GOTO getin8
      END IF
      CALL numtest(i$,i1%,er%)
      IF er%>0 THEN
        CALL printerr("Not numeric",y%,x%)
        GOTO getin8
      END IF
      PRINT TAB(79);""
      LSET custphone$ = MKD$(VAL(i$))
      y% = CSRLIN
      x% = POS(0)
getin9:
      LINE INPUT "enter customer type"; i$
      IF LEN(i$)>1 THEN
        CALL printerr("Too long",y%,x%)
        GOTO getin9
      END IF
      IF LEN(i$)<1 THEN
```

```
        CALL printerr("Too short",y%,x%)
        GOTO getin9
    END IF
    REM -- we have, as an example, set up two customer types, A and__
            C. A customers are dealers, and C customers are retail__
            customers.
    IF i$ = "A" THEN GOTO goodtype:REM -- if type = "A", get out
    IF i$ = "C" THEN GOTO goodtype:REM -- if type = "C", get out
    CALL printerr("Not 1 of the acceptable entries",y%,x%)
    GOTO getin9
goodtype:
        PRINT TAB (79);""
        y% = CSRLIN
        x% = POS(0)
getin10:
    LINE INPUT"enter customer notes"; i$
    IF LEN(i$)>50 THEN
        CALL printerr("Too long",y%,x%)
        GOTO getin10
    END IF
    PRINT TAB(79);""
    LSET custnotes$ = i$
    y% = CSRLIN
    x% = POS(0)
getin11:
    LINE INPUT"enter customer since date"; i$
    i1% = LEN(i$)
    IF i1%>6 THEN
        CALL printerr("Too long",y%,x%)
        GOTO getin11
    END IF
    IF LEN(i$)<1 THEN
        CALL printerr("Too short",y%,x%)
        GOTO getin11
    END IF
    CALL numtest(i$,i1%,er%)
    IF er%>0 THEN
        CALL printerr("Not numeric",y%,x%)
        GOTO getin11
    END IF
```

```
    CALL datest(i$,i1%,er%)
    IF er%>0 THEN
      CALL printerr("Bad date",y%,x%)
      GOTO getin11
    END IF
    PRINT TAB(79);""
    Custsince$ = MKS$(VAL(i$))
    RETURN
putcust:
    PUT 1, f1
RETURN
SUB numtest (n$,lgth%,e%):REM -- n$ is the data, lgth% is the
                          REM -- length of the data item, and
                          REM -- e% is an error flag (0=no error,
                          REM -- 1=error)
    e% = 0:REM -- set the error flag to 0 (no error)
    FOR i% = 1 TO lgth%:REM -- set up a loop to check for numeric
    IF ASC(MID$(n$,i%,1))<48 THEN e% = 1:REM -- test for <0
    IF ASC(MID$(n$,i%,1))>57 THEN e% = 1:REM -- test for>9
    NEXT i%
END SUB
SUB datest (dat$,lgth%,e%):REM -- dat$ is the date, lgth% is the
                          REM -- length of the date, and
                          REM -- e% is an error flag
                          REM -- (0 = no error, 1 = error)
    e% = 1:REM -- set error flag to 1 (we're assuming that until the
           REM -- date passes all the tests, an error has been
           REM -- found).
    IF lgth%<5 THEN GOTO quitdate:REM -- if the length <5 then
                                  REM -- leave the procedure with
                                  REM -- the error flag e% set
                                  REM -- to an error
    IF lgth% = 5 THEN dat$ = "0"+dat$:REM -- make it a six character
                                      REM -- field
    w1% = VAL(LEFT$(dat$,2)):REM -- get the month
    IF w1%<1 THEN GOTO quitdate
    IF w1%>12 THEN GOTO quitdate
    w2% = VAL(MID$(dat$,3,2)):REM -- get the day
    IF w2%<1 THEN GOTO quitdate
    IF w2%>31 THEN GOTO quitdate
```

```
  w3% = VAL(RIGHT$(dat$,2)):REM -- get the year
  IF w3%>90 THEN GOTO quitdate
  e% = 0:REM -- reset error flag to 0 (no errors found)
quitdate:
REM -- just a label to go to
END SUB
SUB printerr (e$,r%,c%): REM -- e$ is the error message
                         REM -- r% is the line number, and
                         REM -- c% is the column number
                         REM -- at which to locate.
  PRINT CHR$(7); e$; TAB(79);"":REM -- ring the bell &
                                 REM -- print error message
  LOCATE r%,c%:REM -- set the cursor at the original location
END SUB
```

1(b). The new part program.

```
REM -- newpart 010190
GOSUB getdate
GOSUB fileopen
GOSUB main
CLOSE
END
getdate:
  d$ = DATE$
  dat$ = LEFT$(d$, 2) + "/" + MID$(d$, 4, 2) + "/" + RIGHT$(d$, 2)
  da$ = LEFT$(d$, 2) + MID$(d$, 4, 2) + RIGHT$(d$, 2)
  da = VAL(da$)
  PRINT dat$; da$, da
RETURN
fileopen:
  OPEN "r", 1, "part.dat", 256
  FIELD 1, 2 AS partnum$, 30 AS partdesc$, 4 AS partretail$, 4 AS_
  partdealer$, 4 AS partcost$, 4 AS partonhand$, 4 AS_
  partminqty$, 4 AS partlastcnt$, 4 AS partonorder$, 4 AS_
  partorderdat$, 4 as partsales1$, 4 AS partsales2$
  FIELD 1, 72 AS partfill1$, 4 AS partsales3$, 4 AS partsales4$,_
  4 AS partsales5$, 4 AS partsales6$, 4 AS partsales7$, 4 AS_
  partsales8$, 4 AS partsales9$, 4 AS partsales10$, 4 AS_
  partsales11$, 4 AS partsales12$
RETURN
errout:
```

```
  REM -- error routine
  PRINT CHR$(7); "*** error"
RETURN
main:
  CLS
  GOSUB getpart: REM -- fileread
  IF i$ = "end" THEN RETURN
  GOSUB disppart: REM -- screenout
  GOSUB getdatain: REM -- process
  GOSUB putpart: REM -- fileout
  GOTO main
RETURN
getpart:
  LINE INPUT "input part number (1-100) , or 'end' to leave program
  "; i$
  IF i$ = "end" THEN RETURN
  f1 = VAL(i$)
  IF f1 < 1 THEN
      GOSUB errout
      GOTO getpart
  END IF
  IF f1 > 100 THEN
      GOSUB errout
      GOTO getpart
  END IF
  GET 1, f1
    partnum% = CVI(partnum$)
    partretail = CVS(partretail$)
    partdealer = CVS(partdealer$)
    partcost = CVS(partcost$)
    partonhand = CVS(partonhand$)
    partminqty = CVS(partminqty$)
    partlastcnt = CVS(partlastcnt$)
    partonorder = CVS(partonorder$)
    partorderdat = CVS(partorderdat$)
    partsales1 = CVS(partsales1$)
    partsales2 = CVS(partsales2$)
    partsales3 = CVS(partsales3$)
    partsales4 = CVS(partsales4$)
    partsales5 = CVS(partsales5$)
    partsales6 = CVS(partsales6$)
    partsales7 = CVS(partsales7$)
```

```
     partsales8 = CVS(partsales8$)
     partsales9 = CVS(partsales9$)
     partsales10 = CVS(partsales10$)
     partsales11 = CVS(partsales11$)
     partsales12 = CVS(partsales12$)
   PRINT "Part description is "; partdesc$
   LINE INPUT "right one, ( y or n ) "; i$
   IF i$ <> "y" THEN GOTO getpart
RETURN
disppart:
   CLS
   PRINT partnum; TAB(8); partdesc$; TAB(40); partretail; TAB(50);__
   partdealer; TAB(60); partcost
   PRINT TAB(8); "Onhand"; TAB(20); partonhand; TAB(40);"Minimum";__
   TAB(50);partminqty; TAB(60); "Lastcount"; TAB(70);partlastcnt
   PRINT TAB(8); "Onorder";TAB(20);partonorder; TAB(40); "Orderdate";__
   TAB(50); partorderdat
   PRINT TAB(8); "Jan"; TAB(20);partsales1
   PRINT TAB(8); "Feb"; TAB(20);partsales2
   PRINT TAB(8); "Mar"; TAB(20);partsales3
   PRINT TAB(8); "Apr"; TAB(20);partsales4
   PRINT TAB(8); "May"; TAB(20);partsales5
   PRINT TAB(8); "Jun"; TAB(20);partsales6
   PRINT TAB(8); "Jul"; TAB(20);partsales7
   PRINT TAB(8); "Aug"; TAB(20);partsales8
   PRINT TAB(8); "Sep"; TAB(20);partsales9
   PRINT TAB(8); "Oct"; TAB(20);partsales10
   PRINT TAB(8); "Nov"; TAB(20);partsales11
   PRINT TAB(8); "Dec"; TAB(20);partsales12
RETURN
getdatain:
   GOSUB getnewpart
RETURN
putpart:
   PUT 1, f1
RETURN
getnewpart:
   y% = CSRLIN
   x% = POS(0)
getin1:
```

```
    LINE INPUT"enter part description"; i$
    IF LEN(i$)>30 THEN
       CALL printerr("Too long",y%,x%)
    GOTO getin1
    END IF
    IF LEN(i$)<1 THEN
       CALL printerr("Too short",y%,x%).
       GOTO getin1
    END IF
    PRINT TAB (79);""
    LSET partdesc$ = i$
    y% = CSRLIN
    x% = POS(0)
getin2:
    LINE INPUT"enter retail price"; i$
    i1% = LEN(i$)
    IF LEN(i$)>7 THEN
       CALL printerr("Too long",y%,x%)
       GOTO getin2
    END IF
    IF LEN(i$)<1 THEN
       CALL printerr("Too short",y%,x%)
       GOTO getin2
    END IF
    CALL numtest(i$,i1%,er%)
    IF er%>0 THEN
       CALL printerr("Not numeric",y%,x%)
       GOTO getin2
    END IF
    PRINT TAB (79);""
    partretail = VAL(i$)
    LSET partretail$ = MKS$(partretail)
    y% = CSRLIN
    x% = POS(0)
getin3:
    LINE INPUT"enter dealer price"; i$
    i1% = LEN(i$)
    IF LEN(i$)>7 THEN
       CALL printerr("Too long",y%,x%)
       GOTO getin3
```

```
        END IF
        IF LEN(i$)<1 THEN
          CALL printerr("Too short",y%,x%)
          GOTO getin3
        END IF
        CALL numtest(i$,i1%,er%)
        IF er%>0 THEN
          CALL printerr("Not numeric",y%,x%)
          GOTO getin3
        END IF
        PRINT TAB (79);""
        partdealer = VAL(i$)
        LSET partdealer$ = MKS$(partdealer)
        y% = CSRLIN
        x% = POS(0)
getin4:
        LINE INPUT"enter part cost"; i$
        i1% = LEN(i$)
        IF LEN(i$)>7 THEN
          CALL printerr("Too long",y%,x%)
          GOTO getin4
        END IF
        IF LEN(i$)<1 THEN
          CALL printerr("Too short",y%,x%)
          GOTO getin4
        END IF
        CALL numtest(i$,i1%,er%)
        IF er%>0 THEN
          CALL printerr("Not numeric",y%,x%)
          GOTO getin4
        END IF
        PRINT TAB(79);""
        partcost = VAL(i$)
        LSET partcost$ = MKS$(partcost)
        y% = CSRLIN
        x% = POS(0)
getin5:
        LINE INPUT"enter on hand quantity"; i$
        i1% = LEN(i$)
        IF LEN(i$)>5 THEN
          CALL printerr("Too long",y%,x%)
          GOTO getin5
```

```
      END IF
      IF LEN(i$)<1 THEN
         CALL printerr("Too short",y%,x%)
         GOTO getin5
      END IF
      CALL numtest(i$,i1%,er%)
      IF er%>0 THEN
         CALL printerr("Not numeric",y%,x%)
         GOTO getin5
      END IF
      PRINT TAB (79);""
      partonhand = VAL(i$)
      LSET partonhand$ = MKS$(partonhand)
      y% = CSRLIN
      x% = POS(0)
getin6:
      LINE INPUT"enter minimum quantity"; i$
      i1% = LEN(i$)
       IF LEN(i$)>5
         THEN CALL printerr("Too long",y%,x%)
         GOTO getin6
      END IF
      IF LEN(i$)<1 THEN
         CALL printerr("Too short",y%,x%)
         GOTO getin6
      END IF
      CALL numtest(i$,i1%,er%)
      IF er%>0 THEN
         CALL printerr("Not numeric",y%,x%)
         GOTO getin6
      END IF
      PRINT TAB(79);""
      partminqty = VAL(i$)
      LSET partminqty$ = MKS$(partminqty)
      y% = CSRLIN
      x% = POS(0)
getin7:
      LINE INPUT"enter date of last count"; i$
      i1% = LEN(i$)
      IF i1%>6 THEN
         CALL printerr("Too long",y%,x%)
         GOTO getin7
```

```
      END IF
      IF LEN(i$)<1 THEN
        CALL printerr("Too short",y%,x%)
        GOTO getin7
      END IF
      CALL numtest(i$,i1%,er%)
      IF er%>0 THEN
        CALL printerr("Not numeric",y%,x%)
        GOTO getin7
      END IF
      CALL datest(i$,i1%,er%)
      IF er%>0 THEN
        CALL printerr("Bad date",y%,x%)
        GOTO getin7
      END IF
      PRINT TAB(79);""
      partlastcnt = VAL(i$)
      LSET partlastcnt$ = MKS$(partlastcnt)
      END IF
RETURN
SUB numtest (n$,lgth%,e%):REM -- n$ is the data, lgth% is the
                         REM -- length of the data item, and
                         REM -- e% is an error flag (0=no error,
                         REM -- 1=error)
    e% = 0:REM -- set the error flag to 0 (no error)
    FOR i% = 1 TO lgth%:REM -- set up a loop to check for numeric
    IF ASC(MID$(n$,i%,1))<48 THEN e% = 1:REM -- test for <0
    IF ASC(MID$(n$,i%,1))>57 THEN e% = 1:REM -- test for >9
    NEXT i%
END SUB
SUB datest (dat$,lgth%,e%):REM -- dat$ is the date, lgth% is the
                          REM -- length of the date, and
                          REM -- e% is an error flag
                          REM -- (0=no error, 1=error)
    e%=1:REM -- set error flag to 1 (we're assuming that until the
         REM -- date passes all the tests, an error has been
         REM -- found).
    IF lgth%<5 THEN GOTO quitdate:REM -- if the length <5 then
                                  REM -- leave the procedure with
                                  REM -- the error flag e% set
                                  REM -- to an error
```

```
IF lgth% = 5 THEN dat$ = "0" + dat$:REM -- make it a six character
                                  REM -- field
w1% = VAL(LEFT$(dat$,2)):REM -- get the month
IF w1%<1 THEN GOTO quitdate
IF w1%>12 THEN GOTO quitdate
w2% = VAL(MID$(dat$,3,2)):REM -- get the day
IF w2%<1 THEN GOTO quitdate
IF w2%>31 THEN GOTO quitdate
w3% = VAL(RIGHT$(dat$,2)):REM -- get the year
IF w3%>90 THEN GOTO quitdate
e% = 0:REM -- reset error flag to 0 (no errors found)
quitdate:
REM -- just a label to go to
END SUB
SUB printerr (e$,r%,c%): REM -- e$ is the error message
                         REM -- r% is the line number, and
                         REM -- c% is the column number
                         REM -- at which to locate.
  PRINT CHR$(7); e$; TAB(79);"":REM -- ring the bell &
                         REM -- print error message
  LOCATE r%,c%:REM -- set the cursor at the original location
END SUB
```

2. Procedure to convert lower case to upper case:

```
SUB upper(i$): REM -- i$ is the string to be converted
  i1% = LEN(i$)
  FOR i% = 1 TO i1%
    w1% = ASC(MID$(i$,i%,1))
    IF w1% > 96 THEN
      IF w1% <123 THEN
      MID$(i$,i%,1) = CHR$(w1%-32)
    END IF
  NEXT i%
END SUB
```

3. Procedure to test for number of days in a month:

```
SUB MOTEST(d,e%): REM -- d is the date, in MMDDYY format, and e%
    is the error indicator (0 = ok, 1 = days are greater than__
    allowed for that month)
```

```
          moda = INT(d/100)
          mo = INT (moda/100)
          da = moda MOD 100
          e% = 0
          IF da >31 THEN
            e% = 1
            goto endmotest
          END IF
          IF mo = 2 THEN
            IF da >29 THEN
            e% = 1
            goto endmotest
          END IF
          IF mo = 4 THEN GOTO thirty
          IF mo = 6 THEN GOTO thirty
          IF mo = 9 THEN GOTO thirty
          IF mo = 11 THEN GOTO thirty
        thirtyone:
          IF da > 31 THEN e% = 1
          GOTO endmotest
        thirty:
          IF da > 30 THEN e% = 1
        endmotest:
        END SUB
```

4. Procedure to check for a minus sign and a decimal point in a number:

```
SUB numtest (n$,lgth%,e%):REM -- n$ is the data, lgth% is the
                    REM -- length of the data item, and
                    REM -- e% is an error flag (0=no error,
                    REM -- 1=error)
  e% = 0:REM -- set the error flag to 0 (no error)
  w2% = 0:REM -- set decimal point counter to 0
  FOR i% = 1 TO lgth%:REM -- set up a loop to check for numeric
    w1% = ASC(MID$(n$,i%,1))
    IF i% = 1 THEN
      IF w1% = 45 THEN
      GOTO nexti
    END IF
    IF w1% = 46 THEN w2% = w2% + 1: GOTO nexti
```

```
    IF w1% < 48 THEN e% = 1:REM -- test for <0
    IF w1% > 57 THEN e% = 1:REM -- test for >9
  nexti:
    NEXT i%
    IF w2% > 1 THEN e% = 1
END SUB
```

CHAPTER 15 EXERCISES

1. Barb's print program:

```
REM -- barblist 010190
GOSUB getdate
GOSUB fileopen
GOSUB main
CLOSE
END
getdate:
  d$ = DATE$
  dat$ = LEFT$(d$, 2) + "/" + MID$(d$, 4, 2) + "/" + RIGHT$(d$, 2)
  da$ = LEFT$(d$, 2) + MID$(d$, 4, 2) + RIGHT$(d$, 2)
  da = VAL(da$)
  PRINT dat$; da$, da
RETURN
fileopen:
  OPEN "r", 1, "part.dat", 256
  FIELD 1,2 AS partnum$, 30 AS partdesc$, 4 AS partretail$, 4 AS partdealer$, 4 AS_
  partcost$, 4 AS partonhand$, 4 AS partminqty$, 4 AS partlastcnt$, 4 AS_
  partonorder$, 4 AS partorderdat$, 4 as partsales1$, 4 AS partsales2$
  FIELD 1, 72 AS partfill1$, 4 AS partsales3$, 4 AS partsales4$, 4 AS partsales5$, 4 AS_
  partsales6$, 4 AS partsales7$, 4 AS partsales8$, 4 AS partsales9$, 4 AS_
  partsales10$, 4 AS partsales11$, 4 AS partsales12$
RETURN
errout: REM -- error routine
  PRINT CHR$(7); "*** error"
```

```
RETURN
main:
  GOSUB fmt
prinnext:
  GOSUB getpart: REM -- fileread
  IF i$ = "end" THEN RETURN
  GOSUB prinpart: REM -- printout
  GOTO prinnext
RETURN
getpart:
  f1 = f1 + 1
  IF f1 < 1 THEN
        GOSUB errout
        GOTO getpart
  END IF
  IF f1 > 100 THEN
        i$ = "end"
        GOTO endget
  END IF
  GET 1, f1
    partnum% = CVI(partnum$)
    partretail = CVS(partretail$)
    partdealer = CVS(partdealer$)
    partcost = CVS(partcost$)
    partonhand = CVS(partonhand$)
    partminqty = CVS(partminqty$)
    partlastcnt = CVS(partlastcnt$)
    partonorder = CVS(partonorder$)
    partorderdat = CVS(partorderdat$)
    partsales1 = CVS(partsales1$)
    partsales2 = CVS(partsales2$)
    partsales3 = CVS(partsales3$)
    partsales4 = CVS(partsales4$)
    partsales5 = CVS(partsales5$)
    partsales6 = CVS(partsales6$)
    partsales7 = CVS(partsales7$)
    partsales8 = CVS(partsales8$)
    partsales9 = CVS(partsales9$)
    partsales10 = CVS(partsales10$)
    partsales11 = CVS(partsales11$)
    partsales12 = CVS(partsales12$)
    IF LEFT$(partdesc$,2) = " " THEN GOTO getpart:REM -- if blank, skip
```

```
endget:
RETURN
REM------------LPRINTS & FORMATS (for Barb)-------------
fmt:
  lin1$ = "\              \                  page ###"
  lin2$ = "            BIKES PEAK Inventory Status (for Barb)"
  lin3$ = "       ITEM                  COST  DEALER  RETAIL  ONHND"
  lin4$ = "###  \          \           ###.## ###.## ###.## #####"
  n1% = 99:REM -- set the line counter to >50, to print the titles
RETURN
prinpart:
  IF n1% < 51 THEN GOTO oneline
  LPRINT USING lin1$; dat$; pagnum: REM -- prints date & page number
  LPRINT lin2$: REM -- prints the report title
  LPRINT lin3$: REM -- prints the column headers
  LPRINT: REM -- space one line
  n1% = 0: REM -- set the line counter to 0
oneline:
  LPRINT USING lin4$;partnum; partdesc$; partcost; partdealer;__
    partretail; partonhd :REM -- this prints one item line
  n1% = n1% + 1
RETURN
```

2. Chuck's print program:

```
REM -- chuklist 010190
GOSUB getdate
GOSUB fileopen
GOSUB main
CLOSE
END
getdate:
  d$ = DATE$
  dat$ = LEFT$(d$, 2) + "/" + MID$(d$, 4, 2) + "/" + RIGHT$(d$, 2)
  da$ = LEFT$(d$, 2) + MID$(d$, 4, 2) + RIGHT$(d$, 2)
  da = VAL(da$)
  PRINT dat$; da$, da
RETURN
fileopen:
  OPEN "r", 1, "part.dat", 256
  FIELD 1, 2 AS partnum$, 30 AS partdesc$, 4 AS partretail$, 4 AS__
  partdealer$, 4 AS partcost$, 4 AS partonhand$, 4 AS__
  partminqty$, 4 AS partlastcnt$, 4 AS partonorder$, 4 AS__
```

```
  partorderdat$, 4 as partsales1$, 4 AS partsales2$
  FIELD 1, 72 AS partfill1$, 4 AS partsales3$, 4 AS partsales4$,__
  4 AS partsales5$, 4 AS partsales6$, 4 AS partsales7$, 4 AS__
  partsales8$, 4 AS partsales9$, 4 AS partsales10$, 4 AS__
  partsales11$, 4 AS partsales12$
RETURN
errout: REM -- error routine
  PRINT CHR$(7); "*** error"
RETURN
main:
  GOSUB fmt
prinnext:
  GOSUB getpart: REM -- fileread
  IF i$ = "end" THEN RETURN
  GOSUB calctot
  GOSUB prinpart: REM -- printout
  GOTO prinnext
RETURN
getpart:
  f1 = f1 + 1
  IF f1 < 1 THEN
          GOSUB errout
          GOTO getpart
  END IF
  IF f1 > 100 THEN
          i$ = "end"
          GOTO endget
  END IF
  GET 1, f1
    partnum% = CVI(partnum$)
    partretail = CVS(partretail$)
    partdealer = CVS(partdealer$)
    partcost = CVS(partcost$)
    partonhand = CVS(partonhand$)
    partminqty = CVS(partminqty$)
    partlastcnt = CVS(partlastcnt$)
    partonorder = CVS(partonorder$)
    partorderdat = CVS(partorderdat$)
    partsales1 = CVS(partsales1$)
    partsales2 = CVS(partsales2$)
```

```
      partsales3 = CVS(partsales3$)
      partsales4 = CVS(partsales4$)
      partsales5 = CVS(partsales5$)
      partsales6 = CVS(partsales6$)
      partsales7 = CVS(partsales7$)
      partsales8 = CVS(partsales8$)
      partsales9 = CVS(partsales9$)
      partsales10 = CVS(partsales10$)
      partsales11 = CVS(partsales11$)
      partsales12 = CVS(partsales12$)
      IF LEFT$(partdesc$,2) = " " THEN GOTO getpart:REM -- if blank, skip
endget:
RETURN
calctot:
   totsales# = partsales1 + partsales2 + partsales3 + partsales4 + partsales5 + __
   partsales6 + partsales7 + partsales8 + partsales9 + partsales10 + partsales 11 + __
   partsales12
RETURN
fmt:
   lin1$ = "\          \                    page ###"
   lin2$ =        BIKES PEAK Inventory Movement (for Chuck)"
   lin3$ = "###\          \  tyr #####      onhd #####"
   lin4$ = "Jan  Feb  Mar  Apr  May  Jun  Jul  Aug  Sep  Oct  Nov  Dec"
   lin5$ = "### #### #### #### #### #### #### #### #### #### #### ####"
   n1% = 99:REM -- set the line counter to >50, to print the titles
RETURN
prinpart:
   IF n1% < 51 THEN GOTO onepart
   LPRINT USING lin1$; dat$; pagnum: REM -- prints date & page number
   LPRINT lin2$: REM -- prints the report title
   n1% = 0: REM -- set the line counter to 0
onepart:
   LPRINT: REM -- space one line
   LPRINT USING lin3$;partnum; partdesc$; totsales#; partonhand__
   LPRINT lin4$
   LPRINT USING lin5$;partsales1; partsales2; partsales3;__
      partsales4, partsales5; partsales6; partsales7; partsales8;__
      partsales9; partsales10; partsales11; partsales12
   n1% = n1% + 4
RETURN
```

CHAPTER 16 EXERCISES

1. The customer lookup program.

```
REM -- lookcust 010190
GOSUB getdate
GOSUB fileopen
GOSUB main
CLOSE
END
getdate:
  d$ = DATE$
  dat$ = LEFT$(d$, 2) + "/" + MID$(d$, 4, 2) + "/" + RIGHT$(d$, 2)
  da$ = LEFT$(d$, 2) + MID$(d$, 4, 2) + RIGHT$(d$, 2)
  da = VAL(da$)
  PRINT dat$; da$, da
RETURN
fileopen:
  DIM custbike$(3), custbike%(3), custbikedol$(3), custbikedol#(3)
  OPEN "r", 1, "cust.dat", 256
  FIELD 1, 2 AS custnum$, 20 AS custlname$, 15 AS custfname$, 30 AS
  custaddr1$, 30 AS custaddr2$, 20 AS custcity$, 2 AS custst$, 9 AS__
  custzip$, 8 AS custphone$, 1 AS custtype$, 50 AS custnotes$, 4 AS
  custsince$, 4 AS custlastmail$, 4 AS custlastpurch$
  FIELD 1, 199 AS custfill1$, 8 AS custthisyr$, 8 AS custlastyr$, 2 AS__
  custbikes$(1), 2 AS custbikes$(2), 2 AS custbikes$(3), 8 AS__
  custbikedol$(1), 8 AS custbikedol$(2), 8 AS custbikedol$(3)
RETURN
errout:
  REM -- error routine
  PRINT CHR$(7); "*** error"
RETURN
main:
  GOSUB fmts
nextcust:
  CLS
  GOSUB getcust: REM -- fileread
  IF i$ = "end" THEN RETURN
```

```
      GOSUB dispcust: REM -- screenout
      GOTO nextcust
RETURN
getcust:
      LINE INPUT "input customer number (1–100) , or 'end' to leave
      program "; i$
      IF i$ = "end" THEN RETURN
      f1 = VAL(i$)
      IF f1 < 1 THEN
        GOSUB errout
        GOTO getcust
      END IF
      IF f1 > 100 THEN
            GOSUB errout
            GOTO getcust
      END IF
      GET 1, f1
      custnum% = CVI(custnum$)
      custphone# = CVD(custphone$)
      custsince = CVS(custsince$)
      custlastmail = CVS(custlastmail$)
      custlastpurch = CVS(custlastpurch$)
      custthisyr# = CVD(custthisyr$)
      custlastyr# = CVD(custlastyr$)
      FOR i% = 1 TO 3
        custbikes(i%) = CVI(custbikes$(i%))
        custbikedol#(i%) = CVD(custbikedol$(i%))
      NEXT i%
RETURN
fmts:
      lin1$ = "           CUSTOMER INFORMATION"
      lin2$ = "#### \        \\          \ type ! phone #########"
      lin3$ = "          \                    \   cust since ######"
      lin4$ = "          \                  \   last mail ######"
      lin5$ = "          \         \ \\\  \"
      lin6$ = "\                                              \"
      lin7$ = "                                    bike purchases"
      lin8$ = "                                    num       date"
      lin9$ = "           total purchases       k1 ###   ######"
      lin10$ = "        this year #####.##      k2 ###   ######"
      lin11$ = "        last year #####.##      k3 ###   ######"
```

```
            RETURN
            dispcust:
              CLS
              PRINT lin1$
              PRINT
              PRINT USING lin2$;custnum;custfname$;custlname$;custtype$;__
              custphone
              PRINT USING lin3$;custaddr1$;custsince
              PRINT USING lin4$;custaddr2$;custlastmail
              PRINT USING lin5$;custcity$;custst$;custzip$
              PRINT
              PRINT USING lin6$;custnotes$
              PRINT lin7$
              PRINT lin8$
              PRINT USING lin9$;custbikes%(1);custbikedol#(1)
              PRINT USING lin10$;custthisyr#;custbikes%(2);custbikedol#(2)
              PRINT USING lin11$;custlastyr#;custbikes%(3);custbikedol#(3)
            RETURN
```

2. The part lookup program.

```
REM -- lookpart 010190
GOSUB getdate
GOSUB fileopen
GOSUB main
CLOSE
END
getdate:
  d$ = DATE$
  dat$ = LEFT$(d$, 2) + "/" + MID$(d$, 4, 2) + "/" + RIGHT$(d$, 2)
  da$ = LEFT$(d$, 2) + MID$(d$, 4, 2) + RIGHT$(d$, 2)
  da = VAL(da$)
  PRINT dat$; da$, da
RETURN
fileopen:
  OPEN "r", 1, "part.dat", 256
  FIELD 1, 2 AS partnum$, 30 AS partdesc$, 4 AS partretail$, 4 AS__
  partdealer$, 4 AS partcost$, 4 AS partonhand$, 4 AS__
  partminqty$, 4 AS partlastcnt$, 4 AS partonorder$, 4 AS__
  partorderdat$, 4 as partsales1$, 4 AS partsales2$
  FIELD 1, 72 AS partfill1$, 4 AS partsales3$, 4 AS partsales4$,__
```

```
   4 AS partsales5$, 4 AS partsales6$, 4 AS partsales7$, 4 AS__
   partsales8$, 4 AS partsales9$, 4 AS partsales10$, 4 AS__
   partsales11$, 4 AS partsales12$
RETURN
errout: REM -- error routine
   PRINT CHR$(7); "*** error"
RETURN
main:
GOSUB fmts
nextpart:
   CLS
   GOSUB getpart: REM -- fileread
   IF i$ = "end" THEN RETURN
   GOSUB disppart: REM -- screenout
   GOTO nextpart
RETURN
getpart:
   LINE INPUT "input part number (1–100) , or 'end' to leave program__
   "; i$
   IF i$ = "end" THEN RETURN
   f1 = VAL(i$)
   IF f1 < 1 THEN
        GOSUB errout
        GOTO getpart
   END IF
   IF f1 > 100 THEN
        GOSUB errout
        GOTO getpart
   END IF
   GET 1, f1
     partnum% = CVI(partnum$)
     partretail = CVS(partretail$)
     partdealer = CVS(partdealer$)
     partcost = CVS(partcost$)
     partonhand = CVS(partonhand$)
     partminqty = CVS(partminqty$)
     partlastcnt = CVS(partlastcnt$)
     partonorder = CVS(partonorder$)
     partorderdat = CVS(partorderdat$)
     partsales1 = CVS(partsales1$)
     partsales2 = CVS(partsales2$)
```

```
        partsales3 = CVS(partsales3$)
        partsales4 = CVS(partsales4$)
        partsales5 = CVS(partsales5$)
        partsales6 = CVS(partsales6$)
        partsales7 = CVS(partsales7$)
        partsales8 = CVS(partsales8$)
        partsales9 = CVS(partsales9$)
        partsales10 = CVS(partsales10$)
        partsales11 = CVS(partsales11$)
        partsales12 = CVS(partsales12$)
RETURN
fmts:
lin1$ =                    "PART INFORMATION"
lin2$ = "####\                    \ ####.## ####.## ####.##"
lin3$ = "       Onhand ##### Min #####        Lastcount ######"
lin4$ = "       Onordr #####              Orderdate ######"
lin5$ = "       SALES"
lin6$ = "       Jan #####"
lin7$ = "       Feb #####"
lin8$ = "       Mar #####"
lin9$ = "       Apr #####"
lin10$ = "       May #####"
lin11$ = "       Jun #####"
lin12$ = "       Jul #####"
lin13$ = "       Aug #####"
lin14$ = "       Sep #####"
lin15$ = "       Oct #####"
lin16$ = "       Nov #####"
lin17$ = "       Dec #####"
RETURN
disppart:
   CLS
   PRINT lin1$
   PRINT USING lin2$;partnum; partdesc$; partretail; partdealer; partcost
   PRINT USING lin3$; partonhand; partminqty; partlastcnt
   PRINT USING lin4$;partonorder; partorderdat
   PRINT lin5$
   PRINT USING lin6$;partsales1
   PRINT USING lin7$;partsales2
   PRINT USING lin8$;partsales3
   PRINT USING lin9$;partsales4
   PRINT USING lin10$;partsales5
```

```
      PRINT USING lin11$;partsales6
      PRINT USING lin12$;partsales7
      PRINT USING lin13$;partsales8
      PRINT USING lin14$;partsales9
      PRINT USING lin15$;partsales10
      PRINT USING lin16$;partsales11
      PRINT USING lin17$;partsales12
RETURN
```

CHAPTER 17 EXERCISES

1. Just write the program with those formulas and print the answers. Notice the difference parentheses make.
2. Write the program using the functions with each number and print or display the results. Compare the difference in the results of each function on the same number, and understand what each function does. For your own edification, make up numbers yourself and print the **INT**, **CINT**, **FIX**, and **CLNG** of them.

3(a). Date conversion (from MMDDYY into YYMMDD) procedure:

```
SUB chgdat(d,d1)
    REM -- the date is in variable name d, the converted date in d1
    d$ = STR$(d):REM -- convert d to a string
    w$ = MID$(d$,2):REM -- get rid of blank sign character
    d$ = w$:REM -- move it back into d$
    IF LEN(w$)<6 then d$ = "0"+w$:REM -- make it 6 characters
    w$ = RIGHT$(d$,2)+LEFT$(d$,2)+MID$(d$,3,2)
    REM -- convert the string into YYMMDD format
    d1 = Val(w$):REM -- convert it into a number
END SUB
```

3(b). Elapsed days procedure:

```
SUB elapsdays (dat1,dat2,elap)
  REM -- dat1 and dat2 are the dates, elap is the elapsed days
  CALL chgdat (dat1,d1)
  CALL chgdat (dat2,d2)
```

```
w$ = MID$(STR$(d1), 2): REM -- make 1st date a string
w1$ = LEFT$(w$, 2): REM -- get the year of 1st date
w2$ = MID$(w$, 3, 2): REM -- get the month of 1st date
w3$ = RIGHT$(w$, 2): REM -- get the day of 1st date
x1 = VAL(w1$)
x2 = VAL(w2$)
x3 = VAL(w3$): REM -- change year, month, and day of 1st date into separate numbers
w$ = MID$(STR$(d2), 2): REM -- make 2nd date a string
w1$ = LEFT$(w$, 2): REM -- get the year of 2nd date
w2$ = MID$(w$, 3, 2): REM -- get the month of 2nd date
w3$ = RIGHT$(w$, 2): REM -- get the day of 2nd date
x4 = VAL(w1$)
x5 = VAL(w2$)
x6 = VAL(w3$): REM -- change 2nd date into separate numbers
w1 = x1 - x4: REM -- subtract the years
w2 = x2 - x5: REM -- subtract the months
w3 = x3 - x6: REM -- subtract the days
IF w3 < 0 THEN
   w3 = w3 + 30
   w2 = w2 - 1
END IF: REM -- if days < 0, add 30 to the days, and subtract 1 from the month
IF w2 < 0 THEN
   w2 = w2 + 12
   w1 = w1 - 1
END IF: REM -- if months < 0, add 12 to the months, and subtract 1 from the year
elap = w1 * 365 + w2 * 30 + w3: REM -- sum the days
END SUB
```

CHAPTER 18 EXERCISES

1. Print every location on your computer screen:

```
FOR i% = 1 TO 24
   FOR j% = 1 TO 80
      LOCATE i%,j%
      PRINT "*";
   NEXT j%
NEXT i%
```

2. Print every location on your computer screen backwards:

```
FOR i% = 24 TO 1 STEP -1
  FOR j% = 80 TO 1 STEP -1
    LOCATE i%,j%
    PRINT "-";
  NEXT j%
NEXT i%
```

3. Create a date table:

```
setmonth:
  DIM motab(12)
  DATA 31,29,31,30,31,30,31,31,30,31,30,31
  FOR i% = 1 TO 12
  READ motab(i%)
  NEXT i%
RETURN
```

4. Creating the train table using **LINE INPUT** statements:

```
DIM traintab$(5,5)
FOR i% = 1 TO 5
  FOR j% = 1 TO 5
    PRINT"Enter the row " + i% + ", column " + j% + " schedule";
    LINE INPUT "";traintab$(i%,j%)
  NEXT j%
NEXT i%
```

5. Creating the train table using **READ** and **DATA** statements:

```
DIM traintab$(5,5)
FOR i% = 1 TO 5
  FOR j% = 1 TO 5
  READ traintab$(i%,j%)
  NEXT j%
NEXT i%
DATA "6:00 AM","6:41 AM","7:14 AM","7:57 AM","8:26 AM"
DATA "7:00 AM","7:41 AM","8:14 AM","8:57 AM","9:26 AM"
DATA "8:30 AM","9:11 AM","9:44 AM","10:27 AM","10:56 AM"
DATA "9:00 AM","9:41 AM","10:14 AM","10:57 AM","11:26 AM"
DATA "10:30 AM","11:11 AM","11:44 AM","12:27 PM","12:56 PM"
```

6. Printing out the train table using a nested loop:

```
FOR i% = 1 TO 5
  FOR j% = 1 TO 5
    PRINT TAB(j%*10); traintab$(i%,j%);
  NEXT j%
  PRINT
NEXT i%
```

CHAPTER 19 EXERCISES

1. The sales/parts receipts program:

```
REM--salesin 010190
GOSUB getdate
GOSUB fileopen
GOSUB main
CLOSE
END
getdate:
  d$ = DATE$
  dat$ = LEFT$(d$, 2) + "/" + MID$(d$, 4, 2) + "/" + RIGHT$(d$, 2)
  da$ = LEFT$(d$, 2) + MID$(d$, 4, 2) + RIGHT$(d$, 2)
  da = VAL(da$)
  PRINT dat$; da$, da
RETURN
fileopen:
  DIM custbike$(3), custbike%(3), custbikedol$(3), custbikedol#(3)
  OPEN "r", 1, "cust.dat", 256
  FIELD 1, 2 AS custnum$, 20 AS custlname$, 15 AS custfname$, 30 AS__
  custaddr1$, 30 AS custaddr2$, 20 AS custcity$, 2 AS custst$, 9 AS__
  custzip$, 8 AS custphone$, 1 AS custtype$, 50 AS custnotes$, 4 AS__
  custsince$, 4 AS custlastmail$, 4 AS custlastpurch$
  FIELD 1, 199 AS custfill1$, 8 AS custthisyr$, 8 AS custlastyr$, 2__
  AS custbikes$(1), 2 AS custbikes$(2), 2 AS custbikes$(3), 8 AS__
  custbikedol$(1), 8 AS custbikedol$(2), 8 AS custbikedol$(3)
  OPEN "r", 2, "part.dat", 256
```

```
    FIELD 2, 2 AS partnum$, 30 AS partdesc$, 4 AS partretail$, 4 AS__
    partdealer$, 4 AS partcost$, 4 AS partonhand$, 4 AS__
    partminqty$, 4 AS partlastcnt$, 4 AS partonorder$, 4 AS__
    partorderdat$, 4 as partsales1$, 4 AS partsales2$
    FIELD 2, 72 AS partfill1$, 4 AS partsales3$, 4 AS partsales4$,__
    4 AS partsales5$, 4 AS partsales6$, 4 AS partsales7$, 4 AS__
    partsales8$, 4 AS partsales9$, 4 AS partsales10$, 4 AS__
    partsales11$, 4 AS partsales12$
RETURN
errout:
    REM -- error routine
    PRINT CHR$(7); "*** error"
RETURN
getcust:
    LINE INPUT "input customer number (1-100) , or 'end' to leave__
    program "; i$
    IF i$ = "end" THEN RETURN
    f1 = VAL(i$)
    IF f1 < 1 THEN
        GOSUB errout
        GOTO getcust
    END IF
    IF f1 > 100 THEN
        GOSUB errout
        GOTO getcust
    END IF
    GET 1, f1
      custnum% = CVI(custnum$)
      custphone# = CVD(custphone$)
      custsince = CVS(custsince$)
      custlastmail = CVS(custlastmail$)
      custlastpurch = CVS(custlastpurch$)
      custthisyr# = CVD(custthisyr$)
      custlastyr# = CVD(custlastyr$)
      FOR i% = 1 TO 3
        custbikes(i%) = CVI(custbikes$(i%))
        custbikedol#(i%) = CVD(custbikedol$(i%))
    PRINT "Customer is"; cust/name$
    INPUT "right one (y or n)", i$
    IF i$ <> "y" THEN GOTO getcust
      NEXT i%
```

```
RETURN
getpart:
  LINE INPUT "input part number (1–100) , or 'end' to leave program__
  "; i$
  IF i$ = "end" THEN RETURN
  f2 = VAL(i$)
  IF f2 < 1 THEN
      GOSUB errout
      GOTO getpart
  END IF
  IF f2 > 100 THEN
      GOSUB errout
      GOTO getpart
  END IF
  GET 2, f2
    partnum% = CVI(partnum$)
    partretail = CVS(partretail$)
    partdealer = CVS(partdealer$)
    partcost = CVS(partcost$)
    partonhand = CVS(partonhand$)
    partminqty = CVS(partminqty$)
    partlastcnt = CVS(partlastcnt$)
    partonorder = CVS(partonorder$)
    partorderdat = CVS(partorderdat$)
    partsales1 = CVS(partsales1$)
    partsales2 = CVS(partsales2$)
    partsales3 = CVS(partsales3$)
    partsales4 = CVS(partsales4$)
    partsales5 = CVS(partsales5$)
    partsales6 = CVS(partsales6$)
    partsales7 = CVS(partsales7$)
    partsales8 = CVS(partsales8$)
    partsales9 = CVS(partsales9$)
    partsales10 = CVS(partsales10$)
    partsales11 = CVS(partsales11$)
    partsales12 = CVS(partsales12$)
  PRINT "Part description is "; partdesc$
  LINE INPUT "right one, ( y or n ) "; i$
  IF i$ <> "y" THEN GOTO getpart
RETURN
main:
```

```
    GOSUB fmts:REM -- define the print lines
    GOSUB gettypedate
nextsale:
  CLS
  GOSUB getcust: REM -- fileread
  IF i$ = "end" THEN RETURN
  GOSUB getpart: REM -- fileread
  If i$ = "end" THEN RETURN
  GOSUB getsales: REM -- process
  GOSUB prinsale: REM -- print transaction
  IF trantype# = "s" then GOSUB putcust: REM -- fileout
  GOSUB putpart: REM -- fileout
  GOTO nextsale
RETURN
fmts:
  lin1$ = "            \              \                    ######"
  lin2$ = "Cust     Cust name      Qty Part  Description        Price"
  lin3$ = "###### \        \#####   ####\                ####.##"
  n1% = 99
RETURN
prinsale:
  IF n1%>50 THEN
    LPRINT CHR$(12)
    LPRINT USING lin1$; t$; trandat
    LPRINT lin2$
    LPRINT
    n1% = 0
  END IF
  LPRINT USING lin3$; custnum; custlname$; tranqty; partnum;__
      partdesc$; tranprice
  n1% = n1%+1
RETURN
gettypedate:
  y% = CSRLIN
  x% = POS(0)
getdat:
  LINE INPUT"enter date of transactions"; i$
  i1% = LEN(i$)
  IF LEN(i$)>6 THEN
    CALL printerr("Too long",y%,x%)
    GOTO getdat
```

```
      END IF
      IF LEN(i$)<1 THEN
        CALL printerr("Too short",y%,x%)
        GOTO getdat
      END IF
      CALL numtest(i$,i1%,er%)
      IF er%>0 THEN
        CALL printerr("Not numeric",y%,x%)
        GOTO getdat
      ENDIF
      CALL datest(i$,i1%,er%)
      IF er%>0 THEN
        CALL printerr("Bad date",y%,x%)
        GOTO getdat
      END IF
      PRINT TAB (79);""
      trandat = VAL(i$)
      tranmo = INT(trandat/10000)
      y% = CSRLIN
      x% = POS(0)
gettype:
      LINE INPUT"enter S for sale, R for parts receipt"; i$
      IF LEN(i$)>1 THEN
        CALL printerr("Too long",y%,x%)
        GOTO gettype
      END IF
      IF LEN(i$)<1 THEN
        CALL printerr("Too short",y%,x%)
        GOTO gettype
      END IF
      IF i$<> "s" THEN
        IF i$<>"r" THEN
      CALL printerr("Bad code"; y%,x%)
      GOTO gettype
      END IF
      PRINT TAB (79);""
      trantype$ = i$
      t$ = "Sales"
      IF trantype$ = "r" THEN t$= "Receipts"
RETURN
putcust:
```

```
     IF partnum <200 THEN
        i% = 1
     END IF: REM -- test for k1 parts
     IF partnum >199 THEN
        IF partnum <300 THEN
        i% = 2
     END IF: REM -- test for k2 parts
     IF partnum >299 THEN
        i% = 3
     END IF: REM -- test for k3 parts
     LSET custbikes$(i%) = MKI$(custbikes%(i%) + tranqty)
     LSET custbikedol$(i%) = MKD$(custbikedol#(i%) + tranprice * tranqty)
     LSET custlastpurch$ = MKS$(trandat)
     LSET custthisyr$ = MKD$(custthisyr# + tranprice * tranqty)
     PUT 1, f1
RETURN
  putpart:
     mult = 1
     IF trantype$ = "r" THEN mult = (-1)
     LSET partonhand$ = MKS$(partonhand - tranqty * mult)
     LSET partsales$(tranmo) = MKS$(partsales(tranmo) + tranqty * mult)
     PUT 2, f2
  RETURN
  getsales:
     y% = CSRLIN
     x% = POS(0)
  getin1:
  LINE INPUT"enter part quantity"; i$
  i1% = LEN(i$)
  IF LEN(i$)>5 THEN
     CALL printerr("Too long",y%,x%)
     GOTO getin1
  END IF
  IF LEN(i$)<1 THEN
     CALL printerr("Too short",y%,x%)
     GOTO getin1
  END IF
  CALL numtest(i$,i1%,er%)
  IF er%>0 THEN
     CALL printerr("Not numeric",y%,x%)
     GOTO getin1
```

```
      END IF
      PRINT TAB (79);""
      tranqty = VAL(i$)
getin2:
    LINE INPUT"enter price"; i$
    i1% = LEN(i$)
    IF LEN(i$)>7 THEN
       CALL printerr("Too long",y%,x%)
       GOTO getin2
    END IF
    IF LEN(i$)<1 THEN
       CALL printerr("Too short",y%,x%)
       GOTO getin2
    END IF
    CALL numtest(i$,i1%,er%)
    IF er%>0 THEN
       CALL printerr("Not numeric",y%,x%)
       GOTO getin2
    END IF
    PRINT TAB (79);""
    tranprice = VAL(i$)
RETURN
SUB numtest (n$,lgth%,e%):REM -- n$ is the data, lgth% is the
                          REM -- length of the data item, and
                          REM -- e% is an error flag (0=no error,
                          REM -- 1=error)
    e% = 0:REM -- set the error flag to 0 (no error)
    FOR i% = 1 TO lgth%:REM -- set up a loop to check for numeric
    IF ASC(MID$(n$,i%,1))<48 THEN e% = 1:REM -- test for <0
    IF ASC(MID$(n$,i%,1))>57 THEN e% = 1:REM -- test for >9
    NEXT i%
END SUB
SUB datest (dat$,lgth%,e%):REM -- dat$ is the date, lgth% is the
                          REM -- length of the date, and
                          REM -- e% is an error flag
                          REM -- (0=no error, 1=error)
    e% = 1:REM -- set error flag to 1 (we're assuming that until the
            REM -- date passes all the tests, an error has been
            REM -- found).
    IF lgth%<5 THEN GOTO quitdate:REM -- if the length <5 then
                          REM -- leave the procedure with
```

```
                                REM -- the error flag e% set
                                REM -- to an error
        IF lgth% = 5 THEN dat$ = "0"+dat$:REM -- make it a six character
                                REM -- field
        w1% = VAL(LEFT$(dat$,2)): REM -- get the month
        IF w1%<1 THEN GOTO quitdate
        IF w1%>12 THEN GOTO quitdate
        w2% = VAL(MID$(dat$,3,2)):REM -- get the day
        IF w2%<1 THEN GOTO quitdate
        IF w2%>31 THEN GOTO quitdate
        w3% = VAL(RIGHT$(dat$,2)):REM -- get the year
        IF w3%>90 THEN GOTO quitdate
        e% = 0:REM -- reset error flag to 0 (no errors found)
    quitdate:
    REM -- just a label to go to
    END SUB
    SUB printerr (e$,r%,c%): REM -- e$ is the error message
                                REM -- r% is the line number, and
                                REM -- c% is the column number
                                REM -- at which to locate.
      PRINT CHR$(7); e$; TAB(79);"":REM -- ring the bell &
                                REM -- print error message
      LOCATE r%,c%:REM -- set the cursor at the original location
    END SUB
```

2. First rename each of the programs (using the **SAVE AS** command), so that they can be called using a name and a number between 1 and 7:

    Rename lookcust to bike1
    Rename lookpart to bike2
    Rename newcust to bike3
    Rename newpart to bike4
    Rename barblist to bike5
    Rename chuklist to bike6
    Rename salesin to bike7

    Now for the menu program:

    ```
    REM--bikemenu 010190
    newscreen:
    ```

```
CLS
LOCATE 3,10
PRINT "Bikes Peak Menu"
LOCATE 3,50
PRINT DATE$;" "; TIME$
LOCATE 6,20: PRINT "1- Customer lookup"
LOCATE 7,20: PRINT "2- Part lookup"
LOCATE 8,20: PRINT "3- New Customer"
LOCATE 9,20: PRINT "4- New Part"
LOCATE 10,20: PRINT "5- Price and availability"
LOCATE 11,20: PRINT "6- Inventory movement"
LOCATE 12,20: PRINT "7- Enter sales/receipts"
LOCATE 15,20: PRINT "end- to end"
LOCATE 20,1: LINE INPUT"Please enter your selection"; i$
IF i$ = "end" THEN GOTO endit
IF VAL(i$)<1 THEN GOTO newscreen
IF VAL(i$)>7 THEN GOTO newscreen
p$ = "bike"+i$
chain p$
endit:
END
```

Last, put this statement in place of the **END** statement in each of those seven programs:

```
CHAIN"bikemenu"
```

Index

A

alphanumeric 84, 95, 211, 222, 223, 330
arrays 319–333
ASC function 264, 265, 269

B

Bikes Peak 14, 66, 67, 273–275
blinking 289, 298
block diagrams 62, 63
block **ELSE** statement 175
block **IF** statement 164
block-line method 24, 27
blocks 24, 27, 106, 110, 116, 117, 121,
    146, 151, 152
blueprint 61–66, 74, 75, 360–363
blueprint to routines 111–113, 116, 366
bottom line 349, 350
Breakpoint 336, 337, 340
Break/Watch menu 73
building-block 8, 35, 106, 110, 116

C

calc (routine) 105, 108, 111, 112
calculations 17, 301, 302, 304–306,
    315, 316
CALL statement 107, 108, 126–128,
    132–135
CHAIN statement 43, 104
change command 147, 148, 149
CHR$ function 239–244, 279, 280, 282,
    293
CINT function 309–312, 316
classic program 104–111, 364, 365
CLNG function 309–312, 316
CLOSE statement 104, 105, 106

CLS statement 294
COLOR statement 288, 289, 296, 297,
    298
commands
    BASIC reserved words 21, 22, 59,
        60, 355, 356
    PowerBASIC environment 113–115
commas 280, 282, 293, 298
compiling a program 347, 348
complex **IF** statement 176–178
concatenating strings 267, 269, 302, 303
concept of files 200–213
continuing a program 340
conventions 19–22
cookbook 5, 11
copy selected text 149, 150
creating a random file 225, 226
CSRLIN statement 244–246, 294, 295,
    298
cut and paste 149, 150
CVD function 224, 225
CVI function 224, 225
CVL function 224, 225
CVS function 224, 225

D

danger of **GOTO** 197, 198
Dartmouth 9, 10
data 15–17, 61–66, 77–92, 95
    editing 231–248
    in files 208–212
    in routines (global and local)
        126–128, 130–135, 140
    using the right types 307
DATA and **READ** statements 326, 327
data dictionary 89–93
data file 200–231
data names 81–89, 95

DATA statement 326, 327
data "window" 132–135
data types 84–86, 95, 307–309
DATE$ function 87
date calculations 313–315
date comparison 313, 314
date swap 314
date testing (editing) 236, 237, 242, 243,
    251–253, 254–256
Debug menu 71, 72, 337, 338
Debugger 334–345
defining a table 321–326
delete selected text 150
design
    blueprint 61–66, 74, 75, 360–363
    file 208–212, 215–223
    printed reports 271–283
    program 98–113, 115–117
    screen layouts 284–299
DIMensioning a table (DIM statement)
    325, 326
Directory Change command
    (PowerBASIC environment) 115
Directory command (PowerBASIC
    environment) 115
disk
    and data files 79, 80, 108, 110,
        214–230
    directory 31
display (on the screen) 284–299
division by zero 303
DO UNTIL command 193–195, 198
dos shell (Os shell) command 115

E

editing
    data 231–248
    keys (PowerBASIC environment)
        144–151
    levels 232, 233
Editor (PowerBASIC) 143–161
elapsed days 314, 315
elements in a table 321–326
ELSE
    block 175, 176
    statement 170–176

and alternative process selection
    171–173
and flow diversion 174, 175
end of the file 195, 196, 226–228, 229
END statement 103, 104
END SUB statement 127, 128, 132, 134,
    136
error
    messages 239–244, 245, 246, 247
    routine 250, 251
everyday, ordinary
    fields 202, 203
    files 201
    records 201, 202

F

F1 94, 95, 96, 145
F2 145, 347
F3 145
F4 337, 338, 340, 341, 342, 343
F5 145, 338, 339, 340
F6 145
F7 335, 336, 337, 338, 339, 341, 342
F8 336, 338, 340, 342
F9 343, 347
F10 338, 341, 343
field 81–84, 202, 203, 209–212
FIELD statement 222–226, 229
file
    layout 210–212
    structures 204–208
    subject categories 208–210
File commands (PowerBASIC
    environment) 113–116, 138–140, 141
File menu 113–116, 138–140, 141
fileout routine 101, 102, 105, 110, 111,
    112
fileread routine 100, 101, 102, 104, 105,
    108, 111, 112
find command 147, 148
find and replace command 148, 149
FIX function 309, 310, 311, 316
FOR (...TO...NEXT) 192, 193
format statement 276–279, 281, 282,
    290–292, 298
functions in BASIC 263–269, 311–316

G

GET statement 215–220, 229
global and local data 130–135
GOSUB statement 122–125, 135, 136, 137
GOTO
    danger of 135–137, 140, 141
    statement 107, 108, 135–137, 140, 141
    with IF statement 165, 166, 167, 169, 174, 184

H

Help
    help on 94–96
    index 94, 96
    specific 94, 96
hidput 61, 62, 64, 65, 75
hints on using the Debugger 343, 344

I

IF EOF THEN GOTO 195, 196
IF statements 53, 162–186
    decision-making rules for 178, 179
IFs and program flow 165–170
implied in this book 7
indenting rule of IFs 182, 183
input (from the keyboard) 231–270
INPUT (LINE INPUT) statement 262, 263
in routines 100–102
instant screen 338, 339, 340
instant watch 337, 338, 341, 342
INT function 309–312
integers 84, 85, 86, 95, 216, 222–225, 330, 331

K

keep it simple! 275, 276, 281, 290, 298

L

label (line) 18, 19, 23, 27
laying out a page 275, 276, 281
LEFT$ function 266–269
LEN function 263, 264, 269
length test 232–235
line
    labels 18, 19, 23, 27
    names 19, 23, 27
    numbers 18, 19, 23, 27
LINE INPUT statement 262, 263
Load command (PowerBASIC environment) 114, 138, 139
LOCATE function 109, 245, 246, 294, 295, 298
locating
    a point on the screen 109, 245, 246, 294, 295, 298
    the elements in a table 321–326
    the right record in a random file 217–219
logic in programs 50–61, 74
long integers 84, 85, 86, 95, 216, 222–226, 330, 331
LOOP statement 192, 193, 194, 198
loop is the logic base 188–191
loops 187–199
LPRINT statement 277–280, 282
LPRINT USING statement 277–280, 282
LSET statement 223–226

M

main control 100–102, 104, 105, 107, 108, 111–113
main routine is the critical loop 196
major routines 100–102, 104–111, 121–125
massage routines 101, 102, 104, 105, 107, 108, 109, 111, 112
math functions 312
memorize (this book) 6, 11
menu program 24–27, 28, 30, 35–44
merge block command (CTL + kr) 145, 151, 152

MID$ function 266–269
minimal testing 179–182
minor tasks 125–128
MKD$ function 223–226
MKI$ function 223–226
MKL$ function 223–226
MKS$ function 223–226
MMDDYY 109, 237, 314
module 114, 115
move text 149–152

N

named lines 19, 23, 27
names (data) 77–93, 95
nature of programming 58–59
New program command (PowerBASIC
    environment) 34, 114, 139
      save a new program 38–40, 139
NEXT (**FOR...TO __ NEXT**) 192, 193
numbered lines 18, 19, 23, 27
numeric
    edit 232, 235, 236, 241, 246
    testing routine 251, 253, 254
numbers, types of 84–86, 95, 211, 216,
    222–226

O

only criterion 297
one-dimensional tables 320
one step at a time 55, 335
OPEN statement 215–217
opening
    a random file 215–217
    an existing program 40, 41, 114,
      138, 139
operators in BASIC 302
Options menu 45–48, 70, 71
organization, program 98–113, 115, 116
out routines 100–102
output
    file 219–226, 228, 229
    print 271–283
    screen 284–299

P

pack 108, 110, 223–226
page layouts 275, 276
paper and pencil 5
parentheses 304–307
patience 3
planning 3
POS function 295
precision of the BASIC language 59, 60
presenting the correct answer 307–309
PRESS 20
Print command (PowerBASIC
    environment) 151
print formats 276–279, 290–292
PRINT statement 291–293
PRINT USING statement 277–280
printed output 271–282
printing out a table 327, 328
printout routine 101, 102, 105, 110,
    111, 112
procedures 125–135
program, classic 104–113
project your own ideas 7
purpose of a program 61–65, 74
PUT statement 220, 221
PowerBASIC
    compiler 346–349
    debugger 334–345
    editor 143–161
    environment 45
    help 94, 95
    limitations 330, 331
    options 45–48

Q

Quit command (PowerBASIC
    environment) 115, 141

R

random file 214–230
range test 233, 238, 243, 244
reading and writing a random file
    219–221
record layout 222, 223

REMark (**REM**) statement 92, 93
repeated tasks 125–128
report
    file 214–230
    printed 271–283
    screen 284–299
reserved words 86, 87, 355, 356
RETURN statement 121–125
right data types 307
RIGHT$ function 266–269
rounding 307–309
routine-selection test 128–130
routines 98–112, 115, 116, 118–137, 140, 141
Run menu 69, 70, 335–344

S

Save command (PowerBASIC environment) 114, 139, 141
saving a program 38–40, 114, 139, 141
screen
    layout 287–290
    mistakes 289, 290
    neatness 245–247
    output 284–299
screenout routine 101, 102, 105, 109, 110, 111, 112
searching (find) 147, 148
secrets of good programming 60, 61
semicolons 280, 282, 293, 298
short integers 84, 85, 95, 216, 222–226, 330, 331
specific help 94, 96
specific value test 233, 238, 244
starting a program 335, 347
starting PowerBASIC 31–33
statement label 18, 19, 23, 27
statement number 18, 19, 23, 27
Stepover command 336
STR$ function 312–316
string functions in calculations 312–316
strings 84, 85, 95, 226, 330, 331
structure, program 98–142
stub 102–107, 111
subcalcs routines 101, 102, 104, 105, 108, 111, 112

subroutines 118–137, 140
subscripts 324, 325

T

TAB function 279, 293
table within a random file record 328
tables 319–333
testing (debugging) a program 334–345
three-dimensional tables 321–326
TIME$ function 87
tools, programming 29, 30
Trace command (PowerBASIC environment) 335
two-dimensional tables 320, 321, 324, 326, 327, 328
TYPE 21
types, variable (data) 84–86, 95, 222, 307
type test 232, 233, 235–238, 241–243, 246, 251, 252, 253–256
typing in a program 33–38

U

underlining 288, 289
unpack 223–225
uses of tables 330

V

VAL function 265, 268, 269
variable (data) names 77–97

W

Watch window 337, 342
what's calculated first 304
WIDTH statement 280, 281
Write to command 115, 140, 141

Y

YYMMDD 314, 315, 316